Political Parties in Post-Communist Eastern Europe

Political Parties in Post-Communist Eastern Europe is the first textbook to survey the course of party developments in eastern Europe as a whole in the post-communist period. Firmly locating the political changes in eastern Europe in a comparative context, this book relates the specifics of the post-communist situation to the broader picture of the early stages of party development in western Europe and also to contemporary models of party organization in established democracies.

After a brief historical introduction to the overall context of post-communist change in eastern Europe the book considers the process of competitive party formation and the sequence of democratic elections that have structured and given impetus to the development of independent parties. Paul G. Lewis examines the types of party that have emerged and their contrasting ideological orientations as well as the striking levels of electoral volatility and parliamentary fragmentation in many parts of the region. Later chapters examine the degree to which stable party systems have evolved in eastern Europe and the contribution that parties make to the emerging democracies of post-communist Europe.

The book reveals that there are indeed identifiable democratic party systems now in east-central European countries; yet the Balkans and the former Soviet Union are still dominated by the institutional legacies of communist rule. Whilst there are some similarities between party systems in eastern Europe and those of established democracies, this book reveals major organizational differences, as well as a higher level of instability which reflects the effects of social transformation. *Political Parties in Post-Communist Eastern Europe* will be an invaluable resource, accessible to undergraduates of politics and European studies, as well as the non-specialist reader.

Paul G. Lewis is Reader in Central and East European Politics at the Open University. He has worked and published extensively on issues of democratization and party development in eastern Europe, and the course of recent historical development. He is the author of *Central Europe since 1945* and has edited an innovative volume on *Party Structure and Organization in East-Central Europe*.

Political Parties in Post-Communist Eastern Europe

Paul G. Lewis

London and New York

First published 2000
by Routledge
11 New Fetter Lane, London EC4P 4EE

Simultaneously published in the USA and Canada
by Routledge
29 West 35th Street, New York, NY 10001

Routledge is an imprint of the Taylor & Francis Group

© 2000 Paul G. Lewis

Typeset in Baskerville by The Midlands Book Typesetting Company,
Loughborough
Printed and bound in Great Britain by Clays Ltd, St Ives plc

British Library Cataloguing in Publication Data
A catalogue record for this book is available from the British Library

Library of Congress Cataloging in Publication Data
Lewis, Paul G., 1945–
     Political parties in post-communist Eastern Europe / Paul G. Lewis.
        p. cm.
     Includes bibliographical references and index.
     1. Political parties – Europe, Eastern. 2. Representative government and
representation–Europe, Eastern. 3. Europe, Eastern–Politics and
government–1989-   I. Title.

  JN96.A979 L49 2000
  324.2′0947–dc21

                                                                00-055321

ISBN 0–415–20181–0 (hbk)
ISBN 0–415–20182–9 (pbk)

To Chantal

Contents

Tables

Preface

More than 10 years have now past since partially contested elections in Poland during the summer of 1989 and the installation of the first non-communist prime minister in eastern Europe since the 1940s. It was following those developments that orthodox communist rule, which derived its credentials from Soviet authority and had strong roots in the Stalinist model that flourished in the Soviet Union, was swept out of the region, and the Soviet Union itself was also, in words coined in a very different context, consigned to the dustbin of history. During this relatively brief period the region as a whole has been a laboratory for a process of far-reaching political change generally, if rather optimistically, characterized as one of democratization.

To the extent that democratic tendencies have prevailed over the temptations of post-communist authoritarianism, competitive parties have been one of the primary organized agencies of political change and the main vehicle for the institutional development of post-communist democracy. As political actors, the contemporary parties do not appear in any heroic light; they are rarely supported or even voted for with any great enthusiasm; their leaders are tolerated rather than acclaimed; and their organizations are generally seen as parasitic and a hospitable workplace for wheeler-dealers rather than dignified supports of a new democratic order. Yet, for all their weaknesses and the mundane problems of survival and operational activity they confront, parties have indeed shaped the main motor mechanism of political change in post-communist eastern Europe and their growth has been one of the key dimensions of democratic development.

A decade of post-communist change, and the holding of three or more contested elections in the more advanced democracies of eastern Europe, offer enough of a perspective and provide a considerable amount of empirical material on which to base a comparative survey of the critical issues of party development that have arisen throughout eastern Europe and the post-communist region as a whole (although Russia itself does not form part of the main discussion). Much has happened in a relatively short period of time, and an enormous number of publications in the area of democratization studies have appeared, many of which involve issues of party development and analyse the impact of party activity in particular areas. This book is designed to offer a broad overview of the process as a whole, and provide a guide both to the course of party development and the nature of east European party activity for the non-specialist reader.

Many colleagues have contributed to an understanding of party development in the different countries of the region and helped with access to material on various aspects of party activity. An early interest in post-communist party development developed within the productive and congenial framework of a research project on Regime Change in East-Central Europe funded by the Economic and Social Research Council, which ran from 1991 to 1995. It was convened by Michael Waller, and also involved Bill Lomax, Geoffrey Pridham and Gordon Wightman, all of whom contributed to a growing interest in east European parties and a better understanding of their activities (Gordon Wightman has been particularly assiduous with help on Czech and Slovak developments). Many other colleagues who participated in this and other projects throughout the first post-communist decade have also been of great assistance during the preparation of this book. It is certainly not possible to mention them all, but particular thanks are due to Radzisława Gortat, Gabriella Ilonszki, Petr Kopecký, Elena Korasteleva and Vello Pettai. Anyone foolhardy enough to attempt a comparative analysis of developments in the numerous and highly diverse countries of eastern Europe automatically offers up innumerable hostages to fortune and commits inevitable inaccuracies, for all of which I apologize in advance. I sincerely hope though, and indeed firmly believe, that the broader benefits of the comparative view nevertheless outweigh the specific shortcomings of its outcome.

PGL

1   Political change in eastern Europe

Introduction

The emergence of independent, competitive parties and the development of party government has been one of the most significant aspects of recent political change in eastern Europe. Political parties appear as one of the most prominent institutions of modern liberal democracy. It is hardly possible, in practice if not in theory, to conceive of a functioning representative democracy without some kind of competitive party system. The development of a range of reasonably effective parties is a prime indicator of the democratization of the former communist countries and the progress they have made towards joining the broad European community of established democratic nations. Parties help anchor the recently established democratic regimes in a broader society and contribute to their stability amidst multiple processes of rapid social and economic change. Effective constitutions and the diverse processes involved in the rule of law are strengthened by the possibilities parties offer for the development of a more active citizenry and the emergence of a robustly democratic political culture. There are also strong reasons to believe that such conditions are conducive to stable processes of economic development and the formation of effective market economies. This book is designed to provide an overview of the critical process of party development in eastern Europe both for those with a special interest in contemporary processes of change in the region and others concerned with the nature of modern political parties more generally.

Firstly, though, it is necessary to define the terms of the survey. Most people have a good idea of what a political party is, although experts find it difficult to agree on a *definition* that sums up its basic characteristics. As social institutions parties can carry different implications and their attributes vary in significance according to social context. Some influential definitions direct attention to a party's primary activity of contesting elections and seeking to place its candidates in public office.[1] Other analysts point out that parties can exist under regimes that do not hold elections, and that otherwise normally constituted parties sometimes choose not to contest a particular election or elections in general.[2] A further criticism of the office-seeking approach is that it provides insufficient grounds for distinguishing between parties and interest groups.[3] Such writers then tend to elaborate on other characteristics and the range of functions parties can perform.

The focus on electoral activity and the ambitions of parties to achieve government office are, nevertheless, of particular importance. In the context of post-communist eastern Europe it can be argued that participation in competitive elections is a major feature of party identity formation and the evolution of such organizations. Party competition is a prominent feature of the contemporary regimes that distinguishes them from the single-party dictatorships of the communist period and provides at the present juncture a natural focus of attention. Consideration of parties that are non-competitive is hardly of great interest here. At the present stage of east European party development, too, the distinction between party and interest group is a difficult one to draw and should not be over-emphasized.

Ranging beyond the question of definition, it must also be recognized that the very *concept* of party and its global scope is problematic. Surveys of parties on a general basis or within a particular region have not been common, and attempts to generalize about them on a comprehensive basis have encountered major conceptual problems. Reasonably stable, well-developed parties tend, quite simply, to be found in established liberal democracies and it is not clear that the parties identified in other contexts are quite the same kind of political institution. Some of the difficulties involved in such comparative exercises could be left to one side in the early stages. The first prominent modern, post-war overview by Maurice Duverger did not pay any attention to the countries that later came to be recognized as the Third World.[4] Leon Epstein was more aware of the problem of scope but acknowledged in his work that discussion of democratic party activity essentially concerned those nations that have participated actively in the 'special Euro-American development' of the last few centuries.[5]

Giovanni Sartori did pay attention to the largely unstructured party activity in Africa and some Latin American countries, although this largely served to emphasize the singularity of the European pluralist model. Von Beyme once more preferred to restrict his focus to parties in western democracies. More recently, Alan Ware has, quite reasonably, been unapologetic in continuing to direct close attention to parties in liberal democratic regimes – although in the context of the 1990s one of the five cases he considers is that of Japan. Discussion of political parties on a general basis has, then, tended to reinforce the focus on established democracies in Europe and associated countries in North America and Australasia. One important work shifted attention to the Third World and dealt with *Political Parties and Political Development*. It tended in this context, however, to emphasize the advantages of one-party regimes – a view that was very much of its time and of limited relevance to the study of parties in contemporary eastern Europe.[6]

In truth, the description and analysis of modern political parties remains rooted in the context of the established democratic regimes of the western world and is by no means necessarily the worse for that. It is certainly the prime reference point for party development in eastern Europe. The one-party regime that evolved within the Soviet dictatorship, and subsequently spread to other parts of Europe and the world, had little in common with the experience of liberal-democratic, competitive party politics. It does not now have a great deal to contribute to the general study of modern party politics.

But that does not mean that the west European and American origins of the party experience, as well as specific implications of the liberal-democratic context, should be ignored in a broader study. In a useful survey of activities outside the liberal-democratic heartland Vicky Randall deplores the prevalence of Euro-centrism and rigid concepts of what a political party should be.[7] The importance of the experience of established liberal democracies for party development and modern party practice overall cannot be ignored – but neither should the specific nature of some of the implications derived from that analysis. Established western practices might well provide the benchmark for modern party activity but, in the context of this study, it would be a mistake to expect the new democracies of eastern Europe either to replicate western models in any detail or to reproduce their party systems within a few years of the ending of dictatorship. Expectations of new democracies often reflect an idealized understanding of western experience and a faulty grasp of the important changes that many established democratic parties are undergoing.

A second major question of definition concerns the region itself. If the idea of the political party itself needs to be examined before being applied to the context of post-communist democracy, so that of eastern Europe also requires some elucidation. Any definition of eastern Europe is firstly, of course, a matter of geography – but also far more than that. The notion of eastern Europe, like that of Europe itself, carries a range of normative overtones and is often associated with particular values. For most of the post-1945 period the definition of the region was quite straightforward. The communist eastern Europe that emerged with the construction of the Iron Curtain was easily defined. From the late 1940s to 1989 it referred to the countries located to the east of the Federal Republic of Germany, Austria and Italy that did not form part of the Soviet Union.

With the removal of the Iron Curtain it now makes sense to revert to an earlier and broader view of eastern Europe – although one that still excludes European Russia, which merits separate treatment by virtue of the Eurasian status of the Russian whole, lingering remnants of its superpower status and special features that mark it off from the smaller countries closer to the democratic European mainstream. The eastern Europe at issue here is, therefore, quite simply defined. It consists of that part of Europe that cannot be described as western – a term with connotations not just geographical but also political (involving an established democratic order and in most cases membership of the European Union and NATO) and economic (capitalist countries with established market economies).

Contemporary eastern Europe thus includes most of post-communist Europe and major portions of the former Soviet Union. The coverage of this book extends to include the Baltic republics, characterized in any case by a firm identification with the countries of central Europe, as well as Moldova with its strong links with Romania. Although more distant from the European heartland, too, Ukraine and Belarus are also broadly European and their status remains reasonably distinct from that of Russia. But such definitions are also contentious and can be highly divisive in political terms. While few would argue with the borders of contemporary eastern Europe being extended to include parts of the former

Soviet Union, many citizens of the pre-1989 eastern Europe, particularly in Hungary, Poland, Slovenia and the Czech Republic, now wish to be known as inhabitants of central Europe, or at least east-central Europe. They have no wish to be identified with the population of any part of the former Soviet Union and assert a distinct cultural, political and economic identity closer to that of western Europe than the regions ruled directly from Moscow until the very end of 1991. Some of them may even feel downright insulted that their rapidly democratizing countries and developing party systems are covered in a book on eastern Europe. It is not the intention here to evoke any such response. My view is just that it is more useful to have a broad view of eastern Europe that encompasses all nineteen post-communist countries of Europe (with the exception of the more ambiguous case of Russia) and, for purposes of comparison and analysis, to direct attention to the marked political, social and cultural differences within that broad category. This survey of the new parties will in any case tend to be more strongly focused on the countries of central (or east-central) Europe that are closer to the west and where party development has generally been more advanced – and which are also countries where the process has been better documented.

It is not just the classification of the different sub-regions that is contentious but also their composition in terms of particular countries. My preferred grouping, and that which will be used throughout this book, distinguishes between the countries of:

• east-central Europe: Hungary, Poland, Slovakia, Slovenia and the Czech Republic;
• the Baltic states: Estonia, Latvia and Lithuania;
• the Balkans: Romania, Bulgaria, Albania and most of the countries of the former Yugoslavia (Bosnia, Croatia, Macedonia, Montenegro and Serbia);[8] and
• former Soviet republics: Belarus, Moldova and Ukraine.

Some political science texts have a slightly different focus. The central Europe examined by Attila Ágh in his recent text, for example, includes not just the countries I describe as east-central European but also Croatia.[9] In a further variant, Keith Crawford includes as constituent parts of east-central Europe all the countries of the former Soviet empire, and includes within it Albania, Bulgaria and Romania.[10] There is no general agreement on what constitutes contemporary eastern Europe or on how the countries that make it up should be grouped.

The classification proposed above is, in my view, somewhat more coherent than the other variants not just in geographical but also in political and economic terms. In line with most east-central European colleagues, indeed, it is difficult not to acknowledge also that these essentially geographical groupings also carry broader social significance. As listed in Table 1.1, the countries of east-central Europe are both further along the democratic path (Freedom Ranking) and richer (GDP per capita). After 1990, Slovenia, for example, rapidly left the 'Balkan' location of the former Yugoslavia to form part of a richer and more democratic east-central

Table 1.1 The countries of contemporary eastern Europe

	Freedom ranking, 1998–99	$GNP per capita, 1998	$GDP in 1998 (1989=100)	Unemploy- ment rate, 1996–97	Population, (millions)
Slovenia	1.5	9,976	104	7.3	1.987
Czech Republic	1.5	5,040	95	4.0	10.304
Hungary	1.5	4,510	95	8.7	10.153
Poland	1.5	3,900	117	11.3	38.650
Estonia	1.5	3,390	76	10.0	1.458
Lithuania	1.5	2,440	65	5.9	3.705
Latvia	1.5	2,420	59	18.3	2.470
Slovakia	2	3700	100	11.6	5.381
Romania	2	1,390	76	6.0	22.570
Bulgaria	2.5	1,230	66	13.7	8.310
Macedonia	3	1,290	72	42.5	1.983
Moldova	3	410	32	1.7	4.310
Ukraine	3.5	850	37	2.8	50.536
Croatia	4	4,520	78	13.4	4.572
Albania	4.5	810	86	15.0	3.324
Bosnia	5	300	–	72.5	3.738
Yugoslavia (Serbia/ Montenegro)	6	2,300	–	26.1	10.597
Belarus	6	2,200	78	2.8	10.215

Sources: Column 2, combined average ranking from 1 to 7 (A. Karatnycky, ed. *Freedom in the World: Annual Survey of Political Rights and Civil Liberties*, New York: Freedom House, 1999), Column 3, World Bank Report (at www. worldbank.org/cgi.bin), Column 4, European Bank for Reconstruction and Development: *Transition Report 1999* (London), Columns 5 and 6, UN Economic Survey of Europe (at www. unece.org/stats/trend/svn.htm).

Europe. In political terms, on the other hand, Slovakia moved away from the more advanced category. Following the break-up of Czechoslovakia it diverged from the broadly democratic path taken by other east-central European countries and continued to show (at least until the elections of 1998) some of the authoritarian characteristics of several of the Balkan and post-Soviet countries. Although former Soviet republics too, the Baltic states entered into fast-track democratization and maintained an economic lead over other former Soviet republics. It is reasonable, therefore, to place them in a separate category.

Contemporary international decisions reinforce the principles underlying this classification. In a further variant of sub-regional fine-tuning, the European Union expressed its own judgement on the pattern of political and economic development in eastern Europe in 1997 by identifying Estonia, Hungary, Poland, Slovenia and the Czech Republic as the countries best suited for early entry to an enlarged community. The fourfold subdivision of eastern Europe is therefore primarily geographical, but also political and economic in some of its broad implications – although these can only be regarded as loose and suggestive in a general sense.

A third, and final, point of definition needs to be added about the term 'post-communism'. This is used to refer to the period after 1989 (in the former eastern Europe) or after 1991 (in the former Soviet Union) when, in the first case, the exercise of Soviet power ceased to be effective and, in the second, the rule of Moscow or the Soviet communist party came to an end and the USSR disintegrated. There is, notes Leslie Holmes, 'no readily identifiable and reasonably specific ideology or even theory of post-communism'.[11] But then there is no particular reason why there should be. Post-communism is simply a condition that exists in countries that have sloughed off communist rule. This common history is indeed likely to leave the countries with important similarities in the immediate post-communist period, but they can be expected to diminish over time rather than forming a distinctive pattern of post-communist evolution. This is precisely what seems to happening in contemporary eastern Europe in terms of levels of democratization and diverging paths of economic development. Nevertheless, for many people the term does carry significant political overtones. The idea of the 'post-communist party' is often used to refer to organizations formed on the basis of former ruling parties not just in a descriptive or historical sense, but also with the distinct implication that they carry over some authoritarian baggage from the former period. In this book any judgements will be based on empirical analysis of the particular party, and the term 'post-communist' will be used in a straightforward descriptive and historical sense rather than in any evaluative way.

Historical background

1989 was a momentous year both for the countries of eastern Europe and the development of a democratic Europe as a whole. Its most striking image might well have been the opening wide of the heavily guarded gates set in the Berlin Wall and the eagerness with which Berliners set about its demolition with pick-axes and crowbars, but in the longer run it was a process of construction that would do most to determine how long and in what form this newly gained freedom would survive. It was not bricks and mortar that were primarily at issue. Central to the process was the building of new political institutions and the establishment of a diversity of parties capable of expressing the interests and aspirations of a modern population. A range of influences bore on the prospects for party development and the capacity of the countries of eastern Europe to produce stable party systems capable of sustaining new democratic systems. One important factor was the region's limited experience of liberal democracy and the relative weakness of party development before the onset of communist rule.

In distinction to the longer established democracies of the west, the newly independent countries of post-communist eastern Europe had little experience of multi-party democracy or the practice of pluralist politics. Even before World War II, when the major portion of contemporary Belarus and the Ukraine already formed part of the Soviet Union, most of the other countries of eastern Europe had little success in preserving or implementing the principles embodied in the democratic constitutions most of them had adopted after the end of the previous war in 1918. Czechoslovakia was the only exception in maintaining a fully democratic regime through to its demise with the Nazi invasion of the already weakened republic in March 1939. Democratic experience elsewhere was very limited, and the different kinds of constitutional order introduced throughout the region were rarely fully implemented.[12] The development of parliamentary democracy was abruptly curtailed in Bulgaria with the overthrow of the Stamboliiski government in 1923, in Poland after a coup d'état in 1926, and in Yugoslavia with the proclamation of a royal dictatorship in 1929. In Hungary there was little in the way of democratic development at all, the brief Soviet Republic of Béla Kun in 1919 being followed by a series of administrations under the overall supervision of Admiral Horthy until his removal in 1944. Apart from a brief extension of the franchise in 1920, the Hungarian electorate also remained restricted to 27.5 per cent of the adult population, so the limited degree of party competition was further restricted in its democratic reach in terms of popular representation.

Although early democratic aspirations – let alone practices – generally gave way to authoritarianism and varying degrees of dictatorship, the east European regimes were still distinct from the totalitarian system created in the Soviet Union. Political rule might well have been dictatorial and repressive in many cases, but it was by no means as tyrannical or monolithic as that established in Stalin's Russia. Unlike the situation within the resolutely one-party system installed in the Soviet Union, parties and elections did make some input to eastern Europe's public life and democratic processes retained some political significance. Thus, within the strongly monarchical system of rule that persisted in Romania, the National Peasant Party won a major electoral victory in 1928 and embarked on a series of reforms; Bulgaria, too, saw a People's Bloc of diverse party forces voted into power in reasonably free elections in 1931 to cope with the effects of the Depression. The Polish election of 1928 offered a fair degree of political choice and it was only after the passage of a new constitution and the death of Marshal Piłsudski in 1935 that dictatorial currents gained real strength. While the limits placed on party activity and the maintenance of a restricted franchise might mean that inter-war east European political life bore little resemblance to the practices of modern democracy and the party systems of the west, it at least saw a semblance of the institutional pluralism and competitive politics wholly absent from the territories that made up the Soviet Union.

As the region emerged from the ravages of the Nazi dictatorship after World War II, former parties were re-established and some features of party competition again came to the fore. Not surprisingly, the resurgence of party politics was more solidly based and longer lasting in Czechoslovakia, where the communist party gained a respectable 38 per cent of the vote in free elections held in 1946. Free elections were also held during November 1945 in Hungary, and here the communists gained a more modest 17 per cent and were soundly beaten by the anti-communist Smallholders' Party. In the region as a whole, though, the picture was a mixed one and the short phase of renewed pluralism more evident in some countries than in others. Party competition and organized opposition had little chance to develop in Romania, Bulgaria or Poland, where the Soviet Union had shown a strong determination to impose its political will from the outset. The power of non-communist forces during the short-lived coalition phase of post-war Hungarian political life was also soon sliced away by the 'salami' tactics famously adopted by the nation's communist leaders.

Soviet influence was less decisive for developments in Yugoslavia and Albania where the communist movement had stronger domestic roots. A Communist People's Front rapidly took control in Yugoslavia and gained 91 per cent of the vote in federal elections held during November 1945, with a negligible number of ballots being cast in a combined residual 'opposition' urn. Communist leader Josip Broz Tito enjoyed considerable political support as commander of the partisan forces that had played a major role in liberating the country, but he too had little sympathy for parliamentary democracy and no inclination to tolerate the activity of competing political parties. The three Baltic states and the republic of Moldova (which had formed part of pre-war Romania) remained in the possession of the Soviet Union, as they had briefly been before Germany's invasion of Russia in 1941, and thus saw no part of this brief phase of patchy pluralism in eastern Europe.

Such elements of democracy and party competition that had emerged were soon eliminated as Soviet forces strengthened their grip over the region. Even in Czechoslovakia, the tenuous phase of post-war pluralism only lasted until the communist coup of February 1948, by which time the consolidation of communist power had involved the elimination of all elements of liberal democracy elsewhere in the region. From that year on Soviet control was maintained over most of eastern Europe (Yugoslavia and Albania remained the exceptions) and communist party rule persisted without facing any institutionalized challenge until just before its demise with the Polish elections in 1989.[13] Popular revolt erupted on occasion, but no formal political opposition or alternative parties were ever permitted. The closest eastern Europe came to this was during the period of Solidarity's initial legal existence during 1980–81 in Poland, but the organization's leaders paid some lip-service to Soviet requirements and continued to insist that it was an independent trade union and not a political body.

Once more, though, political life in communist eastern Europe differed from the Soviet Union and the monolithic character of the Soviet system was never fully replicated. The worst excesses of totalitarian rule were only approached during the early years of communist rule before Stalin's death in 1953, and even then were never fully applied in a country such as Poland. Bulgaria, Czechoslovakia and Poland even had a range of formally established political parties, although the non-communist 'puppet' organizations had no political independence and were unable to act as an opposition or to contest elections (they stood on a joint platform with the communist party when the largely ritual elections were held). In further distinction to Soviet practice, a range of social institutions enjoyed considerable autonomy in some countries and exercised a corresponding degree of public influence. Diverse social, cultural and religious organizations were allowed to exist and, although not essentially political in character, they often exerted considerable public pressure and impinged on the political sphere, representing elements of pluralism within the overall uniformity of the communist system. The role of the Catholic Church in Poland was the most striking example of this tendency. Political life in eastern Europe was more diverse and consistently showed more signs of incipient pluralism than the Soviet Union, although still to a much lesser extent than in western Europe and other liberal democracies.

It was also underpinned by the existence of a more advanced, differentiated and generally freer society. A greater freedom of association and elements of a civil society both reflected and reinforced existing levels of national tradition and public awareness. This enabled some countries to sustain a relatively high degree of social independence in the face of the bureaucratic political monopoly embodied by the communist party. To varying degrees its influence also affected leading members of ruling communist bodies, who often showed more political acumen and greater sensitivity to the public mood than their senior comrades in the Soviet elite. There were overt signs of political pluralism within the party organization, which sometimes took the form of inner-party factionalism and further qualified the monolithic quality of communist party rule in eastern Europe.[14] This was most prominent in Hungary and, particularly, Poland where it undoubtedly contributed to the successive leadership crises and instability of communist rule in that country. Factional tendencies were less apparent in Czechoslovakia, although a movement for inner-party reform came dramatically to the fore in the developments that led to the Prague Spring of 1968. These features of east European communist rule helped prepare favourable conditions for pluralist party development when the regional political climate changed. Such experiences also strengthened the capacity of former ruling parties to transform themselves into social democratic bodies capable of acting with considerable political skill in the post-communist democracies.

The historical background for party formation and development in post-war eastern Europe in 1989 was, then, quite a differentiated one. None of the countries in the area had experienced democratic politics or the relatively free operation of independent parties during the preceding 40 years of communist rule, although background social conditions and the character of communist rule differed significantly throughout the region. The brief interregnum between Nazi dictatorship and the consolidation of communist rule had provided some opportunity for party activity. But in most countries this was very limited and even in a more positive case such as Czechoslovakia the period concerned was only short. It was only in that country that the 20 years or so of inter-war independence had seen the relatively successful operation of a democratic system and the conduct of party politics in ways that had tended to sustain effective government, contribute to political stability and maintain the integrity of a newly established multi-ethnic state. The inter-war experiences of the other independent states in the region were less conducive to the establishment of any kind of democratic tradition, but the experience of national independence itself helped create the basis for a modern political community and was generally a positive factor for subsequent processes of post-communist democratization. The experience of Belarus and Ukraine, most of whose territory had formed part of the Soviet Union from the outset, was quite different in this respect.

In these countries questions of state formation and primary definition of the political community were faced for the first time when the Soviet Union ended in 1991. This clearly impinged on processes of post-communist democratization and party development, as basic issues of civic identity and political representation had to be faced from the outset. There was little sense of such identity in Belarus and limited faith either in its statehood or capacity to develop as an autonomous political community, particularly on the part of its president, Aleksandr Lukashenka. Much of the early political agenda in independent Moldova was similarly dominated by issues of national identity and pressures to merge its territory with neighbouring Romania. In such cases questions of whether a state should exist at all crowd out those concerned with how it should develop and the objectives its government should pursue, matters that are the normal stuff of party politics. Ukraine showed more confidence about its national identity, but parties in the early phase of post-communist independence rarely spanned the divide between the western area that formed part of pre-war Poland and an east that was long ruled by Russia. Political life in Latvia and Estonia was similarly characterized by a major gulf between native inhabitants and the sizeable Russian population, which continued to act as a major obstacle to the formation of an inclusive political community.

Neither had all conflicts about the national bases of other east European states and the essential character of the political community been settled during the inter-war period of independence. Problems of state formation and political integration remained to dog the post-communist period in some areas. Many key problems of state formation and violently conflicting claims on the territories of eastern Europe had been placed on the agenda with the break-up of the Ottoman, Russian, German and Austro-Hungarian empires at the end of World War I but were never fully settled or, even by the end of the communist period, moved sufficiently down the political agenda to maintain anything more than a temporary political stability.[15] During the communist period such tensions were generally suppressed rather than brought to any clear resolution.

Questions surrounding the ethnic character of the inter-war state had been particularly prominent in Yugoslavia, where they were tackled with considerably less success than in Czechoslovakia. This had predictable consequences for the fate of the country's democratic regime, which collapsed in 1929, while nationality issues were also very prominent in Hungary, Romania and Poland. The fault lines that ran through the original Kingdom of Serbs, Croats and Slovenes at the time of its formation in 1918 (it only took the name Yugoslavia with the failure of the original regime in 1929) thus remained to dash any hopes of a peaceful post-communist transition in the early 1990s. Amongst the former Yugoslav republics it has only been post-1989 Slovenia, which is ethnically homogenous and thus not subject to the conflicts seen elsewhere, that has escaped the threat of inter-community violence and developed a reasonably effective party system to channel its conflicts and political tensions. Even Czechoslovakia, the unique success story of inter-war eastern Europe in terms of democratic development and the fairly harmonious relations between Czechs and Slovaks (although not with the Sudeten Germans), failed to survive once the straitjacket of communist rule was removed. But at least in this case it was properly conducted elections that helped define the nature of the issue, with constitutional procedures being followed when the federal state was dissolved at the end of 1992.

Processes of post-communist democratization and party development have thus been overlaid with unresolved problems of state formation and conflicting ethnic claims even where stronger democratic traditions existed and there was considerable experience of constitutionally based politics. The very definition of what a nationality was remained fluid in modern eastern Europe as different kinds of regime sought to identify their own social base.[16] State formation and the restructuring or consolidation of existing territorial units emerged as fundamental tasks to be confronted concurrent with those of democratization and regime change. Competing parties had little chance of emerging, as in the west, within reasonably well-established and constitutionally defined nation states. Historical conditions have not been particularly favourable to party development in many parts of the region and it is significant that it is in the countries of east-central Europe, where ethnic tensions are weaker and the problems of state formation and consolidation less pressing, that democratization and the development of party systems have made most progress.

The transition from communism

Aspects of more recent history have also shaped the political landscape of contemporary eastern Europe and helped create the conditions under which independent political parties have developed. The particular path from communism taken by individual countries and the nature of the transition to, in most cases, some form of democratic regime have been of particular importance. The origins of the transition from communism in eastern Europe can be traced to two major factors. One was the changing situation in the Soviet Union and shifts in Kremlin policy towards the region after leadership was assumed by Mikhail Gorbachev in March 1985. The second concerned the situation in eastern Europe itself and the changing context in which communist rule was exercised (discussion here refers to the countries of post-1945 eastern Europe which lay outside the borders of the Soviet Union).

The first factor was mostly related to the changing nature of Soviet influence within the region. Communist rule had been largely imposed by force of Soviet arms after World War II and maintained by the threat of military intervention in the years that followed (events in Hungary and Czechoslovakia in 1956 and 1968 respectively showed that the threat was not an empty one). But the conditions under which that rule was exercised changed significantly over the years.[17] The acquiescence of east Europeans in communist rule was increasingly achieved by a mixture of relative affluence and partial tolerance of political diversity. This, however, was an uncertain basis for Soviet dominance. The fate of independent forces in Poland during 1981 and the imposition of a domestically organized military regime showed both the restricted capacity of east European economies to buy popular acquiescence and the continuing limits of Soviet tolerance. It was the shift in policy under Gorbachev that prompted changes opening the way to fundamental political transformation and the regime change that spelt the end of Soviet-sponsored communist rule.

The 'new thinking' in the area of regional policy introduced by Gorbachev radically transformed the basis of communist rule in eastern Europe. His initial response to the general problems of economic stagnation and political alienation throughout the Soviet bloc was based on established principles of social discipline and central control. But within a few years of Gorbachev's accession to the leadership the Soviet position on eastern Europe changed from one of promoting modernization and reform through tighter regional integration to a more relaxed policy that permitted the various allies to choose their own path of development and a resignation from enforced orthodoxy. Military force had been used to support communist rule from the outset, but it soon became clear that Gorbachev had dispensed with this option. He did not seem to envisage the abandonment of communism, but neither was it fully ruled out. His initial view seemed to be that where it had been established communism had considerable potential for development in both economic and cultural terms. The problems and instability in eastern Europe that had emerged were, in Gorbachev's early view, attributed to 'miscalculations by the ruling parties' rather than to more fundamental causes.[18] First indications of elements of a new political approach were made known to some east European leaders as early as 1985, although the change in policy was only confirmed – and then just to leading officials – during the following year.[19]

But it took some time for the apparent shift in the Soviet approach to be reflected in the policies of the east European regimes, and more radical departures from established policy did not become apparent until 1988. The stakes after all were high – and there had been sincerely held hopes in Hungary of avoiding conflict with the Soviet Union in 1956, while the 1968 reform movement in Czechoslovakia had been carefully planned so as not to provoke Soviet intervention. There had, too, been real fears of Soviet forces invading to crush Solidarity's freedom in Poland during 1980–81, and the domestic imposition of martial law was often presented as an alternative to Kremlin action. East European leaders thus exercised considerable caution in testing the limits of Gorbachev's new policy. But pressures within eastern Europe were steadily growing as awareness of the relative failure of the communist economic model became widespread and various political shortcomings emerged as the subject of more open discussion. Forces of political opposition and more general social dissatisfaction had surfaced on occasion throughout the period of communist domination, but, in the final analysis, could always be constrained so long as Soviet forces were available to reinforce the domestic organs of repression. Short of these extreme measures it was the capacity of the communist system in eastern Europe to deliver economically that was counted on to maintain stability, defuse opposition and secure the persistence of the Soviet-sponsored regimes. By the mid-1980s major limitations in its capacity to achieve these objectives had become apparent.

It was failure in this area that emerged as the second main factor in the east European transition from communism. Economic slowdown accompanied the weakening of political authority in a looming crisis of the communist regime as a whole. Levels of socio-economic development had certainly risen over the decades and national wealth had greatly increased since the immediate post-war years of material devastation and widespread impoverishment. But increases in wealth and the maintenance of relative stability had not succeeded in generating much popular support for the east European regimes or in establishing their legitimacy. Several factors were responsible for the continuing unpopularity of the Soviet-sponsored regimes. One was the continuing example of western Europe and the democratic capitalist world more generally, where economic performance was far more impressive and the level of civic freedom considerably higher. Neither did the relaxation of dictatorship and repressive practices after Stalin's death in 1953 improve the situation much in this respect. Liberalization was too limited to satisfy popular demands but sufficient to permit freer communication and a degree of contact with the west that only made awareness of relative failure of the communist system that much sharper. The weakening performance of the east European economies and the failure of successive reform initiatives had the effect not just of underlining this contrast, but also of destroying the faith of much of the political establishment and leading cadres in the system they were administering. This had particular significance for the dynamism and survival potential of the elite-dominated dictatorships and contributed to the near-universal erosion of the ideology that was central to the operation and continuing survival of the regime.[20]

The problematic consequences of the communist model for patterns of economic development, particularly as it applied to eastern Europe, had been apparent at an early stage. Early corrections had been made in 1953, just after Stalin's death. But the changes permitted within the orthodox communist model were insufficient to ensure radical change and the relative status of the eastern economies had steadily worsened, leading to diverse outcomes in terms of substantial foreign indebtedness in the case of Hungary and Poland and a swingeing regime-imposed austerity programme in Romania. The policy that gradually took shape under Gorbachev opened up new possibilities for the stricken east European countries. Radical measures were first envisaged in Hungary and Poland, where what appeared to be a new framework of regional relations could be used to invigorate the flagging reformist impetus. More effective measures were envisaged to cope with the enormous foreign debts burdening the economy and the political resentment still reflected (at least in Poland) in significant underground opposition and free trade union activity. Elsewhere the radical nature of the Soviet changes was not fully recognized, or just ignored by ageing, conservative leaders with little interest in contemplating extensive long-term change. One early sign of change in the higher echelons of the east European political leadership was the unconventional replacement of Hungarian party leader Janos Kádár in May 1988 without direct Soviet involvement. This was a sign both of east European rejuvenation in the most literal sense and of the possibility of radical system change more generally. Such opportunities were soon taken up elsewhere.[21]

In Poland, further industrial strikes broke out in the summer of 1988 and again involved the participation of Solidarity activists. As the repression of the free trade union in 1981 had never been fully effective, the party leadership now felt able under Gorbachev's new regional dispensation to consider a more promising solution. They agreed to propose negotiations with Solidarity representatives about prospects for trade union pluralism and restoration of the organization's legal rights. Round-table negotiations were opened between union delegates and representatives of various opposition groups. Agreement between the different groups was reached early the following year on, among other things, the re-legalization of Solidarity (it was finally registered in April 1989) and elections in which at least some seats would be open to free competition. Partly because of miscalculations by the party leadership, but also to the growing swell of political opposition, the communist party failed to maintain its overall political dominance and Solidarity representative Tadeusz Mazowiecki was installed as prime minister in August 1989. At the beginning of the year and seeing the way the wind was blowing the Hungarian party elite, too, had already disavowed its traditional insistence on communist party leadership in February and also embarked on consultations with opposition forces. This resulted in a number of agreements that gained constitutional force in October 1989. Free elections were scheduled to be held in early 1990. In East Germany and Czechoslovakia opposition took longer to gain momentum, but once it got under way the established leadership and the communist elite quickly collapsed and the communist regime itself crumbled.

By the end of 1989, then, after initially cautious moves towards reform and regime change in Poland and Hungary, full-scale retreat from orthodox communism and a major process of transition had begun throughout eastern Europe. Change was slower to get under way in the Balkans, and its consequences were less decisive for the end of communist rule. In Bulgaria a more restricted path of change was followed as a place coup secured the dismissal of incumbent leader Todor Zhivkov in November 1989 and a reformist communist group assumed power. In neighbouring Romania, mass demonstrations preceded the overthrow and execution of the Ceausescus on Christmas Day, and their removal was followed by extensive fighting and sharp-shooting in the streets. In Albania, isolated from direct Soviet influence, it was only towards the end of 1990 that an alternative Democratic Party was founded and the possibility of free elections began to be contemplated (they were finally held in March 1991). Despite the very different pace and pattern of developments in Czechoslovakia, Hungary and Poland, a major overhaul of the political system was soon set in train and an extensive overhaul of the ruling elite occurred. In Bulgaria and Romania, however, power was not assumed by representatives of such an opposition. In Bulgaria it was primarily reform-minded groups within the party leadership, and in Romania a more ambiguous association of reformists in the party establishment and dominant military groups in broad opposition to the security apparatus (the Securitate).

The dynamics of political change in Yugoslavia were also different, and here the transition from communism to such forms of democratic or other forms of regime as finally emerged was set in a broader pattern of political transformation. As in the case of Poland, 1980 had been a major political turning point. The implications of Tito's death in May of that year had never been fully worked out as individual republics tended to pursue their own interests and the workings of the fragile federal economy led to increasing regional inequality, inflation and ethnic friction. The latter factor in particular was increasingly exploited by Serbian leader Slobodan Milošević. Starting in 1987 he increasingly directed Serbian frustration along ethnic lines, firstly against the Albanian population of Kosovo and then against the other Yugoslav republics in a bid to restore the federation's stability on the basis of Serbian supremacy. Rather than a transition from communism to an alternative political system, the strategy followed by Milošević represented more the effort of a communist leader to strengthen his power base by harnessing nationalism in pursuit of his ambitions.

But as it soon led to the break-up of the Yugoslav federation, with different consequences for the individual republics, it nevertheless spelt the demise both of the communist Yugoslavia that had been formed in 1945 and of any notion of orthodox communist rule in its constituent parts.[22] The transition from communism, such as it was, did not generally create the conditions for any viable form of pluralist political life. Only in Slovenia was a liberal democracy comparable with those in the north of the region established. Elsewhere Serbia and Croatia were soon at war, often on the territory of the Bosnian republic, and different forms of authoritarianism and political violence tended to thrive rather than any drive for democracy. Montenegro had few resources of its own and remained closely allied with Serbia in a rump Yugoslavia, whereas Macedonia – whose very existence and claim to independence as a nation-state was as much denied by its 'western' neighbour Greece as its former Yugoslav partners – succeeded only in maintaining a precarious stability, although it did manage to sustain several democratic features.

The dissolution of another federal state, the Soviet Union, provided the context for the course of regime change in the last group of countries. Again, there were significant differences within the group that made up the original union. The pressure for change was strongest in the Baltic states. They showed the greatest enthusiasm to escape from the rigours of Soviet control and pursue political reform, although independence and national liberation rather than democratization per se were the dominant objectives. The Baltic states had experienced national independence during the inter-war period and were only incorporated into the Soviet Union in 1940, just a year before Hitler's army launched its thrust to the east. Although limited in time, this experience of independent statehood contributed to a strong sense of cultural identity and national community. By 1988 national cultural associations were being formed, previously banned national flags were again flown and the Baltic languages were given official status. In 1989, Lithuania in particular (where the Russian population was far smaller than in Latvia and Estonia) was moving close to a final break with the Soviet Union, a process that gathered pace the following year.

The movement was still bitterly contested by some elements in the Soviet leadership during the first half of 1991. The greatest violence in the Baltic region took place in January 1991 when thirteen people died as Soviet troops stormed the television station in Vilnius, Lithuania's capital. In response, a national referendum to demonstrate the popular desire for independence was organized, although it failed to gain any positive response from the Soviet leadership. When Gorbachev was away on holiday in August 1991 a coup was launched by conservative elements in the leadership to hold back the course of change and prevent further loosening of the Soviet federation. It was badly conceived, poorly executed and gained little popular support, collapsing ignominiously within a few days. Its failure spelt the end of the Soviet state in December 1991, although the consequences for the Baltic states were more immediate. Independence was granted all three republics in September 1991 as soon as failure of the coup was confirmed.

Ukraine, Moldova and Belarus remained part of the Soviet Union until its demise at the end of the year although – as in the case of Russia itself – the transition from communist dictatorship began some time earlier.[23] Cultural, nationalist and human rights groups had begun organizing in Ukraine and were more developed than in most other Soviet republics although, unlike the situation in Russia, the Ukrainian Communist Party as a whole remained strongly conservative and resistant to most democratic tendencies. There were also significant divisions within the country, western Ukraine being more nationalist and subject to the influence of a relatively strong Uniate Church. Traditions of anti-Soviet separatism survived from the pre-war period (west Ukraine having formed part of inter-war Poland) in contrast to a more Russified east and south. A Democratic Bloc won significant representation, but not an overall majority in Ukraine's Supreme Council in the elections of March 1990, and at the time of the 1991 coup overall power was still in the hands of Leonid Kravchuk, a seasoned communist party leader. In line with the accelerating flow of events and the general tendency to escape from Moscow's control, though, he led Ukraine along a clearly nationalist – if relatively moderate – path of development towards full independence.

Belarus and Moldova developed far less of an opposition movement than either Ukraine or the Baltic republics and produced few pressures for democratic change. Belarus had virtually no separate national identity and remained resolutely committed to Moscow. Even when the end of the Soviet Union was formally declared at the end of 1991, much of the Belarussian population was not ready to accept the divorce from Moscow or envisage the creation of an alternative regime – let alone one that contemplated the development of a liberal society that was governed on democratic principles. Moldova, too, was firmly Russified and the pace of early change slow, although a democratic nationalist current became prominent in 1989 and a reform faction strengthened within the CP.

The character of the transition from communist rule within eastern Europe was therefore highly differentiated and the progress made towards liberal democracy quite diverse – if any movement at all towards such a general goal could be identified or even realistically conceived. Movements of democratic opposition were far stronger in some countries than others and, while the pace of political change accelerated throughout the region, the direction in which it was heading and the objectives of key players were by no means easily defined. What was at least clear was that the system of orthodox communist rule – essentially that created by Stalin and only modified rather than transformed since his death in 1953 – had been changing fast and completely fell apart in the wake of the failed Soviet coup of August 1991. This created a wholly new political situation, whose consequences were quite uncertain.

The course of post-communist transition in which the process of party development was set was a complex one. The context of post-communist party development was historically specific, but in many ways remained quite fluid. Independent parties did not emerge, as in the west, within reasonably well-established and constitutionally defined nation-states. In broad terms the transition was in fact a triple one,[24] as alongside the substitution of democratic rule for communist dictatorship and the reformation – or in some cases – establishment of new state structures there was also the parallel need to dismantle what remained of the former command economy and construct almost from scratch a capitalist market system. This broad transformation had profound effects throughout eastern Europe. Existing economic processes were severely disrupted and most countries experienced a major drop in national wealth during the critical period of political change while unemployment levels rose (see Table 1.1). This put further strain on east European political life.

The pattern of radical political change that emerged in the transition had its deepest roots in non-Soviet eastern Europe. The immediate impetus for change had come from the Soviet Union with Gorbachev's increasingly determined revision of both domestic and foreign policy. But it was not in the Soviet Union that the move away from communism progressed with greatest speed or was guided by the strongest commitment to democratic objectives. As the pressures for change built up throughout the region, different conditions for the subsequent process of post-communist change and pluralist party development had been created in different countries. The struggle to maintain some form of communist rule that sought to accommodate the diverse national pressures with what were understood to be the continuing requirements of the Soviet leadership created a range of new political relations within the east European regimes during the 1980s. As Gorbachev's new thinking evolved and it became clear how far political change could now be taken, such arrangements rapidly became transformed into different models of transition from orthodox communist rule.

In Hungary and Poland a reform movement was well established in the communist party, and transition progressed through negotiation and the conclusion of political pacts between representatives of opposition forces and the communist establishment. Where the ground was not prepared in this way the mass opposition that erupted in 1989 led straight to the collapse of the communist regime and the wholesale substitution of the communist leadership, as happened in Czechoslovakia and East Germany. In the less developed Balkan countries the later start of the transition process involved more limited initial change (Bulgaria, Romania, Albania). It is possible, therefore, to identify a wide range of transitions in terms of negotiation (Poland), evolution (Hungary), transition jump-started by implosion or collapse (Czechoslovakia), change under conditions of moderate violence (Romania), or violent transition with ethno-linguistic conflict and territorial separation (Yugoslavia).[25]

Such structural differences between the east European countries can also be related to the broad models of democratic transition derived from south European and Latin American experience. Where authoritarian regimes are confronted and roundly defeated by opposition forces (as happened in Portugal during 1974), transition takes place through rupture or replacement. Where existing regimes retain considerable power and are able to guide the processes of reform, the process is one of transaction or transformation (Spain and Brazil being major cases here). It is also possible to identify an intermediate mode of extrication or transplacement in which the rules of the authoritarian regime are abandoned but governments retain sufficient power to preserve some of their advantages and negotiate a political retreat.

A model of east European change can be drawn up on this basis, with Bulgaria and Romania experiencing regime transformation rather than replacement, and Hungary and Czechoslovakia seeing a more clear-cut dismantling of the old regime. Against a background of lengthy conflict with the Solidarity movement in Poland and an early decision to initiate round-table negotiation while the structures of communist power remained intact, the Polish transition was best defined as a process of extrication.[26] The mode of transition has major consequences for later developments, the formation of new parties and the nature of the parties in the course of further evolution. The sharper break with the communist regime in Hungary and Czechoslovakia provided a firmer base for pluralist party formation. More evolutionary processes of transformation or extrication, on the other hand, created conditions for the survival of authoritarian forces within partially reformed socialist parties with greater potential to block the emergence of a coherent opposition.

Democratization and parties: comparative perspectives

Political parties did not play a major part in the institutional framework within which the critical changes of the early democratization period took place, nor were they prime movers in the initial phase of political transition. The early dynamic behind the reform measures that paved the way for eventual regime change came from a policy shift within the Soviet leadership, a move that elicited a decisive elite response in some east European countries and significant mass action in others – or varying mixtures of the two in different countries. Parties of a pluralist nature – i.e. those distinct from a communist party establishment that was solely concerned with the exercise of monopoly power – were generally absent and, in most countries, none had been formed at all.

Signs of their emergence were most clearly evident in Hungary, where opposition currents were able to coalesce at an early stage. A Hungarian Democratic Forum was established as early as September 1987, and it was registered as a party in 1988. It would be misleading, though, to draw a direct line from the founding meeting of 1987 to the party system of post-communist Hungary or to identify this organization too closely with the party that formed the democratic government of 1990. Members of alternative opposition groups as well as representatives of the reform wing of the ruling party were also present, and the gathering was very much one composed of those opposed to the orthodox ruling establishment as a whole. The 1987 meeting in Hungary was followed in 1988 by the emergence of other associations that soon took the form of more formally organized political groups, as well as the resurrection of the former, 'historic' parties. Signs of pluralism were also increasingly evident on the establishment side, as the Hungarian Socialist Workers' (communist) Party renounced its claim to permanent leadership and declared for the development of a multi-party system, in which leaders of the reformist wing felt their chances of survival and political victory to be quite strong.[27]

The Hungarian pattern of evolutionary regime change in which a range of organized groups began emerging at such an early stage was unique. Elsewhere in eastern Europe evidence of tendencies suggestive of party development were largely absent, which was not surprising in view of the general weakness of democratic forces at this stage. In most countries there was no legal provision for the registration of independent parties and, under the continuing practices of communist dictatorship, spontaneous party formation on the basis of free association also remained out of the question. Measures of liberalization and the steps taken towards democracy were elite-led in most countries and often a response to developments in countries such as Poland and Hungary that led the movement away from authoritarianism.

Parties, indeed, generally formed after or during the first elections rather than preceding these fundamental democratic initiatives or playing much of a role in channelling the pressures that led to them being held at all. Even in Poland, where the liberalization of communist rule paralleled that of Hungary and Gorbachev's initiatives met an equally positive political response, there was little inclination amongst those active in the opposition to embark on party formation. The party leadership agreed in principle during August 1988 to open negotiations with the opposition, but it was not until January 1989 that they actually got going.[28] It was finally agreed to allow Solidarity to register legally as an independent trade union and the movement, mostly operating underground since 1981, took on a public identity after registration in April 1989. The round-table negotiations provided for a measure of electoral choice, and the communist leadership agreed to leave 35 per cent of seats in the legislature open to competition in June 1989. Nevertheless, the Citizens' Committees set up to organize non-party, opposition forces were identified wholly with Solidarity as an independent trade union and social movement and explicitly excluded the small groups and proto-parties already in existence.[29] Some years on, the resistance to party activity was no less strong in Ukraine, where political change took far longer to get under way. As late as 1994, when the independent state's first elections were held, the majority of votes cast went to independent candidates and only 34 per cent were cast for those standing on a party platform.

It was the social movement and broadly-cast umbrella organization that was the most prominent form within which the new opposition and infant democratic forces situated themselves throughout eastern Europe. This was to a large extent a response to the overwhelming dominance of the east European political space by the communist party and the monopolistic system of rule it maintained in each of the east European countries. It was a natural consequence of the way in which opposition formed and was able to operate within the tightly constructed institutional edifice of the Soviet-designed system. The only political opposition that could emerge was primarily one of society against the state, and its organization took the form of social informality in contrast to the officialdom and patterns of authority set by party bureaucracy. The general absence of political parties was a characteristic feature of the transition from communism in eastern Europe, and this initial condition raises questions about the subsequent role of parties in the democratization of the region.

Parties may be central to the operation of a modern democracy, but they are by no means always necessary for the establishment of a democratic order and have not been major agents in all transitions. Different views have been expressed on this issue, but that of Gábor Tóka is quite unequivocal: 'Historically, political parties have played little or no role in transitions to democracy, and the case of Eastern Europe has been no different'.[30] The pre-eminence of parties in any particular case owes much to the way democratization develops and the extent to which other actors have been excluded from or discredited by the previous authoritarian experience. Political parties came to dominate the process in Italy after World War II partly because they mobilized within the resistance movement and grew gradually stronger as the institutions that operated under the fascist regime progressively weakened. They were considerably less prominent in Spain some 30 years later, not least because of the existence of other areas of stability such as the monarchy or statesmen who were able to transcend lines of party division and lacked particular institutional affiliation.[31]

If, too, democratization is understood as the overall process of regime change that embraces both the transition to liberal democracy and its subsequent consolidation, parties may be considerably more central to the consolidation phase than to the earlier transition period. G. Pasquino has indeed robustly stated 'Not all the processes of transition have been party dominated; but all processes of democratic consolidation have indeed been party dominated'.[32] He is not the only one to stress the importance of stable party systems for the consolidation of a new democracy.[33] Final judgement on consolidation and the role of east European parties in this respect is still some way off, but it is clear that their role in the earlier stage of transition from communism was indeed limited.

From a preliminary survey of the role of the democratization process and the restricted nature of their contribution to the early stages of transition, the question also arises of whether conditions in eastern Europe have been particularly unfavourable to the emergence and development of political parties. Several characteristics of transition and democratization in post-communist countries can be distinguished, some of which have a particular bearing on party development. Five ways in which the challenges confronting post-communist countries differed from those faced by other authoritarian regimes during the process of democratization have been identified.[34] They are:

- high levels of ethnic complexity which produce separate communities claiming special political rights within a given territory and impede the emergence of an authentic civil society;
- a relatively high level of socio-economic and industrial development that was nevertheless rooted in old-fashioned and generally dysfunctional structures devised by former Soviet leaders;
- the dual-track nature of post-communist transitions, involving the simultaneous attempt to construct both pluralist democracy and a market economy (in some cases a triple transition was also clearly involved);
- the influence of the international environment, which may be relatively strong but is also more uncertain and potentially unfavourable for democratic transition than it was, for example, for the countries of southern Europe during the 1970s under Cold War conditions; and
- doubts about the resilience of civil society in eastern Europe and the capacity of political and social organizations to act responsibly within an established institutional framework.

Some of these features have already been identified as characteristic of the transition from communism, and they are also likely to have specific consequences for party development. There were few ethnically complex societies with sharp lines of division in the 'third wave' democratization in southern Europe and Latin America. Their presence in some parts of eastern Europe, and particularly the Balkans, provides fertile soil for the emergence of ethnically defined parties that fuel bitter political or physical conflict that sometimes cannot be contained within a single state structure at all.

Other features, such as the dual-track nature of the east European transitions that combine regime change and economic transformation at a relatively high level of socio-economic development, leave an extensive if outmoded infrastructure to overhaul and wide-ranging welfare expectations to cope with. These are likely to have less direct influence on the actual role of parties than major consequences for the specific content and direction of party activity. The context of marketization thus produces a range of socio-economic groups with divergent interests and expectations that do not correspond to the distinctive political cleavages and range of parties generally seen in western democracies.[35]

The international context of the east European transitions and the region's close links with western Europe have also been influential. The global economic context has had increasing importance, whereas the impact of the Cold War political divisions that had an effect on party alignments in the new democracies of earlier periods was now absent. It is likely that western Europe has exerted a particular influence on developments in the post-communist democracies. Growing popular disillusion with traditional parties and declining support for them in established democracies during the 1980s may well have strengthened the general east European antipathy to the political party and contributed to the formation and growing strength of the social movement or free-standing interest groups. Non-party human rights groups and single-issue movements such as that for European Nuclear Disarmament took special care to establish links with groups in eastern Europe and exerted an influence on the growth of opposition in the 1980s. After the critical events of 1989, though, the established parties of western Europe and the international organizations associated with them offered considerable (although largely undocumented) material and technical support.[36]

But of the five features identified, it is the relative weakness of civil society that emerges as one of the most important conditions for party development. The critical factor here seems to be not so much the development or preservation of spheres of social autonomy, but more their capacity to interact and co-ordinate activity in a relatively spontaneous and unconstrained fashion within the framework of a liberal-democratic system. In this the somewhat paradoxical role of civil society in eastern Europe assumes considerable importance. Apparently resilient enough in some areas to withstand the depradations of communist rule and stand up to the authoritarian state, it has also been argued that it provides only a weak base for institutional development and the establishment of effective political organizations. This observation corresponds directly with observed contrasts between southern Europe and Latin America in terms of democratization and the development of parties as components of a consolidated democratic system. The more solid start of the south European transitions in relation to those in Latin America has been directly linked to the differing configuration of civil society in the two regions and its greater strength in southern Europe.[37]

An equally little developed civil society in eastern Europe, associated with relative backwardness in terms of socio-economic development and its archaic industrial structure, may well contribute to the continuing weakness of party development. The wealthier countries have certainly enjoyed more favourable conditions in this respect. As a fairly exceptional case, the vigour with which the developed Czech Republic emerged from the stringencies of post-1968 normalization and proceeded with the construction of a relatively robust party system underlines the importance of a context of social modernity in sustaining the framework of civil society. Firm conclusions about the role of civil society in democratization and party development are nevertheless difficult to establish, partly because of the broadness of the concept and the ambiguities inherent in most definitions. Even where civil society is relatively strong, for example, it is by no means clear that it always strengthens democratic tendencies and sustains stable processes of party government.[38] But in broad terms the relative weakness of civil society in eastern Europe is likely to have had a negative impact on the prospects of democratic party government.

The position of civil society in eastern Europe has by no means been the only point of difference from other regions identified with respect to party development. Specific factors of state structure are also involved. The authoritarian regime within which the transition began was distinctive in that it contained strong elements of a totalitarian structure in contrast to the corporatist systems that predominated in early cases of transition like Spain and Brazil.[39] The totalitarian institutions around which the communist political system was organized were arguably less favourable to the compromises and political pacts that fostered democratization processes elsewhere. The experience of eastern Europe beyond the borders of the Soviet Union was different from that engendered by the classic examples of totalitarian development such as China and the Soviet Union, although only in Poland was there any kind of institutionalized societal organization in the form of Solidarity and the Church. Even in this case anti-communist forces grouped very much within a social movement rather than forming an institutional opposition. It was, arguably, an outcome decidedly less favourable to the development of strong organization and the emergence of an institutionalized leadership that could negotiate effective pacts and regulate the processes of regime change. The weak organizational capacity inherent in east European communist society deriving from the established state structure has therefore also been identified as a factor holding back party development and processes of democratization more generally.

The nature of the communist state in cases like Hungary and Poland nevertheless diverged considerably from that implied by the classic totalitarian model. Specific forms of national development in eastern Europe militated against the strong impact of the totalitarian tendencies implicit in communist rule. Their relative weakness encouraged more liberal forms of party leadership and affected the degree of unity it was able to maintain in the face of social pressures. These were factors that favoured the emergence of opposition, facilitated a process of differentiation within it and assisted the formation of independent groups. Opposition unity and the maintenance of a strong umbrella organization was encouraged in situations where the communist party was perceived as united and strong rather than fractionalized and split in groups with different policy approaches.[40] This was certainly true of Czechoslovakia and East Germany on one hand and Hungary on the other, although the fractionalized nature of the Polish party by no means prevented opposition unity during the critical phase of transition in that country. In that case, however, the main vehicle of political change in the form of Solidarity was formed in 1980 under quite different political conditions and in a regional context of determined Soviet supremacy that may well have formed strong behavioural patterns that persisted through to the end of the decade.

In truth it must be acknowledged that national tradition and historical experience created considerable diversity throughout eastern Europe both during the communist period and the democratization that has succeeded it. The shared experience of communist rule provided a similar starting point, but national characteristics played a very important part. A comparative perspective suggests that conditions for party development in eastern Europe were not particularly favourable, although opportunities for novel forms of organization and diverse political initiatives have not been lacking. The rapid collapse of the communist system left a relatively unstructured political space in which a wide range of responses to the challenge of democratic rule emerged and different kinds of party have been able to form. The application of different models of party to east European developments may be useful in helping to grasp the nature of change in this context. The understanding of post-communist politics will benefit from analysis of the extent to which the new forms of party politics follow west European patterns and models derived from the experience of established western democracies.

Early observation, for example, suggested that the mass democratic party that has been so influential in the west was unlikely to provide a dominant model of post-communist development.[41] This was a theme that had certainly dominated much early analysis of west European development.[42] But, as in western democracies, and established democracies more generally, the model of a mass membership party that played such a large part in early theoretical discussion of the political party now appears increasingly to be rooted in the experience of the nineteenth century, and was of decreasing relevance to the democratic politics of the late twentieth century either in the east or west. The weak links of many new parties with well-defined social groups and the increasingly professional approach taken to the critical task of winning elections suggest the growing association of east European parties with variants of the catch-all and electoral-professional party.[43] Strong dependence on the state and its financial resources have equally directed attention to the recently launched concept of the cartel party.[44] Such conceptual issues will also inform the analysis pursued in this book and contribute to the comparative perspective taken on the development of the new parties in post-communist eastern Europe.

2 Party origins and party development

Parties and movements in the founding elections

Parties are only one amongst a range of political actors in post-communist systems, and they have by no means always been the most important ones. They were largely absent in the early stages of change and political transition in eastern Europe, and their role has been still further limited in the countries less advanced in the process of democratization. There was still only a 'fledgling multi-party system' fragmented into thirty-eight parties in Ukraine after the 1994 elections.[1] Many deputies remained unaffiliated to any party. Neither did the ongoing struggle of the Belarussian parliament with the strongly authoritarian tendencies of President Lukashenka provide a helpful framework for party development, and most of the new deputies elected at the end of 1995 in that country were registered as independents. These areas of the former Soviet Union stood at the low-point of the scale for party development in eastern Europe.

But neither did parties develop much more robustly elsewhere. A distinct situation of 'overparticization' was identified in east-central Europe but this, paradoxically, reflected the very weakness of parties as their leaders have assiduously tried to dominate the formal political space precisely because of their parties' slender organizational resources and shallow roots in society.[2] Party development in eastern Europe has generally been slow and the early processes of transition were clearly dominated by other forces such as social movements and the umbrella organizations associated with them. Movements do not necessarily fall outside the electoral and office-seeking definition of parties proposed in the Introduction (Chapter 1), but they tend to share a number of features (particularly those that tie them more to symbolic political representation than power-seeking) that distinguish them from the structurally developed party as it evolved in the west.[3]

Elections have been particularly important in eastern Europe's democratization, not just because of their obvious role in helping to choose the most popular candidates for major political positions in newly established pluralist systems, but also by establishing the democratic credentials of the post-communist states, helping them acquire legitimacy in the eyes of the international community, and providing the context for early party development. But, because of their relatively late emergence and the dominance of less formally organized movements, parties were not generally major forces in the historic 'founding' elections of post-communist Europe, even if their role was a greater one in later stages.

The Polish elections of June 1989 occupied an ambiguous place at the beginning of the sequence in this respect and, while they undoubtedly set the ball rolling in terms of ultimately leading to the replacement of communist rule with a pluralist order, they were not even contested by the small number of parties already in existence. There was nevertheless a strong element of competition, not just for the 35 per cent of legislative seats formally open to non-party candidates but also for others not filled on the first ballot, although the actual electoral battle was fought by the placement of the communist establishment and candidates of the Solidarity movement rather than by representatives of independent parties. In this situation Solidarity remained intimately related to the communist order, if only by defining its identity primarily with reference to the Soviet-backed antagonist and adopting a stance of vehement opposition towards it. The 'High Noon' poster stuck up throughout Poland by Solidarity activists portrayed the election very much as the final showdown with Soviet communism that the election turned out to be. In this sense the 1989 election was as much a contest between forces generated by communism as one between the pluralist forces characteristic of a liberal-democratic system. It was this hybrid and unique election that led to the collapse of communist rule not just in Poland, but also throughout eastern Europe. From early 1990 a sequence of less constrained 'founding' elections was held throughout eastern Europe, although by no means all of them saw the immediate defeat of communist forces (see Table 2.1).

The first free election in an independent post-communist state took place during mid-March 1990 in East Germany (a country not generally covered in this book as unification with the Federal Republic later that year took the former Soviet dependency out of eastern Europe altogether), and was soon followed by the second in Hungary at the end of the month. It was contested by the several major parties founded in 1987–88 as the liberalization of east European politics gathered pace: the Hungarian Democratic Forum (HDF), Alliance of Free Democrats (AFD) and League of Young Democrats (FIDESZ).[4] The Socialist Party, founded after the dissolution of the communist party, as well as two historic parties – the Independent Smallholders' and Christian Democratic People's Party (reactivated or refounded respectively in 1988 and 1989) – also participated. All of them, together representing three different types of party – some newly formed, others revived from the past, and one built on the former ruling party, won seats in the new parliament.

It was only in the exceptional case of Hungary that communist leaders had the region foreseen and accepted the installation of a democratic pluralist system in eastern Europe and took measures in the early weeks of 1989 to facilitate its birth – on the assumption that they would soon be able to play a leading political role within the new framework. Much of the leadership elsewhere in eastern Europe either failed to recognize the extent of the change that was in the making or resolutely set their face against it, neither approach providing much in the way of conditions for pluralist party development. Nationalist candidates in the Baltic

Table 2.1 First liberalized or multi-party elections in the countries of eastern Europe

4 June 1989	Poland	Semi-democratic elections held as outcome of round-table talks, with 35 per cent of seats in lower house open to competition.
24 February 1990	Lithuania	Competitive elections held within continuing framework of USSR (republican commitment to a multi-party system from December 1989).
25 February 1990	Moldova	Competitive elections to Supreme Soviet in most of republic's constituencies.
18 March 1990	Estonia	Independence pressures less strong than in Lithuania, but relatively free competition in elections to Supreme Soviet in Estonia.
18 March 1990	Latvia	Independence pressures less strong than in Lithuania, but relatively free competition in elections to Supreme Soviet and Latvia.
25 March 1990	Hungary	First democratic, multi-party elections – preceded in former Soviet Europe only by East Germany (18 March).
8 April 1990	Slovenia	Effectively democratic multi-party elections, although independence not yet declared.
22 April 1990	Croatia	First competitive, multi-party elections.
20 May 1990	Romania	First multi-party elections.
8 June 1990	Czechoslovakia	Democratic, multi-party elections.
10 June 1990	Bulgaria	First multi-party elections.
9 November 1990	Macedonia	Competitive, multi-party elections.
18 November 1990	Bosnia	Competitive, multi-party elections.
9 December 1990	Serbia	Competitive, multi-party elections.
9 December 1990	Montenegro	Competitive, multi-party elections.
31 March 1991	Albania	First multi-party elections.
27 October 1991	Poland	Fully democratic multi-party elections.
20 September 1992	Estonia	First democratic election as independent state.
25 October 1992	Lithuania	First democratic election as independent state.
5 June 1993	Latvia	First democratic election as independent state.
27 February 1994	Moldova	First democratic election as independent state.
27 March 1994	Ukraine	Democratic election with some features of party competition.
14 May 1995	Belarus	Formally democratic elections with limited elements of party competition.

states, too, had achieved considerable success in elections to the Congress of People's Deputies in March 1989 held throughout the Soviet Union, and the popular fronts of the three countries exercised a major influence on the outcome of the republican elections held in February and March 1990. Considerable influence was also exerted by the Moldovan Popular Front in that republic's elections. But a full transition to democracy in the republics of the Soviet Union only occurred after the coup of August 1991 and the emergence of independent states within the framework of the former federation.

Between the two rounds of the Hungarian elections a ballot was held in Slovenia. Although independence was not formally declared until October 1991, the elections were indicative of the strong currents supporting the formation of an independent, democratic Slovenian state. Links between the republics of the Yugoslav federation had weakened considerably after Tito's death in 1980, and the national communities had become more diverse both in economic and political terms. Amongst the republics of the surviving federation Slovenia was notable for being a highly developed and westernized republic and had visibly developed a 'civil society more vibrant than any other in the entire communist world'.[5] On this basis, the development of independent political parties was considerably advanced and 55 per cent of votes were cast for the Democratic Opposition (DEMOS), a centre-right coalition of six parties. Unlike the situation in Poland and Hungary (and for that matter East Germany), the Slovenian election did not produce an outcome suggesting the overwhelming preponderance of anti-communist sentiments among the electorate – in the sense of a rejection both of the former regime and those most closely associated with it. In a contest held at the same time as the legislative elections the incumbent republican president, Milan Kučan, was returned to the post by a comfortable majority and a process of effective cohabitation set in train.

Elections were also held in neighbouring Croatia 2 weeks later. Party development was considerably less advanced there and had only got under way in 1989. Nationalist sentiments were also very strong in the ethnically mixed republic, directed primarily against Serbia and its domination of the Yugoslav federation. Here, too, a six-party coalition (the Croatian Democratic Union) won the election. In contrast to Slovenia, the communists won a sizeable share (35 per cent) of the vote, boosted to a significant extent by the support they gained from the minority Serb population. Free elections were held in most of the now fully independent states of eastern Europe the same year, and their outcome also showed that links with the officially defunct communist system were by no means fully severed.

Romania held its elections in May and, in an apparent reflection of the earlier victory of the Solidarity movement in Poland rather than the success of the more differentiated and formally constituted parties in Hungary, returned candidates of a National Salvation Front in a striking majority with 66 per cent of the vote. Founded amidst the tumult of the preceding December, however, apparently just after the execution of the Ceausescus, its political identity was quite ambiguous. The NSF was dominated by former senior communists and military personnel and led by Ion Iliescu and Petre Roman (formally elected as president and prime minister respectively in May 1990), who had occupied equivalent interim leading roles as soon as the overthrow of Ceausescu's personal dictatorship had been achieved in December 1989. But it also presented itself as the authentic representative of revolutionary forces, calling for the introduction of political democracy and pluralism as well as the separation of powers on an effective constitutional basis.[6]

In accordance with its original claim to be a revolutionary force the NSF declared that it would not turn itself into a political party or compete in the forthcoming elections, a position it soon retreated from. Conditions in Romanian society at this stage were not at all conducive to party development and the NSF faced little effective challenge (although 80 parties and other political groups actually competed in the May contest), leaving it free to win the election with a sweeping majority. The most effective opposition to the NSF was mounted by the Hungarian Democratic Union of Romania, which nevertheless received no more than 7 per cent of votes in the election. An even smaller proportion of votes was taken by the two 'historic' parties revived in time for the May election: the National Liberal Party and the Christian Democratic National Peasants' Party.

Elections followed in Czechoslovakia during early June. As in Poland, a broad anti-communist front in the guise of Civic Forum (in the Czech lands) and Public Against Violence (in Slovakia) won 46 and 47 per cent of the vote respectively for the two chambers of the Federal Assembly (although this translated into effective majorities of 58 and 55 per cent of seats). In contrast to Solidarity traditions in Poland, Civic Forum itself had only been formed as an opposition alliance in November 1989 and had little chance to build on grass-roots support or develop any broader form of organization prior to the collapse of communist rule, although this did little to hamper its initial electoral success. In keeping with its strong inter-war and immediate post-war record, the communist party still managed to secure 14 per cent of the vote and came out just in front of the allied Christian Democratic Union and Christian Democratic Movement – the latter emerging as a particularly strong force in Slovakia. Other smaller opposition groups were based on the regionally-oriented Society for Moravia and Silesia and the Slovak National Party.

The final election in the sequence held in the region of former Soviet domination during the first half of 1990 was that in Bulgaria where, with considerably less ambiguity than in Romania, the Bulgarian Socialist Party (created directly out of the former ruling communist party in April 1990) won 47 per cent of the vote in June elections. The main opposition was mounted by a United Democratic Front, organized in December 1989 on the lines of Solidarity and Civic Forum to group together the diverse anti-communist forces, but unlike its parallels in Poland and Czechoslovakia, it achieved – with 38 per cent of the vote – neither an electoral nor a more general political victory.

Democratization and pluralist development was significantly slower in Yugoslavia's southern republics than in Slovenia. When the first round of multi-party elections in Macedonia and Bosnia-Herzegovina were held in November 1990, the overwhelming issue was still the fate of the federal union. Conditions in neither republic were conducive to the development of democratic institutions and procedures. Macedonia was extremely poor and generally backward, whereas Bosnia had experienced the rule of a particularly conservative communist leadership. Ethnic considerations were ominously prominent in both cases, with the division in Bosnia between Muslims, Serbs and Croats being directly translated into relations between the three leading party groups in the new parliament.

Macedonia's national identity and political status was no less contested and the fate of the territory it now occupied had been a major bone of contention as far back as the Balkan wars of 1912–13, the attention of neighbouring Greece still being sharply focused on the issue. In this context it was not very promising that a majority of seats was won by a party standing as the Internal Macedonian evolutionary Organization (IMRO), as a similarly named organization had reaked terroristic havoc in the Balkans in the inter-war period and bedevilled, in particular, Bulgaria's precarious steps towards constitutional government in the 1920s. But, in fact, a reasonable degree of political stability survived under President Gligorov in post-communist Macedonia, and it was Bosnia that fell prey to the resurgence of violence initially mounted by Serbs against sovereign Bosnian (and, by now, necessarily Muslim) authority.

If the hold of former communists over the levers of power had remained strong in Romania and Bulgaria, elements of continuity were even more pronounced in Serbia. While multi-party elections were held during December 1990, political control of the republic remained firmly in the hands of ex-communist Milošević. Even if the election itself was conducted fairly (which is open to some doubt), alternative forces and independent parties had little chance to organize although nearly a hundred separately constituted parties contested it.[7] They were, however, subject to major restrictions in terms of campaign activity and media access. Growing Serbian nationalism also ran in Milošević's favour and his reconstituted Socialist Party won 194 of the parliament's 250 seats. Elections in Montenegro, traditionally the Yugoslav republic politically closest to Serbia, were also held in December. Here, too, the orthodox League of Communists won 83 of the 125 seats in the National Assembly, although at the beginning of 1989 a significant degree of renewal had taken place within the party as a new and more reform-minded generation established itself in the leadership.

In Albania, the last bastion of Stalinist orthodoxy, any signs of a break with established communist rule came even later. It was not until March 1991 that multi-party elections were held and, with opposition parties only permitted to organize in December 1990, the established Party of Labour succeeded in winning a decisive victory. In line with the tardy process of party formation in the longer-established former Soviet republics, the organization of anything such as free elections on their territory also followed with considerable delay. In the republican elections of March 1990, the Moldovan Popular Front and its allies won a decisive majority on lines similar to those set in the Baltic republics. But communist forces prevailed in both Ukraine and Belarus, and slow progress towards the establishment of a pattern of pluralist party politics was evident in the subsequent elections of 1994 and 1995 respectively.

The formation of political parties in eastern Europe as a whole thus only really began during 1990, and even where the organization of viable parties did get under way the process was a patchy and generally limited one. Few parties capable of mobilizing much support existed in eastern Europe before the prospect of holding free elections suddenly appeared. Only in Hungary were reasonably well-established parties in a position to contest the founding elections and even in Slovenia, where parties had also been developing quite freely, anti-communist forces presented themselves to the electorate as a coalition rather than as independent competitive forces in the republican elections of 1990.

Elsewhere it was broad anti-communist and nationalist movements, which were capable of appealing to a broad social constituency but otherwise had no

Table 2.2 Victorious forces in first free elections

	Movement / Party	Percentage votes	Percentage seats
Poland, June 1989	Solidarity (Senate)	64	99
Lithuania, February 1990	Sajudis-approved candidates	–	80
Moldova, February 1990	Popular Front	–	c 33
Estonia, March 1990	Popular Front	–	9
Latvia, March 1990	Popular Front	–	5
Hungary, March 1990	Democratic Forum	25	43
Slovenia, April 1990	DEMOS	55	47
Croatia, April 1990	Democratic Alliance	42	54
Romania, May 1990	Salvation Front	66	66
Czechoslovakia, June 1990	Civic Forum	53	68
	Public Against Violence	68	19
Bulgaria, June 1990	Socialist Party	47	53
Macedonia, November 1990	IMRO	–	32
Bosnia, November 1990	Democratic Action (Muslim)	–	36
Serbia, December 1990	Socialist Party of Serbia	–	78
Montenegro, December 1990	League of Communists	–	66
Albania, March 1991	Party of Labour	56	68
Ukraine, March 1994	Old left (estimate)	–	44
Belarus, May 1995	Unaffiliated (pro-Lukashenka)	–	48

clearly defined political identity or formal organization, that emerged as the major opposition to the communist establishment. Such forces dominated in Poland, Czechoslovakia, Croatia, Moldova and the Baltic states (see Table 2.2). Where neither opposition parties nor independent movements were capable of mounting much opposition, the former establishment prevailed in formally democratic (though hardly fully competitive) elections following partial reformation, sometimes having removed the old communist figurehead (Ceausescu and Zhivkov in Romania and Bulgaria respectively) and in other contexts with an aggressive leader having strengthened the existing political base in order to perpetuate leadership in the new situation (Milošević in Serbia). The only formal parties winning the early elections in these areas were, therefore, those representing the old ruling communist organizations.

The context and process of party formation

When parties did come into existence in post-communist eastern Europe they were formed under conditions that differed considerably from those that characterized previous cases of democratization or redemocratization. The region's recovery after World War II and continued modernization had produced conditions, particularly mass education and extensive urbanization, that are generally thought to be favourable to democratization and stable party growth. But in other ways conditions were less promising, and processes of party development faced major structural obstacles. Little had existed by way of organized political opposition to the communist establishment and even the development of independent associations of a non-political character had been very limited. Unlike the situation in many countries confronting the prospect of party development in Latin America and the Third World in the 'third wave' of democratization, links with any pre-authoritarian past were very distant and extremely limited, and promised little in the way of any direct contribution to contemporary process of regime change.[8] Civil society was particularly weak in some parts of post-communist Europe and had no opportunity to pluralize before the early organization of competitive elections, conditions eminently suited for major portions of the former establishment to safeguard their position and use the ballot box to defeat the immature threat presented by an undeveloped opposition.[9]

The processes of democratization and party development in late twentieth-century eastern Europe had in many ways an *ab initio* character and could in some ways be compared more with those of nineteenth-century Europe than new democracies in other parts of the world. The situation in eastern Europe was a specific one in which the process of post-communist democratization, the nature of the electorate and the parties that did exist, the context of competition and the pattern it was tending to take were all different from other cases – and generally in ways that impeded rather than assisted in processes of effective party development.[10] In other ways the structural context in eastern Europe was actually less favourable for party formation than it had been in the west a century or more earlier. Unlike earlier developments in the more favoured countries of nineteenth- and early twentieth-century Europe, such as Britain and France, the emergence of pluralist party systems open to all members of the public was not occurring within a context of pre-existing – if limited and elitist – 'party democracy'.[11] The experience of those European countries where such elements of elite democracy had been lacking showed the dangers inherent in later processes of political development. The fate of Germany during the first half of the twentieth century demonstrated the importance of such structural factors and the consequences they could have for the development of mass democracy.

Although qualified by internal conflict and factionalism, and sometimes accompanied by a formal pluralism represented by the existence of organizationally separate but wholly powerless auxiliary parties, communist rule also remained virtually monolithic until the end and devoid of any significant features of institutional diversity. While, too, the population had been mobilized within an extensive network of political and social organizations during the communist period, these had generally been tightly controlled and gave the citizenry little decision-making power or effective sense of political participation. East Europeans were presented in 1989 and the years immediately following with initial opportunities for democratic political activity in a situation generally devoid of any pluralist institutions or participatory organizations – and, with the singular exception of inter-war Czechoslovakia, very little practical experience of either. The early stages of post-communist democratization and party-building took place, then, in a largely unstructured situation where the institutions of the communist period had lost much of their meaning and function (if not all their organizational resources) and many of the social conditions conducive to political pluralization were lacking.

But, while many east Europeans were eager to reject communist rule and much of what it represented, and seemed equally delighted to embrace the general principles of liberal democracy (and often the structures of the free market with which western democracy is intimately associated), there was also little enthusiasm to seize the opportunities for independent political activity and participation in the independent structures that could now be established quite legally. Politics was a sphere of activity that many rejected and were often mistrustful of – as, indeed, they often were in established western democracies. More specifically, it was often observed that the compulsory participation in political activities organized by communist party officials gave many east Europeans a pronounced aversion to the very notion of the political party and the activities it conventionally engages in.

Surveys have suggested that parties are among the most distrusted of contemporary east European institutions, with fewer than one person in seven actually expressing any trust in them.[12] Average figures for east European respondents on such issues of party trust and commitment were significantly lower than those for west Europeans, on average no more than half the British level. For many people, too, the immediate situation was often one of economic crisis and material hardship, which further diverted attention from the political sphere. Under such conditions, particularly in the harder hit post-Soviet countries, commitment to the idea of a multi-party system was itself limited. In 1994, only 36 per cent of Ukrainians thought that one was necessary in their country, and the proportion declined yet further in subsequent years.[13]

The learning process that the liberation of the political space engendered also brought with it a 'new alienation' from politics reflected in decreasing voter turnout for elections and, it has been claimed, an increasing danger of populism.[14] The sheer pace of change was certainly disorienting and provided little by way of a solid basis for organized public action. Movements of national unity based on diffuse, if strongly held, sentiments of anti-communism and social autonomy were far more in keeping with the spirit of this period and, if not the well-known and professionally organized groups benefiting from lengthy communist experience, it was these associations that attracted most votes in the early elections. Their role was prominent but temporary, providing a bridge to the period of more pluralistic politics and more concerted processes of party formation and institution-building. The process of party formation was, therefore, an unsteady one in many parts of eastern Europe. It produced organizations that had weak links with social constituencies, often little sense of ideological certainty or clarity, and frequently pushed to the fore a range of contending leaders who desperately sought the means of adequate institutional and social support within a crowded political space. This often led to the voicing of strongly populist appeals, high levels of irresponsibility and the articulation of extreme political programmes.

Under the conditions of social flux and systemic change that characterized the beginning of the post-communist period, questions of party formation, institutionalization and organizational durability became particularly important. Experience suggests that major factors in such processes are the acquisition by a party of a stable constituency, the construction and articulation of a consistent party platform and the growth of internal consensus within the organization.[15] Background conditions identified in the literature for the emergence of viable political parties and their development within a stable democratic system, on the other hand, tend to be very general and emphasize the importance of the overall trust of citizens in political institutions (without which the establishment of viable party system becomes particularly difficult) and the importance of regular free elections being held, which provides the conditions for parties to gain pre-eminence as intermediary institutions and creates a climate in which civic trust can grow.

Such a degree of trust could not be assumed in eastern Europe, and the speed with which the initial elections were held often favoured existing communist organizations rather than new pluralist parties. The existence of conditions favourable to democratic party formation even in relatively developed countries can by no means be assumed, as the experience of failed democracy in Germany, Italy and Spain prior to their eventual installation of a more successful democratic order testifies. With little history of pre-communist democracy (Czechoslovakia as the main example) and limited experience of national independence in many cases, neither historical background nor the contemporary domestic conditions of eastern Europe were particularly promising in the early post-communist period.

The more developed countries of east-central Europe were clearly better placed to meet such conditions for democratic party development. They were able to hold competitive elections before most other parts of the region (Table 2.1), independence movements and representatives of the democratic opposition in east-central Europe and the Baltic states succeeded in defeating regrouped or otherwise surviving communist forces at the first electoral opportunity and thus made a sharp break with the former regime (Table 2.2), and they tended to display somewhat higher levels of popular trust in parties and identification with them (Table 2.3) – although Poland did not fully fit with this pattern, as subsequent levels of electoral turnout and party membership confirmed. But while these factors were more positive for party formation and subsequent institutional development than conditions elsewhere in the region, major challenges still faced east-central Europe in this area. The conditions under which parties formed varied throughout the region, but they were nowhere very positive.

Apart from the problems involved in moving beyond the loosely organized and diffuse aims of the movement (which could nevertheless be the focus of passionate conviction) to the more differentiated and interest-based vehicle of the party, fundamental uncertainties of political identity also had to be addressed in most countries. One basic question of statehood was solved with the dissolution of federal Czechoslovakia into its two constituent parts at the end of 1992, but the strong mixture of nationalism and anti-communism embedded in the movements of democratic independence movements in most countries left other problems of collective identity still to be solved, too.[16]

The inauguration of a sequence of fully competitive elections nevertheless

Table 2.3a Attitudes to parties in eastern Europe (1993–96)

Percentage of respondents:	Czech Republic	Slovakia	Hungary	Ukraine
considering themselves as a supporter of a political party	37	33	28	13
very favourable to one or more of named parties	31	29	35	18
at least favourable to one or more named party	88	87	83	59
do not believe that any existing party meets/ represents their interests/views	35	54	66	71
Average visibility of parties (percentage viewing parties favourably or unfavourably)	56	54	50	37

Source: W.L. Miller, S. White and P. Heywood, *Values and Political Change in Post-communist Europe*, Basingstoke, Macmillan, 1998, pp. 169–70.

Table 2.3b Percentage of people – (1) feeling close to a party or movement, 1995, or (2) expressing trust in parties, 1994

	1	2
Czech Republic	–	24
Romania	41	19
Slovakia	–	16
Belarus	–	13
Hungary	39	11
Slovenia	22	11
Bulgaria	–	11
Ukraine	–	8
Poland	18	7

Sources: (1) Rose and Mishler, 'Negative and positive partisanship', p. 10; (2) R. Rose, 'Mobilizing demobilized voters in post-communist societies, *Party Politics*, 1995, **1**: 551.

accelerated a number of political tendencies already in existence and provided a major stimulus to party development. This was obviously the case in the run-up to the elections as competing forces organized themselves and sought to maximize the chances of achieving their objectives. The outcome of representative parliaments and responsible governments itself produced a lively environment for party formation where this had not been possible before elections were held. A primary mode of party formation was that which took place within the recently elected parliaments and involved the rapid dissolution of the recently triumphant anti-communist movements. Within a short period the demands of government office, policy making and a rapidly evolving political situation – as well as normal processes of conflict within a large and diverse group – produced extensive differentiation and political fragmentation. Links with particular social groups and institutions (such as the Church and the different groups associated with the Solidarity union in Poland) began to replace the former unity and provided a fertile environment for political differentiation and, in some cases, reasonably effective party formation. It was a situation strongly reminiscent of the 'internal' origins of modern parties that Duverger argued had been the primary mode of party formation in the western democracies until around 1900.[17]

This route was typified by developments in the parliaments of Poland and Czechoslovakia, where deputies sponsored by Solidarity and those originally associated with the Czech Civic Forum soon developed more differentiated political views and group affiliations. Such pluralist tendencies nevertheless had extensive roots that could be traced back to the 1970s in the case of KOR (Workers' Defence Committee)/Solidarity in Poland and Charter 77 in Czechoslovakia (see Table 2.4). Signs of later party tendencies could in particular be identified in Poland's extensive and widely differentiated dissident movement, which continued to have ramifications in the Solidarity-based coalition that dominated the parliament elected in 1997. The Confederation for an Independent Poland had formed as a party as far back as 1979, but this was a very singular case. Even in the case of new parties formed under conditions of immediate post-communist flux there were significant continuities not just in terms of individual actors and political orientations, but also certain organizational features.[18] In other countries democratic parties were formed or reformed quite rapidly with the coalescence of diverse individuals and groups without much benefit of prior organized dissidence or proto-opposition experience.

Other forms of democratic choice and different kinds of election also played a part in the process. While Poland's 'contract' parliament established on the basis of agreement with the communist authorities during 1989 lasted until the autumn of 1991, the country's communist president felt constrained to resign in September 1990 and opened the way to competitive elections for the post. It was in this context that a major process of party formation in Poland got under way, a Centre Alliance having formed first to promote the candidature of Lech Wałęsa for the post and then a Citizen's Movement emerging by way of opposition, both developments soon leading to the establishment of formally constituted parties.

A second mode of party formation was apparent as former ruling parties abandoned the authoritarian trappings of Marxist–Leninist ideology and reconstructed themselves (to varying degrees) as democratic parties, some of them eventually succeeding in establishing a new political authority in fully competitive elections. Those that clung on to power and fought off the challenge of a weak democratic opposition in the early phase of post-communist transition were less inclined to contemplate their major democratization as political parties. A far greater degree of continuity with the former regime was involved in these cases. The Bulgarian party was the prime example of this, with those of Romania, Serbia, Montenegro and Albania very much in the same camp. Their performance in office and the more fundamental changes that took place in late 1996 and 1997 in some countries showed that the original transformation during the transition of 1989–90 was considerably less than complete.

The Bulgarian Socialist Party (BSP) was formed after the communist establishment removed Todor Zhivkov from office and commitments were made to free elections and political pluralism (although the leadership showed some reluctance to ditch a number of the Marxist principles that had been espoused by the former organization). As a result of the weakness of anti-communist opposition forces at this stage the BSP won the 1990 election with a hefty majority. The transformation of much of the Romanian communist establishment into a National Salvation Front seemed to promise more radical change, but its performance in power also showed major continuities with the former regime (although without the personal excesses associated with Ceausescu's rule). The renamed Serbian Party of Socialists equally showed itself to be no less of a vehicle for the perpetuation of the power of Slobodan Milošević. Having lost their hold on the machinery of power and failed in early elections, other former ruling parties reconstructed themselves in more radical fashion, some returning to power after a relatively short period (Lithuania and Poland) and, after a somewhat longer interval, Hungary. The initial attempt of the Hungarian communists to reposition themselves in the changing political situation was a failure and could not prevent their removal from power in 1990. The subsequent performance of all three parties showed that reconstruction of the former authoritarian organization during a period out of power produced a far more thoroughgoing transformation. As the case of the Slovak Party of the Democratic Left showed, though, the path of political reform was no guarantee of parties emanating from former ruling organizations returning to power.

Other parties that formed in the immediate context of regime change and political transition lay between these two categories. Some were based on the auxiliary parties that had also formed part of the communist establishment but lay outside from the central locations of party–state power, operating more as social transmission belts for the communist authorities than as political institutions in their own right. The Polish Peasant Party was a prime example of the development of such a hitherto marginal organization. Other parties sprang not so much from the civil society and institutions of communist rule as from the period before the communist take-over in the late 1940s.

'Historic' parties were reactivated and in some cases political figures returned from emigration to lead them, although they rarely achieved a great deal of success. The Czech Social Democratic party was one successful party based on a pre-communist organization, but its contemporary success owed more to skilful contemporary leadership than to more distant roots. Another historic party, the Hungarian Smallholders', has secured a regular but less prominent parliamentary presence. Such modes of party formation were not always mutually exclusive, and the Polish Peasant Party was rooted not just in the former communist ally, but also assimilated elements of the historic peasant movement with considerable success. Other historic parties with roots in inter-war political life or the immediate post-war period were reformed even though their links with contemporary eastern Europe were distant and their purchase on post-communist political life limited. Most remained on the margins of the developing party system. Those

Table 2.4 Conditions and processes of party formation

	Dissident groups	Anti-communist movement	Party formation	Basic party legislation
Poland	Prevalent since 1976 with formation of KOR, free union movement	Solidarity active 1980–81, returns as major force in summer 1988	CIP formed in 1979, but major contemporary parties formed from 1990	Solidarity legal from April 1990, party law in August, revised May 1997
Czechoslovakia	Limited, although Charter 77 maintains a significant presence	Civic Forum (CF) and Public Against Violence formed in November 1989	Parties registered from early 1990, parties emerge in CF autumn 1990	Main law adopted January 1990
Hungary	Numerous groups and diverse informal opposition from early 1980s	Single-issue groups in 1980s, environmentalists particularly prominent	Democratic Forum founded 1987, other major groups from 1988	Legal amendments November 1988, multi-party system from March 1989
Slovenia	Liberal climate supports thriving cultural pluralism throughout 1980s	Human Rights committee formed in 1988, focus for independence movement	Peasant Union 1988, more emerge from Human Rights committee	Pluralism accepted March 1989, multi-party system from December
Lithuania	Catholic rights movement from 1970s, some civil rights activists	Sajudis formed June 1988 with support of independent communists	More opposition and factionalism in Sajudis from early 1992 with full independence	CPSU authority disavowed December 1989, party legislation September 1990
Latvia	Environmentalism strong from mid-80s, nationalist movements to the fore in 1988	Popular Front and National Independence Movement founded in 1988	Numerous groups formed 1988–90, but formal party organization follows later	Multi-party system accepted by communists in January 1990
Estonia	Strong nationalist impetus develops from early 1970s	Popular Front founded 1988 as first in USSR, led by reform communists	Organizational pluralism from 1988 and party formation from 1990	Stricter rules for party registration in 1994
Croatia	Reform/nationalist movement strongly repressed from 1960s	Pan-Yugoslav liberal movement founded February 1989	1989 May: Social Liberal Party, June: nationalist CDU	Multi-party system established late 1989
Bulgaria	Very limited individual dissent	No movement as such, UDF formed after opposition legalized in December 1990	Continuing factionalism in BSP and, particularly, UDF from 1990	Legislation in April 1990

Romania	Cautious signs of dissent in 1989, reformist views expressed by former leaders	National Salvation Front a vehicle for former establishment	First parties formed 1990, but remain generally weak and factionalized	Initial declaration of NSF Council January 1990
Serbia	Diverse currents of nationalism strengthen throughout 1980s	Ambiguous anti-bureaucratic revolution launched by Milošević	Spring 1990: begins with Serbian Renewal Party as major opposition party	Opposition parties legalized August 1990
Montenegro	Generally parallels Serbian developments	Full participant in Milošević's anti-bureaucratic movement	Resistance to Milošević grows, DPS driven into opposition in 1998	Democratic Party of Socialists formed after 1990 elections
Bosnia	Continuing repression of Muslim groups in 1980s	Strengthening ethnic identification	Groups formed from beginning of 1990, ethnic representatives predominate	Original 1990 ban on ethnic parties overruled by Constitutional Court
Macedonia	Little specific to the republic, but Albanian activism feared	Growing resistance to Serbian nationalism	Generally under way from early 1990	Stricter laws on registration introduced 1995
Albania	Politically quiescent until demonstrations in December 1990	No public manifestations, but mass emigration in 1990	DP and other groups formed just before 1991 election, APL reconstituted after election	Independent parties legalized December 1990, new electoral law 1992
Ukraine	Restricted nationalist and Helsinki-based movements emerge in 1970s	Partial coalescence of groups, mostly on nationalist base, in 1990	Weak party groups begin to emerge in 1990, communists relegalized 1993	Restrictive rules for registration prior to 1994 elections, revised 1997
Belarus	A single anti-Soviet dissident (M. Kukabka) identified	Popular Front formed 1988, but influence quite limited	Popular Front struggles to survive, little further growth	CP relegalized February 1993, harsh election regulations
Moldova	1987: dissident activity in Writers' Union	Democratic Movement formed 1988, basis for Popular Front of Moldova (PFM)	PFM officially recognized June 1989, growing links with reform communists in early 1990	Open competition for 1990 Supreme Soviet elections

appealing to the traditional values of the rural population tended to have more success – such as the Independent Smallholders in Hungary, Bulgarian Agrarian National Union and the Polish Peasant Party.[19]

Two main kinds of proto-party or movement thus prevailed in the first elections. One was the anti-communist and nationally-oriented democratic movement, and the other was composed of communist forces deriving from the former establishment, but subject to varying degrees of reform and adaptation to suit the new political situation and its electoral requirements. In the eighteen different countries that made up eastern Europe at this time, elections in eleven were broadly won by anti-communist forces and seven by organizations or candidates deriving from the former communist establishment. If communism was on its death-bed in eastern Europe between 1989 and 1991 its condition, at least in the short term, was by no means immediately terminal and many of its supporters found ways to survive under the new conditions. This had a major influence on the formation of democratic parties and prospects for their subsequent development throughout the region.

Party development across the region

The two kinds of outcome that emerged in the founding elections, mostly throughout 1990 but also in 1989 (Poland) and considerably later in Ukraine and Belarus, were not distributed equally throughout eastern Europe. Relatively stable parties and structures of party government were quicker to emerge in the east-central European countries (Poland, Czechoslovakia – until its division into two separate countries at the end of 1992 – Hungary and Slovenia), either in the very early stages of transition or after the brief dominance of movements of anti-communist opposition. In the context of party development it is therefore useful to focus on the different areas that make up eastern Europe as a whole.

In *east-central Europe* turmoil developed in the Polish Solidarity camp soon after the original victories of 1989, whilst a gradual process of consolidation took place on the now marginalized left. The presidential campaign and an intensifying 'war at the top' within the Solidarity leadership were major factors that contributed to the polarization of the movement as parties began to form. A much debated Law on Political Parties came into force in August 1990 as the struggle for the presidency intensified. It was in this context that a Centre Accord was founded in May 1990 to promote Wałęsa's campaign for the presidency, the association being transformed into a formal party in March 1991. An equivalent party was set up by Mazowiecki supporters in December 1990 as the Democratic Union. Processes of party formation were more advanced amongst Solidarity's former protagonists. The old 'communist' party dissolved itself in January 1990 and established a new Social Democracy of the Polish Republic.

Parties established on the foundations of the ruling bodies of the former regime had undoubted advantages and maintained a significant political presence, whereas the fate of most other parties across the centre and right-wing was more mixed. The Democratic Union was renamed the Freedom Union following a merger with the Congress of Liberal Democrats in 1994 and survived more successfully than most other parties, performing well in the 1997 elections. More right-wing, populist parties generally did less well in the early 1990s although the Confederation for Independent Poland, founded by dissident activist Leszek Moczulski as far back as 1979, won some parliamentary seats both in the first fully competitive elections of 1991 and those held in 1993 elections. The sheer number of parties formed did not help the initial emergence of a stable party system. Over a hundred existed in early 1991 and around seventy-five had been formally registered.[20] Until new legislation some years later, a party only needed fifteen members to qualify for registration, a minimal requirement that contributed to party proliferation.[21] The number of officially recorded parties did not necessarily present an accurate reflection of anything like the number of effective organizations in existence, though. By 1997, when new legislation had been passed, as many as 370 parties were supposed to exist but in early 1998 only forty had been registered under the new regulations.[22] The others were deregistered and passed from the scene altogether. But the field was still open for the formation of important new organizations. Solidarity was resurrected as an organized electoral force (SEA) only in June 1996 and went on to win the elections held in September the following year.

In Czechoslovakia the early post-communist period was similarly dominated by the presence of Civic Forum (in the Czech lands) and Public Against Violence (in Slovakia) as broad and closely allied social movements. Some small groups and parties had begun to spring up as signs of the imminent collapse of communism emerged and more were set up in December, including a Green Party, Farmers' Party, Christian Democracy, and a revived Social Democratic Party. A new law was adopted in January 1990 to encourage party formation, having first given formal recognition to Civic Forum and Public Against Violence, as well as to the Communist Party of Czechoslovakia and the former auxiliary parties that had re-established their independence after the November revolution.[23] In March 1990, thirty-eight parties were registered with the Interior Ministry and by June, when the first democratic elections were held, there were a total of seventy-nine – with twenty-seven having been rejected for failing to meet formal criteria (such as providing full list of officers).[24] The groups participating in the initial elections were nevertheless primarily those forming part of the original regime-change movement and were generally speaking proto-parties rather than distinctive political organizations, and only twenty-three political groups were formally registered as participants in the June elections.

By the autumn of 1990 a distinct process of differentiation could be seen in Civic Forum, which had won around half of all votes cast in the Czech areas. Václav Klaus was elected Civic Forum's first chairman in October and argued for the transformation of the Forum into a right-wing party, the Forum splitting in April to form in April a right-wing Civic Democratic Party and more centrist Civic Movement. In Slovakia, the dominant figure was Vladimìr Mečiar, who had been appointed republican prime minister in June 1990 but was dismissed in April 1991 and led his supporters out of PAV to found the Movement for a

Democratic Slovakia, which espoused leftist economic and social policies but also a nationalism more characteristic of the radical right. He created a form of political dominance that persisted, largely on a personal rather than party basis (and not without a spell outside government in 1994), until the September 1998 elections and the victory of the democratic opposition.

In Hungary there was no broad social movement such as those seen in Poland and Hungary, and more distinctive political groupings began to emerge at an early stage. From one perspective, indeed, the onset of multi-party politics could be dated from 1985–86 with the entry into parliamentary of a number of independent rather than regime-endorsed deputies.[25] Equally, certain kinds of proto-party began to emerge on the basis of competing policy lobbies within the party–state establishment from the early 1980s. The activity of independent political organizations was formally accepted by the government at the end of 1988 and in March 1989 the creation of a multi-party system was endorsed. One immediate outcome was the establishment of an 'Opposition Round Table' (ORT) with the involvement of seven parties on the pattern of negotiations already taking place in Poland.[26] They included the Independent Smallholders', Social Democrats (HSDP), People's Party (HPP) and the Christian Democratic People's Party, all of which were 'historic' organizations active before the communist take-over of the country. Both the HSDP and HPP had been revived in late 1988. Representing the new parties (although with historic roots in earlier groupings and established cultural tendencies) were the Hungarian Democratic Forum, Free Democrats and FIDESZ. The HDF had been established as far back as September 1987, and AFD and FIDESZ in November and March 1988 respectively.

Following the elections of March/April 1990 a reasonably representative party spectrum emerged in the country, with all but two of the ORT parties being represented in parliament. The new parliament produced the region's most stable party system, which sustained the freely elected government for its full 4-year term. The balanced and relatively restricted party system that emerged in the 1990 parliament was achieved by strict requirements for candidates that demanded quite substantial party representation in the country as a whole. Many minor parties were effectively eliminated, and while sixty-five parties had been registered by the time of the elections only thirty actually presented candidates, most of whom failed to gain a place on the national list.[27] The ferment of early party formation continued and by 1996, 176 parties were registered.[28]

In Slovenia it was outspoken opposition to the policies of Belgrade that prompted the emergence of an increasingly strong democratic movement and the creation of embryonic parties.[29] A mass demonstration was held when four Slovenes were put on trial in June 1988 for possession of a military document, an act that raised questions about the protected status of the strongly Serb-influenced federal military organization as well as contentious issues of free speech. A widely supported human rights committee formed, and this was soon followed by the establishment of a number of parties. They included a Social Democratic Alliance, Slovenian Democratic Union, Christian Socialist Movement, and a

Green Party. A Peasant Union that had come into existence before the trial also grew rapidly, and had 25,000 members by September 1989. Closer to the existing establishment, the League of Socialist Youth and Socialist Alliance of Working People displayed greater independence and showed signs of becoming proper political parties.

The ruling League of Communists of Slovenia soon followed the democratizing trend and in March 1989 published a Programme of Renewal that endorsed the introduction of political pluralism, although it was not until December that a congress of the League formally agreed to introduce a multi-party system within the republic and scheduled elections for April 1990. A large majority was won by the democratic opposition, DEMOS, with 55 per cent of the vote. Once independence had been achieved, further elections in 1992 reflected a more fragmented party spectrum as the different organizations that had initially combined to form DEMOS stood on their own account, with the Liberal Democrats gaining the largest proportion of the votes at 23 per cent.

Pressures for democracy and the impetus for the formation of independent parties were also strong in the *Baltic states*. Although forming part of the Soviet Union and subject to correspondingly greater restrictions on their independence than the countries of east-central Europe, they had only formed part of the communist federal state since 1940, so memories of national independence were little more distant than those of their western neighbours and the desire for its restoration was no less strong. The prominence of the national factor was demonstrated by the leading part taken by Lithuania in this process, as only in that country did ethnic nationals make up as much as 80 per cent of the population (Estonia's population was approximately one-third Russian, and Latvians only made up a half of that country's population). One of the region's most prominent organizations was Sajudis (or Movement), founded in Lithuania during June 1988 (seventeen of whose thirty-six founding members actually belonged to the communist party).[30]

After republican Supreme Soviet elections in March 1990 national independence was declared, although it did not receive international recognition until first accepted by the Soviet authorities in September 1991. A new law on parties was nevertheless formulated and passed on 25 September 1990 (requiring the registration of 400 members, a party programme and the holding of a founding congress), although 'public movements' were also allowed to contest elections. In December the authority of the Communist Party of the Soviet Union in Lithuania was abolished, and it became the first Soviet republic to establish a multi-party system.[31] Its pattern of political development tended to remain more structured than that of its Baltic neighbours, and it was a Sajudis-based party in the form of the Homeland Union that went on to win the election of 1996.

In what was called the 'third awakening' (1988–91) in Latvia there was also a major organizational transformation of national political life prior to the achievement of full independence after the failed August coup in the Soviet Union. The communist party was split into moderate and pro-Moscow factions after the vote of the Supreme Council (as the Supreme Soviet was now called) on independence, and an Independent Communist Party of Latvia was formed in April 1990. In September it renamed itself the Democratic Labour Party of Latvia.[32] Parties closed down by the pre-war dictatorship in 1934 were revived. These included Social Democrats (re-established in 1989) and the Agrarian Union (April 1991).[33] Lists were presented by twenty-three groupings and parties in the first free elections held in 1993, but they often had little sense of a clear political identity or distinctive political platform.

The institutional status of some major groupings also remained somewhat uncertain. Dominant on the right, for example, were the National Independence movement which was founded in July 1988 but only formally registered as a party in June 1994, and the Popular Front (also founded in 1988 and not established as a party organization until 1994 – by which time many supporters had moved to better organized party formations). Also represented on this side of the party spectrum were Fatherland and Freedom as well as For Latvia (an ambiguous nationalist formation led by an activist with German nationality). The political centre and government more generally was dominated from 1993 by Latvia's Way, an electoral coalition also formally established as political party only in October of that year. The left faced even greater problems in preventing fragmentation and achieving political respectability.

In similar fashion, parties had also begun forming in Estonia during 1988, with that country's Popular Front securing a particularly strong showing in elections to the Soviet Congress of People's Deputies in 1989 and the Estonian Supreme Soviet in March 1990. A fuller range of parties came into being in 1990, particularly on the right wing (Christian Democrats, Entrepreneurs Party, United Republicans), although a broader Social Democratic Party combining a number of smaller groups was also formed. Party identification nevertheless remained low, organizational development was not very advanced and the spectrum of political groupings was a wide one – with registration being made more stringent in 1994.[34] This did not greatly advance the consolidation of the relatively unformed party system, where fractions frequently split and recombined to present themselves to the electorate as partly reconstituted organizations made up of largely familiar political forces. Estonia could therefore be presented as the archetype of an 'anti-party system' in which political competition remained largely non-institutionalized.[35] Specific measures were taken to limit this tendency prior to the 1999 elections, but they had a relatively limited effect.

The process of forming independent parties and the passage to democratic party government was a generally slower process in the *Balkans*. Neither independent parties nor democratically inclined nationalist movements emerged as prime actors in the process of transition. The next country to hold multi-party elections after Slovenia was the neighbouring Yugoslav republic of Croatia, which was more developed and considerably wealthier than other parts of the Balkans (see Table 1.1) but also possessed more serious obstacles to democratic development than Slovenia. The rise of independent movements in Croatia and initial moves towards party formation faced a more conservative and far less sympathetic communist party leadership than in Slovenia, and the interests represented by new independent groups were correspondingly more resolutely anti-communist and emphatically nationalist (drawing on strongly rooted anti-Serb sentiments) than in the neighbouring republic. Following steps to found a liberal movement at the beginning of the year the Croatian Democratic Union (CDU), led by prominent dissident Franjo Tudjman, was launched in June 1989. When elections were held in late April and early May 1990, the CDU won a decisive majority over the three dozen or so other parties that had registered to compete in the ballot. On 30 May, Tudjman was elected president by a similarly decisive parliamentary majority and henceforth dominated independent Croatia's political life on a personal basis and, for the early years, as military leader during the conflicts in Bosnia and adjacent areas.

In Bulgaria, a broad democratic movement – the Union of Democratic Forces (UDF) – came into existence, but this was as much associated with the prior weakness of opposition forces as with the political resurgence of any strong social formation. The removal of long-established communist dictator Todor Zhivkov on 10 November 1989 by more liberal members of the leadership was followed by the legalization of opposition groups. In January 1990, the party opted for principles of democratic socialism and was transformed in April 1990 into the Bulgarian Socialist Party. Numerous alternative parties and movements also sought official recognition after Zhivkov's ouster and at least fifty were registered in the early weeks of the new regime, although none had the status to present itself as an effective alternative to the communist establishment. On 7 December 1989, therefore, ten organizations formed the Union of Democratic Forces, and a further six bodies joined before elections to a Grand National Assembly were held in June 1990. A new law on political parties was passed by the existing National Assembly on 3 April. On this basis around forty-five parties were registered by the time of the June elections.[36] To the surprise of many in the UDF, and in distinction to the recent electoral outcomes in Hungary and Czechoslovakia, the socialists came top of the poll and won over half the parliamentary seats. Factionalism soon developed in both of the two main political formations, although the Socialist Party appeared to be the most coherent and effective organizations until the onset of major economic crisis of 1996.

In Romania, Ceausescu's dictatorship had a highly dogmatic, personalized nature and was overthrown violently in December 1989. Tentative signs of intellectual opposition and dissent had surfaced in Romania during 1989, but they did not make much political mark. In this context it was not surprising that historic, pre-war parties were unusually prominent in Romania's particular form of 'post-communist' democratization.[37] The precise nature of the 1989 'revolution' is still somewhat uncertain, and it was members of the communist establishment that stepped forward to assume power within a National Salvation Front. The NSF claimed to represent a decisive break with communism, and committed itself to a multi-party system and free elections. But some of its leading figures did not welcome the creation of parties and denied that party competition was necessary whilst the Front permitted factionalism and internal pluralism.

Immediately after Ceausescu's overthrow, though, some former parties were re-established, with the National Peasant Party soon merging with a new Christian Democratic group to form the National Peasant Christian and Democratic Party, which became the backbone of the opposition. The speed with which elections (held on May 20) were organized disadvantaged all new parties and the National Salvation Front gathered two-thirds of the entire vote. The NSF soon split and Iliescu established the Democratic NSF, later renamed Social Democrats, which maintained overall political supremacy until the elections of 1996.

Military operations in what had been until 1991 the Federal Republic of Yugoslavia meant that conditions in Serbia were equally antithetic to the development of party government and a viable democracy, although this was by no means the only political obstacle involved. Slobodan Milošević, chair of the Serbian League of Communists, had made highly effective use of nationalist themes since 1987 and embraced pluralist principles with reluctance, permitting the legalization of opposition parties only in August 1990. In July the League merged with the Socialist Alliance of the Working People of Serbia to form a new Socialist Party and succeeded in attracting significant numbers of new members, winning 46 per cent of the vote in free elections held on 9 December. This represented a decisive victory over the opposition Serbian Renewal Party of Vuk Drašković, formed in the spring of 1990. Milošević's position was reinforced by the outbreak of war with Croatia in June 1991, hostilities that lasted in various forms for 4 years. Foreign intervention was generally counter-productive for Serbia itself and only helped consolidate support for Milošević. But war was not the only obstacle to democratic development. Nationalism had been a major channel for the dissatisfaction throughout the 1980s and it has been argued that Serb attitudes just did not support a democratic culture.[38]

A residual Yugoslavia continued to be formed by Serbia with the small republic of Montenegro, ruled by an orthodox Democratic Party of Socialists until 1998. The early party spectrum largely replicated that of Serbia, although Muslim and Albanian parties also participated in elections. An indigenous People's Party did little to strengthen opposition to the ruling Democratic Party, and the first democratic elections were actually won by an unreconstructed League of Communists.[39] Opportunities for democratic party development were even less propitious in the former Yugoslav republic of Bosnia, where Croatian and Serbian military forces were both active until 1995. With the collapse of the Yugoslav League of Communists at its extraordinary congress in January 1990 the Bosnian leadership permitted the formation of opposition parties with the proviso that they were not based on ethnic principles, an exclusion that was soon overruled by the Constitutional Court. During the rest of 1990 at least forty parties or equivalent organizations were formed, although only thirteen put candidates forward for election in November.[40] The campaign was predictably dominated by three major ethnic parties who, rather than concentrating on forming alliances with non-national groups, concluded a formal partnership but then proceeded to pursue basic national interests, a strategy that fitted all too well with the growing ethnic conflict within Yugoslavia as whole and did nothing to slow its advance in independent Bosnia.

Macedonia's status was equally contested and state legitimacy fundamentally challenged, a situation hardly conducive to effective democratization or the formation of a stable party system. In December 1990, a multi-party election was held in which more than twenty parties participated. A contemporary version of the historic nationalist Internal Macedonian Revolutionary Organization won 32 per cent of seats, although it failed to form a government and a largely non-political administration emerged. A major unifying influence was exerted by President Kiro Gligorov, a seasoned Yugoslav politician without minority ethnic affiliations, who beat the IMRO candidate and survived as the leading figure of the independent state, heading a further left-wing coalition to win further elections in October 1994.

Albania, as one of the most authoritarian countries of the region, also saw no anti-communist opposition until the very end. Independent parties were finally permitted to come into existence after extensive demonstrations in December 1990.[41] A Democratic Party (DP) was soon organized and registered on 17 December. Later that month the ruling Albanian Party of Labour (APL) also committed itself to support a multi-party system and four more opposition parties formed before elections were held in March 1991. The former ruling party was well placed to perpetuate its dominance in hurriedly organized free elections, although formal victory was no longer sufficient to sustain rule in the new political context and a multi-party coalition was needed to sustain the government until new elections were won by the Democrats in 1992.

In countries of the *former Soviet Union* conditions for party formation were also generally unfavourable. The authorities in the Ukraine continued to harass opposition activists throughout 1989 when official attitudes in Russia had already softened. Limited movements of dissent in the 1970s were closely linked with diverse nationalist currents that strengthened as opposition groups began to coalesce in 1990. The delayed onset of democratization in the Ukraine helped give the communists a decisive majority in that year's republican elections. Of the seventy-eight deputies elected within the Democratic Bloc forty belonged to Rukh, the Ukrainian People's Movement for Perestroika originally conceived as broad coalition based on the model of the Polish and Baltic democratic independence movements. More numerous than any other non-communist party representatives were, in fact, the bloc of eighty-seven unaffiliated and formally independent deputies. While numerous parties were formed overall membership was scanty, actually 'bordering on insignificance'.[42] This lack of social linkage enhanced the elite's freedom of action, already solidly established during the communist period. After the coup of August 1991 the highly conservative party elite embraced the cause of national independence as a means of safeguarding its power, a move that was positively received by the nationalist opposition and helped former party secretary Leonid Kravchuk become independent Ukraine's first president.

With the support both of the old elite and much of the opposition Kravchuk's position was quite secure, and only in late 1992 did Rukh split to produce an opposition fraction under Viacheslav Chornovil. The strengthening of presidential powers in line with similar tendencies in Yeltsin's Russia did not produce conditions favourable for party organization. Further obstacles to independent party development also remained. Electoral laws prior to elections in March 1994 greatly favoured incumbent deputies and independent candidates, whereas party registration procedures were extremely demanding and the candidates they proposed subject to extensive controls. Of party-affiliated mandates in 1994 most were won by communists and only a minority by candidates of pluralist parties. Changes in the electoral mechanism helped structure the parliamentary centre on party lines in 1998, although no real signs of party system consolidation were yet in evidence.[43]

Independence posed different problems for Belarus, where nationalism was prominent by its virtual absence. Signs of political opposition during the Soviet period were also minimal until the nuclear accident at Chernobyl in 1986. Coinciding with the extension of *glasnost'* throughout the Soviet Union, the accident itself and the unsatisfactory response of the authorities gave ample grounds for the rise of opposition, and in October 1988 a Belarussian Popular Front for Perestroika was founded.[44] But it gathered little popular support and did not develop much of an organization. A certain level of worker unrest in 1991 did nothing to change this situation. The communist party of Belarus remained resolutely conservative and only went so far as to accept the BPF's demands for political and economic independence in the wake of the August coup – but rejected that for national independence. The continuity of communist rule was maintained unchanged for some years, as the deputies elected to the republican Soviet in March 1990 remained in post until 1995. The influence and membership of the BPF did see some growth, but other opposition groups remained very small. A new constitution opened the way for presidential elections in June and July 1994 won by Alyaksandr Lukashenka, who showed ever-strengthening authoritarian tendencies that had disastrous consequences for Belarus's sickly democracy and further possibilities of party development. Signs of fundamental constitutional crisis grew in subsequent years as conflict persisted about the legitimacy of Lukashenka's extended tenure as president and his reluctance to hold further elections.

A contentious legacy of national identity also affected post-communist development in Moldova and was responsible for the strongly conservative policy imposed on the republic by the Moscow leadership. Reformist currents only surfaced in 1987 and centred on issues concerning the writers' union. The following year saw the formation of two reformist groups, after which the Popular Front of Moldova was established and in June 1989 gained official recognition.[45] Divisive ethnic issues soon came to the fore as the republic's sizeable Russian minority founded its own movement, Edinstvo, and conflict increased within the communist party, some of whose members moved closer to the Popular Front. It gained around a third of the seats in Supreme Soviet elections in February 1990, although was able to command an overall majority with the support of reformist communists. On this basis, former party secretary Mircea Snegur was elected president.

In contrast to other republics, the Moldovan leadership denounced the August coup and declared the formation of an independent republic – while analogous steps within Moldova itself were taken by the Russian and Gagauz minorities in the areas they dominated, full-scale civil war breaking out with the rebel Transdniestrian Soviet Republic in 1992. Despite the rapid cessation of open hostilities, the Transdniestr conflict remained a major complicating factor in relations with both Russia and Romania. Within the Moldovan leadership moves were made to reduce the power of strong nationalists. Although the influence of radicals in the Popular Front tended to grow, the strongly pan-Romanian Mircea Druc was replaced as first prime minister in May 1991, and elections called for February 1994 confirmed the declining influence of the Popular Front, whose ranks had become highly differentiated over a number of ethnic and reform issues – which weakened the strong pan-Romanian sentiments originally held by much of the population.

Party families in eastern Europe

Parties have, therefore, developed hesitantly and incompletely throughout much of eastern Europe – and in some countries to no great extent at all. Such political organizations that can be identified may be differentiated in various ways. One obvious starting point that emerges on the basis of the survey just presented is that of party origin, which is, further, the starting point for an influential contemporary theoretical view of party development.[46] Parties may be distinguished by their links with the social movement or umbrella organization that represented the forces of anti-communist opposition in many countries of eastern Europe, or by the origin of parties in relation to organizations of the communist or pre-communist period (so-called 'historic' and 'post-communist' parties).

These distinctions cannot always be easily drawn. The Polish Peasant Party was largely derived from the auxiliary party of the former establishment, but also successfully assimilated some attributes of the old historic agrarian party (not least its name), whereas the contemporary Czech Social Democrats are formally based on an historical organization but have largely reinvented themselves and developed as a new political formation. Parties emanating from the ruling parties of the communist period vary enormously in outlook and political style. Socialist and social democratic parties of Hungary and Poland fit in well with the west European community of democratic left-wing organizations, whereas the Serbian Socialists under Milošević remain closely wedded to their authoritarian origins. Others throughout the Balkans show an uneasy mix of characteristics of both categories that reflects the partial advance towards democracy made in those countries. Equally, the direct descendants of the anti-communist opposition and the former social movements have undergone major changes or largely disappeared in some countries (such as, for example, the Czech Civic Forum or Hungarian Democratic Forum). Yet another leading movement, Polish Solidarity, apparently disintegrated only to re-emerge as an electoral force in rather different form in 1996.

As time passes, moreover, differentiation in terms of origin becomes less help-ful in providing guidance to the range of contemporary east European political organizations. As parties developed or, more frequently, failed to do so and faded out of the scene altogether their origins became less important and attri-butes in terms of contemporary presentation and performance more prominent. Many of the parties that emerged in the different countries as outlined in the pre-ceding section seemed, indeed, to fall into recognizable groups not wholly differ-ent from those seen in established democracies: old communist and reformed social democratic parties, and a range of liberal, Christian Democratic, conserva-tive, nationalist and Green parties reminiscent of the party spectrum in western democracies (see Table 2.5 for a summary listing all major parties currently represented in east European parliaments).

Several major points emerge from an overview of party representation in con-temporary east European parliaments.

- First, just a few major parties (two or three in most cases) now succeed in capturing the majority of votes in the more democratically advanced coun-tries, which suggests that, general political conditions permitting, a reason-ably balanced party system representing new democratic forces may be in the process of emerging.

- This is most obviously *not* the case in the more backward republics of the former Soviet Union (Table 2.5d), where relatively traditional communist parties continue to gain most support and competing parties have not been able to gain much of a foothold amongst the electorate (especially in Belarus, where further elections have not been held at all).

- The process of party formation is by no means complete and, as can be seen in the column with dates of formation, new parties continue to emerge and score highly in the contemporary electoral process; in many cases they emerge more as electoral coalitions or blocs of parties rather than as coher-ent political organizations.

- In association with the fluidity of party organization and shifting patterns of party allegiance, many parties have quite few members; outside the more developed countries of east-central Europe and the Baltic region such numerical indicators are that much more difficult to obtain and are likely to be still lower.

- Increasingly, though, a distinctive range of parties has emerged that goes way beyond the initial conflict between communist establishment and anti-communist opposition often seen in the early stages of the east European transformation; parties have developed political characteristics that enable them generally to be compared with the west European spectrum of political parties.

This summary overview of major east European parties shows that their ideologi-cal character and political programmes have increasingly crystallized and come to characterize different groups of parties whose origins and degree of 'partyness'

Table 2.5a Parliamentary parties in east-central Europe

Country and date of last election	Percentage of votes	Date of formation	Membership	Party family
Czech Republic, June 1998				
Czech Social Democratic Party	32.3	1878/1989	13,000	Soc. Dem.
Civic Democratic Party	27.7	April 1990	22,000	Liberal Cons.
Communist Party of Bohemia and Moravia	11.0	March 1990	137,000	(Post-) Com.
Christian Democratic Union	9.0	Dec. 1989	60,400	Christ. Dem.
Freedom Union	8.6	Jan. 1998	3000	Liberal Cons.
Hungary, May 1998				
FIDESZ: Hungarian Civic Party	28.2	1988/1995	15,000	Liberal Cons.
Hungarian Socialist Party	32.3	Oct. 1989	37,000	Post-Com.
Independent Party of Smallholders	13.8	1909/1988	60,000	Agrarian
Alliance of Free Democrats	7.9	Nov. 1988	32,000	Liberal
Hungarian Justice and Life Party	5.5	Nov. 1993	7000	Nationalist
Hungarian Democratic Forum	3.1	Sept. 1987	25,000	Cons./Ch. D
Poland, September 1997				
Solidarity Elector. Action (Soc. Movement)	33.8	1996 (1998)	30,000	Cons./Ch. D.
Democratic Left Alliance (SDRP/SLD)	27.1	1990/1999	60th/80th	Post-Com.
Freedom Union	13.4	1990/1994	22,000	Liberal
Polish Peasant Party	7.3	May 1990	120,000	Agrarian
Movement for Reconstruction of Poland	5.6	Nov. 1995	20,000	Conservative
German Minority	0.6	1990		Ethnic
Slovakia, September 1998				
Movement for Democratic Slovakia	27.0	June 1991	34,000	Nat, Post-Com.
Slovak Democratic Coalition	26.3	July 1997	39,000+	Lib -SD-Ch.D.
Party of Democratic Left	14.7	Oct. 1990	48,000	Post-Com.
Hungarian Coalition	9.1	1992 (1998)	36,000	Ethnic
Slovak National Party	9.1	Feb. 1990	7000	Nationalist
Party of Civic Understanding	8.0	Feb. 1998	6500	Liberal
Slovenia, November 1996				
Liberal Democracy of Slovenia	27.0	1990/1994	5300	Liberal
Slovene People's Party	19.4	May 1988	44,000	Cons, Agrarian
Social Democratic Party of Slovenia	16.1	Feb. 1989	20,000	Soc. Dem.
Slovene Christian Democrats	9.6	March 1989	36,600	Christ. Dem.
United List of Social Democrats	9.0	April 1993	23,000	Post-Com.
Democratic Party of Retired People	4.3	1990	26,000	Soc. Dem.
Slovene National Party	3.2	March 1991	5800	Extreme Right

Table 2.5b Parliamentary parties in the Baltic states

Country and date of last election	Percentage of votes	Date of formation	Membership	Party family
Estonia, March 1999				
Estonian Centre Party	23.6	1993	2500	Soc. Dem.
Estonian Reform Party	16.0	Nov. 1994	1000	Liberal Cons.
Fatherland Union	16.0	Dec. 1995	1100	Conservative
Moderates	15.1	1996	1100	Soc. Dem.
Coalition Party	7.6	1993	1200	Liberal
Country People's Party/Rural Union	7.2	1994/1992	2100	Agrarian
United People's Party	6.1	1994	1100	Soc. Dem.
Latvia, October 1998				
People's Party	21.2	Dec. 1997		Liberal
Latvia's Way	18.4	Oct. 1993	700	Liberal
Cons. Union for Fatherland and Freedom	14.7	Jan. 1995	1000+	Conservative
National Harmony Party	14.2	Feb. 1994	400	Soc. Dem.
Latvian Social Democratic Alliance	12.9	1997		Soc. Dem.
New Party	7.3	1998	1000+	Soc. Dem.
Lithuania, October 1996				
Homeland Union – Conservatives of Lithuania	29.8	May 1993	16,000	Conservative
Lithuanian Christian Democratic Party	9.9	1904/1990	8500	Cons. Ch. D.
Lithuanian Democratic Labour Party	9.5	Dec. 1990	8000	Post-Com.
Lithuanian Centre Union	8.2	1992		Liberal
Lithuanian Social Democratic Party	6.6	1896/1989		Soc. Dem.

may otherwise differ. Precisely how such differences may be described and the range of contemporary parties characterized is debatable – ideology implies a degree of structuration and theoretical support that is generally lacking, whereas formal programmes rarely give a fully reliable guide to the nature of parties. But west European party experience certainly provides some guidance. One starting point for establishing differences between the parties may be derived from the influential schema of the different *familles spirituelles* proposed for west European democratic parties by K. von Beyme.[47]

With some variation the classification may also be applied to eastern Europe, and von Beyme himself has identified eight equivalent kinds of party in this context, although one of these is the forum (or movement-based) party, which is generally a rather different kind of organization and, we have suggested here,

Table 2.5c Parliamentary parties in the Balkans

Country and date of last election	Percentage of votes	Date of formation	Party family
Albania, July 1997			
Socialist Party of Albania	52.8	June 1991	Post-Communist
Democratic Party of Albania	25.7	Dec. 1990	Conservative
Human Rights Unity Party	2.8	Feb. 1992	Ethnic (Greek)
Democratic Alliance of Albania	2.8	July 1992	Liberal
Social Democratic Party of Albania	2.5	March 1991	Social Democratic
Bosnia and Herzegovina, September 98			
Coalition for Single and Demo. Bosnia	40 (seats)	1998	(Multi-)ethnic
Croatian Democratic Union	14	Aug. 1990	Ethnic
Sloga (Unity) Coalition	10	1998	Serb (Soc. Dem.)
Serb Democratic Party	10	July 1990	Ethnic
Bulgaria, April 1997			
Union of Democratic Forces	52.3	Nov. 1989	Liberal-Conservative
Bulgarian Socialist Party	22.1	April 1990	Post-Communist
Alliance for National Salvation	7.6	1997	Ethnic
Euro-Left	5.5	Feb. 1997	Soc. Dem.
Bulgarian Business Bloc	4.9	1992	Liberal-Populist
Croatia, January 2000			
Social Democrats/Social Liberal Party	47.0	1990/1989	Post-Com., Liberal
Croatian Democratic Union	30.5	June 1989	Conservative-Nat.
Peasant Party-led coalition	15.9	1999	Conservative
Croatian Rights' Party	3.3	Feb. 1990	Nationalist
Macedonia, October 1998			
IMRO – Democratic Party	28.1	1894/1990	Conservative Nat.
Social Democratic Union of Macedonia	25.2	1991	Post-Communist
Albanian Coalition	19.3	1998	Ethnic
Democratic Alternative	10.1	1998	Conservative
Liberal Democrats	7.0	1990	Liberal
Montenegro, May 1998			
For a Better Life coalition	48.9	1997	Post-communist led
Socialist National Party	35.6	1997	Post-communist
Liberal Union of Montenegro	6.2	1990	Liberal
Serb People's Party	1.9	1995	Ethnic
Democratic Union (Albanian)	1.6		Ethnic
Romania, November 1996			
Democratic Convention of Romania	30.2	1992	Liberal-Conservative
Romanian Party of Social Democracy	21.5	1993	Post-Communist
Social Democratic Union	12.9	1996	Soc. Democratic
Hungarian Democratic Union of Romania	6.6	Dec. 1989	Ethnic
Greater Romania Party	4.5	May 1991	Nationalist
Romanian National Unity Party	4.4	1992	Nationalist
Serbia, September 1997			
Joint (Left) List	44 (seats)	1997	Post-Communist led
Serbian Radical Party	33	Jan. 1990	Extreme Right
Serbian Renewal Movement	18	Aug. 1990	Nationalist

Table 2.5d Parliamentary parties in the former Soviet Republics

Country and date of last election	Percentage of votes	Date of formation	Party family
Belarus, 1995			
Communist Party	21.2 (seats)	1993	Traditional CP
Agrarian Party	16.7	1992	Post-Communist
United Civic Party	4.5	1995	Liberal
Party of National Accord	4.0	1991	Liberal
Supreme Council dissolved 1996 but no further free elections held			
Moldova, March 1998			
Communist Party of Moldova	30.1	1994	Traditional CP
Democratic Convention of Moldova	19.2	1997	Liberal-Cons. (presidential)
Bloc for Democratic and Prosperous Moldova	18.2	1997	Liberal
Party of Democratic Forces	8.8	1995	Conservative
Ukraine, March 1998			
Communist Party of Ukraine	24.7	1993	Traditional CP
Rukh	9.4	1989	Nationalist
Socialist and Peasant Bloc	8.5	1997	Pro-Communist
Green Party	5.5	1990	Green
Ukrainian National-Democratic Party	5.0	1996	Centrist
Hromada	4.7	1994	Conservative
Social Democratic Party of Ukraine	4.0	1990	Social Democrat
Progressive Socialist Party	4.0	1995	Social Democrat

belongs more to the pre-party phase of political development than to the group of contemporary party families itself.[48] His classification of east European parties excludes from the original west European scheme conservative parties and right-wing extremist organizations, although elsewhere in his discussion he does note the role of nationalists and various functional groups. In fact, the identities of new east European parties follow the west European model more closely than might have been anticipated.

The lengthy experience of communist authoritarian rule nevertheless gives a specific meaning to contemporary east European conservatism. On one basis it might be argued that in terms of the origins of east European parties it is the various kinds of communist or communist-successor organization that best represent conservative forces.[49] This is broadly what has happened with the Communist Party of Bohemia and Moravia in the Czech Republic, the small orthodox communist offshoots of the old parties in other east-central European countries, and major parts of the old establishment in the Balkans and republics of the former Soviet Union. In other developed states of east-central Europe, such as

Hungary and Poland, major segments of the post-communist parties have rapidly established themselves as credible social democracies. Broadly similar transformations have occurred in Slovenia and Lithuania. But neither variant of the post-communist party is fully conservative in normal political terms and all such successor organizations are clearly identified by voters as left-wing forces. There is clearly room for some kind of more conventional right-wing conservative category even under the specific conditions of post-communist eastern Europe.

If east European conservatism cannot be identified with the old communist establishment, neither can it be fully subsumed by new currents of free-market liberalism. There is, indeed, also a confusing contemporary overlap between conservatism and liberalism in western democracies.[50] Some conservative tendencies fit well with the free-market principles of post-communist liberalism, whereas others are more comfortably allied with organizations committed to traditional religious values or varieties of nationalism. It is equally clear that the Christian Democrat category (which occupies an important place on the right of the political spectrum in some west European countries) is not sufficiently broad to encompass all kinds of right-wing conservative forces in eastern Europe. Although separate Christian Democrat parties do exist in several countries they are mostly small and relatively marginal, and they by no means encompass the right wing as a whole.

Even in Poland, where religious forces have a strong political impact, Church-oriented groups occupy only a limited political space in the broad right-wing association of the Solidarity Electoral Action. It provides a general conservative umbrella as much as one based on either religious or trade union values. The initiative to found a Social Movement on the basis of the Solidarity Action after the 1997 election was indeed hailed as the first attempt to found a proper Christian Democratic Party in Poland, but developments during the year that followed did not support the view that an authentic process of party development was really under way.[51] A further complicating factor in eastern Europe more generally is that self-defined Christian Democrats are by no means generally accepted as such by the broader west European Christian Democratic community. The new east European parties were often more conservative and authoritarian than the west European variants and it was, for example, the Hungarian Democratic Forum that was first recognized by the west European association rather than the equivalent Hungarian CD party.[52] To the extent that sizeable and reasonably well-defined Christian Democratic parties have been absent from the east European party spectrum, their combination with representatives of a broad conservative category seems to be that much more appropriate. The more free-market oriented conservatives, on the other hand, are better linked with contemporary liberals.

More extreme right-wing and nationalist forces require a separate category, although they also tend to shade into other types of party.[53] Such forces have occupied a distinctive place in a number of post-communist parliaments. The extremist Republican Party of Czechoslovakia gained a parliamentary presence after the elections both of 1992 and 1996 but failed to overcome the threshold for entry in 1998. During the same year, though, the Hungarian Justice and Life Party (an extremist offshoot of the HDF) overcame the threshold and showed itself to be more popular than its maternal party. Extremist nationalist parties also showed considerable staying power in Romania and other Balkan countries. Such radical forms of nationalism seem to have a permanent place in the east European party spectrum, even if its role has remained a relatively limited one in the more developed east-central European democracies.

The identification in the east European context of a range of party families on the west European model seems, therefore, to provide a useful initial guide to the current party spectrum – although the relevance of west European categories and the precise identity of some east European parties certainly require some examination. The sevenfold classification presented in Tables 2.6 covers all main variants while retaining a reasonable degree of economy.[54] It dispenses with ecological and green parties, who now generally appear in some electoral alliances and as currents within parties rather than as parliamentary forces in their own right (the Ukrainian legislature of 1998 was one exception, however). It encompasses the following groups:

- communist successors;
- social democrats;
- liberals (and market-oriented conservatives);
- ethnic groups;
- agrarians;
- Christian Democrats/traditional conservatives; and
- nationalists.

Rather surprisingly, too, the well-established form of political differentiation that developed in western societies between left- and right-wing groups has also retained considerable resonance in post-communist Europe. An important recent finding is that the established left-right party differentiation is indeed valid and has widespread meaning in contemporary eastern Europe, and that party families can be roughly distributed in line with analysis of the political space conducted on this basis. People throughout the region can generally locate parties on a left-right spectrum and also identify themselves in these terms, although the elements that enter into such a definition may be quite diverse and the likelihood of a one-dimensional left-right distinction dominating the political arena is low.[55] This particular analysis also confirms that the liberal category is a particularly broad one in contemporary eastern Europe and ranges quite far to the right, making it feasible to extend it to encompass a number of quite conservative forces with a strong right-wing identity. Nationalist forces, on the other hand, are by no means always identified as right-wing forces in eastern Europe and are often associated with a broadly populist centre.

The location of east European parties on a left-right scale is, therefore, highly tentative and designed only to provide a rough guide to the political orientation

Table 2.6a Party families in east-central Europe and the Baltic states

	Post-Communist	Social Democrat	Liberal/Conservative	Ethnic	Agrarian	Christian Dem./Conservative	Nationalist
Czech Republic	Communist Party of Bohemia and Moravia	Czech Social Democratic Party	Civic Democratic Party, Freedom Union			Christian Democratic Union	
Hungary	Hungarian Socialist Party		FIDESZ, Alliance of Free Democrats		Independent Party of Smallholders	Hungarian Democratic Forum	Hungarian Justice and Life Party
Poland	Democratic Left Alliance (Social Democracy of Republic)		Freedom Union	German Minority	Polish Peasant Party	Solidarity Electoral Alliance (Soc. Movement), Movement for Reconstruction of Poland	
Slovakia	Party of the Democratic Left		Slovak Democratic Coalition	Hungarian Coalition		Movement for Democratic Slovakia	Slovak National Party
Slovenia	United List of Social Democrats	Social Democratic Party of Slovenia	Liberal Democracy of Slovenia		Slovene People's Party	Slovene Christian Democrats	Slovene National Party
Estonia		Centre Party, United People's Party	Coalition Party, Moderates	Our Home is Estonia	Rural Union, Rural Centre	Reform Party, Fatherland Union, Rightists	
Latvia		Social Democratic Alliance, National Harmony Party, New Party	Latvia's Way, People's Party			Conservative Union for Fatherland and Freedom	
Lithuania	Lithuanian Democratic Labour Party	Social Democratic Party	Centre Union			Homeland Union, Christian Democrats	

Left-right alignment of parties at head of table indicative and intended only to give idea of divergent location of parties in different countries, although the suggested range does reflect the relative location of party supporters (see Markowski, 'Political parties and ideological spaces').

Table 2.6b Party families in the Balkans and former Soviet Republics

	Post-Communist	Social Democrat	Liberal/Conservative	Ethnic	Agrarian	Christian Dem./Conservative	Nationalist
Albania	Socialist Party	Social Democratic Party	Democratic Party	Human Rights Unity Party			National Front
Bosnia		Sloga	Coalition for Single and Democratic Bosnia	(Coalition, Croat DU, Serb DP)			Croatian Democratic Union, Serb Democratic Party
Bulgaria	Bulgarian Socialist Party	Euro-Left	Bulgarian Business Bloc, Popular Union	Alliance for National Salvation	Bulgarian Agrarian Union	Union of Democratic Forces	
Croatia	Social Democratic Party		Croatian Social Liberal Party		Peasant Party, People's Party		Democratic Union, Rights Party
Macedonia	Social Democratic Union of Macedonia	Socialist Party	Liberal Democratic Party	Albanian Coalition, Roma Alliance			IMRO
Montenegro	Democratic Socialists, Socialist National Party	Social Democratic Party	Liberal Union of Montenegro	Democratic Union			Serb Radical Party
Romania	Romanian Party of Social Democracy	Social Democratic Union		Hungarian Democratic Union of Romania		Democratic Convention of Romania	Greater Romania, National Unity Party, Radical Party, Renewal Movement
Serbia	Socialist Party of Serbia						
Belarus	Communists	Social Democratic Grammada	Civic Unity Party		Agrarian Party		
Moldova	Communists		Democratic Convention, Democratic and Prosp. Moldova		Free Farmers	Party of Democratic Forces	
Ukraine	Communists, Socialist Party	Social Democrats	National Democratic Party, Greens		Peasant Party		Rukh

of new east European parties. The conditions under which parties emerged in post-communist eastern Europe and early processes of party development nevertheless soon produced relatively well-defined political identities. A key part in this evolution was played by the sequence of elections held in many countries, and it is this aspect of post-communist change that we now consider.

3 Parties, elections and parliaments

Elections and party development

Elections have played a crucial role in advancing the growth and development of some democratic parties in post-communist eastern Europe, and pronounced a sentence of death on the political prospects or survival of those unsuccessful in their confrontation with the electorate. Yet other parties have presented at successive elections and maintained a limited if precarious existence on the margins of democratic parliaments and post-communist political life. Elections propel the leaders of some parties into positions of governmental responsibility, but consign others to political oblivion. Electoral success generally strengthens the commitment of supporters to their chosen party, whilst confronting the organization with the challenge of delivering on its commitments and moving it on from the abstract realm of promise and political aspiration to that of more practical government responsibility. The electoral contest thus provides parties with the prime opportunity to advance to a further phase of development and political growth, and lead some of them into the complex arena of responsible parliamentary action and towards further structural evolution. Some parties clearly cope with these challenges more successfully than others, and major aspects of the flux of early post-communist political life in eastern Europe have been clarified by a range of elections that have advanced the institutional careers of the chosen few parties represented in parliament and banished to the margins the unsuccessful many.

Entry into parliament, as D.M. Olson put it, brought 'some order out of chaos' in early post-communist Europe by introducing a measure of consistency in relations between the major parties and clarifying the identity of the different political organizations.[1] Amongst all the differences that can be drawn between east European parties the most important, according to Polish writer S. Gebethner, is that between parliamentary organizations and those whose prime objective of parliamentary status has yet to be achieved (or do not even share this goal).[2] A focus on elections is a prime component of what J. Bielasiak identifies as the process approach to new party systems in post-communist Europe, and places major emphasis on the developmental patterns emerging in the region and the dynamic properties of the transition process. Electoral and parliamentary activities thus 'serve as a filter for the management of political space, acting as a screening device that elevates some political contenders to prominent roles, marginalizes other party formations, and eliminates altogether most aspiring parties'.[3]

This prime aspect of democratization under contemporary conditions was established quite successfully during the first decade of post-communist eastern Europe. Multi-party elections have been held regularly throughout the region and mostly conducted according to agreed constitutional procedures, although major disputes emerged over these matters in Belarus and some other countries subject to relatively strong authoritarian rule. Three reasonably standard elections have been held in most countries, a situation that permits an overview of party development and electoral practice under the new conditions. A relatively small number of parties have emerged as the major players in the new political order and only a few are real contenders for governmental power, although there are important differences between the different countries and areas of the region (Table 3.1).

The process has, not surprisingly, advanced furthest in the more developed countries of east-central Europe. In Hungary, Poland, the Czech Republic and – in 1998 – Slovakia two major parties or electoral associations emerged as the leading contenders for power with the capacity to mobilize the support of around 30 per cent of voters, with one or more second-rank parties establishing themselves with sufficient parliamentary strength to present themselves as viable coalition partners for the formation of reasonably stable governments. In these countries at least, a situation that approaches a reasonably balanced competitive party system has emerged following the acclamatory elections of the early years that in many countries endorsed broad anti-communist forces and the newly organized but only loosely structured democratic organizations.

Conditions for multi-party elections

For elections to achieve this effect in eastern Europe certain conditions had to be fulfilled. First, they had to be held at regular intervals in accordance with constitutional provisions. Civil peace and a reasonable degree of public order are necessary for any kind of normal politics to develop. Warfare is a prime factor that destroys the conditions of normal social life and civic stability that are required for elections to be held in the first place. Only in Bosnia has warfare been so destructive of the political community in eastern Europe that elections were not held at all between 1990 and 1996, as any prospect of resolving ethnic conflicts through the means of the ballot box disappeared once war broke out in April 1992. But war can affect the prospects for effective electoral competition in less direct ways. Even where the extent of physical destruction and social disruption was more limited, as in Croatia and Serbia, involvement in military activities strengthened government authority and had the effect of de-legitimizing opposition. Such tendencies were already well established in the authoritarian-inclined nationalist regime of Tudjman in Croatia and the only partially transformed dictatorship of Milošević in Serbia – neither of whom were readily inclined to tolerate electoral defeat and even minor opposition victories at local level when they occurred. Although several contested elections were held in Serbia during the early 1990s (three for the Serbian authorities themselves and one for the new

Table 3.1a Election results in east-central Europe

Czech Republic 1992–98 (percentage of vote for parties represented in 1998)

Party	1998	1996	1992
CSDP: Czech Social Democratic Party	32.3	26.4	6.5
CDP: Civic Democratic Party	27.7	29.6	29.6
CPBM: Communist Party of Bohemia and Moravia	11.0	12.3	14.0
CDU: Christian Democratic Union	9.0	8.1	6.3
FU: Freedom Union	8.6	–	–

88.6 per cent of electorate represented by parliamentary parties in 1998, 88.9 per cent in 1996, 80.1 per cent in 1992.

Hungary 1990–98 (percentage of first round vote and number of seats for parties represented in 1998)

Party	1998		1994		1990	
FIDESZ (Alliance of Young Democrats)/ Hungarian Civic Party	28.2	148 seats	7.5	20 seats	8.9	21 seats
HSP: Hungarian Socialist Party	32.3	134	32.6	209	10.9	33
ISP: Independent Party of Smallholders	13.8	48	8.5	26	11.8	44
AFD: Alliance of Free Democrats	7.9	24	19.5	70	21.4	92
HJLP: Hungarian Justice and Life Party	5.5	14	*1.6	–	–	–
HDF: Hungarian Democratic Forum	3.1	17	12	37	24.7	164

*Failed to gain parliamentary representation; 90.8 per cent represented in 1998, 90 per cent in 1994, 89 per cent in 1990.

Poland 1991–97 (percentage of vote for parties represented in 1997)

Party	1997	1993	1991
SEA: Solidarity Electoral Action	33.8	–	–
ChNU: Christian National Union (Fatherland/CEA)		*6.4	8.8
CIP: Confederation for Independent Poland		5.8	7.6
NBSR: Non-Party Bloc to Support Reform	5.4	–	
S: Solidarity		*4.9	5.8
CA: Centre Alliance		*4.4	8.7
DLA: Democratic Left Alliance	27.1	20.4	12.0
FU: Freedom Union (Democratic Union)	13.4	10.6	12.3
PPP: Polish Peasant Party	7.3	15.4	8.6
MPR: Movement for Polish Reconstruction	5.6	–	–
German Minority	0.6	0.7	1.5

*Failed to reach threshold for parliamentary representation of 5% or 8% (for coalitions); 87.3 per cent of electorate represented in 1997, 65.6 per cent in 1993, 93.8 in 1991.

federal Yugoslav parliament), an atmosphere of war hysteria prevailed and the elections were largely sham in nature.[4] When relative peace prevails, though, parties have at least some opportunity to campaign and mobilize support, and electors can cast their vote relatively freely.

Table 3.1a continued

Slovakia 1992–98 (percentage of vote for parties represented in 1998)

Party	1998	1994	1992
MDS: Movement for Democratic Slovakia	27	35.0	37.3
SDC: Slovak Democratic Coalition	26.3	–	–
CDM: Christian Democratic Movement		10.1	8.9
DU: Democratic Union		8.6	–
DP: Democratic Party		3.4	3.3
SDP: Social Democratic Party		(PDL)	4.0
GPS: Green Party of Slovakia		(PDL)	2.1
PDL: Party of Democratic Left	14.7	10.4	14.7
HC: Hungarian Coalition	9.1	10.2	7.4
SNP: Slovak National Party	9.1	5.4	7.9
PCU: Party of Civic Understanding	8.0	–	–

Slovenia 1990–96 (percentage of vote for parties represented in 1996)

Party	1996	1992	1990
LDS: Liberal Democracy of Slovenia	27.0	23.5	14.5
SPP: Slovene People's Party	19.4	8.7	12.6
SDPS: Social Democratic Party of Slovenia	16.1	3.3	7.4
SCD: Slovene Christian Democrats	9.6	14.5	13.0
ULSD: United List of Social Democrats	9.0	13.6	17.3
DPRP: Democratic Party of Retired People	4.3	(ULSD)	0.4
SNP: Slovene National Party	3.2	10.0	–

Table 3.1b Election results in the Baltic states

Estonia 1992–99 (percentage of vote for parties represented in 1999)

Party	1999	1995		1992
Estonian Centre Party	23.6		14.2	–
Estonian Reform Party	16.0		16.2	–
Fatherland Union	16.0	(as alliance)	7.8	–
Fatherland (Isamma)				22.0
National Independence Party				8.8
Moderates (SD and Rural Centre)	15.1		6.0	12.9
Coalition Party	7.6	(with Country People's)	32.2	17.8
Country People's Party/Rural Union	7.2		–	–
United People's Party	6.1	(Rightists: 5.0) –		

Table 3.1b continued

Latvia 1993–98 (percentage of vote for parties represented in 1998)

Party	1998	1995	1993
People's Party	21.2	–	–
Latvia's Way	18.4	14.6	32.4
Conservative Union for Fatherland and Freedom	14.7	–	–
National Conservative Party		6.3	12.4
Fatherland and Freedom		11.9	5.4
National Harmony Party	14.2	5.6	12.0
Latvian Social Democratic Alliance	12.8	*4.6	–
New Party	7.3	–	–

*Below threshold for parliamentary representation.

Lithuania 1990–96 (percentage of vote for parties represented in 1996)

Party	1996	1992	1990
Homeland Union – Lithuanian Conservatives	29.8	18.4	(seats) 63.8
Lithuanian Christian Democratic Party	9.9	12.0	1.4
Lithuanian Democratic Labour Party	9.5	46.6	22.0
Lithuanian Centre Union	8.2	–	–
Lithuanian Social Democratic Party	6.6	5.7	6.4

Table 3.1c Election results in the Balkans

Bulgaria 1990–97 (percentage of vote for parties elected in 1997)

Party	1997	1994	1991	1990
Union of Democratic Forces	52.3	24.2	34.4	35.6
– Bulgarian Agrarian People's Union		6.5	(under 4)	8.1
Bulgarian Socialist Party	22.1	42.5	33.1	47.9
Alliance for National Salvation	7.6	–	–	–
– Movement for Rights and Freedom		5.4	7.6	5.9
Euro-Left	5.5	–	–	–
Bulgarian Business Bloc	4.9	4.7	–	–

Second, to be effective, elections in a liberal democracy must be genuinely contested and voters permitted to make their choice without coercion or intimidation. This condition has generally been met in east European elections, which have been subject to extensive outside scrutiny and broadly conducted with less corruption and intimidation than many such activities in the early stages of democratic development in western Europe. Criticism of electoral arrangements has, however, not been absent and the presence of foreign observers permitted a number of reservations to be logged. Bulgaria and, particularly, Romania were

Table 3.1c continued

Romania 1990–96 (percentage of vote for parties elected in 1996)

Party	1996	1992	1990
Democratic Convention of Romania	30.2	20.0	10.5
Christian and Democratic National Peasants' Party		(DC)	2.6
National Liberal Party		2.6	6.4
Romanian Party of Social Democracy	21.5	–	–
Democratic National Salvation Front		27.7	(NSF: 60.4)
Social Democratic Union	12.9	–	–
Democratic Party: National Salvation Front		10.2	(NSF: 60.4)
Hungarian Democratic Union of Romania	6.6	7.5	7.5
Greater Romania Party	4.5	3.9	–
Romanian National Unity Party	4.4	7.5	2.6

Albania 1991–97 (percentage of vote for parties elected in 1997)

Party	1997	1996	1992	1991
Socialist Party of Albania	52.8	20.4	25.7	67.9 (% seats)
Democratic Party of Albania	25.7	55.5	62.1	30.1
Human Rights Unity Party	2.8	4.0	2.9	2.0
Democratic Alliance of Albania	2.8	–	–	–
Social Democratic Party	2.5	(under 2)	4.4	–
National Front	2.3	5.0	–	–
Republican Party of Albania	2.3	5.7	3.1	–

Croatia 1992–2000 (percentage of vote for parties elected in 2000)

Party	2000	1995	1992
Social Democratic Party/		8.9	5.5
Croatian Social Liberal Party	47.0	11.6	17.5
Croatian Democratic Union	30.5	45.2	43.2
Peasant Party-led coalition	15.9	18.3	14.0
Croatian Rights' Party	3.3	5.0	6.8

Macedonia 1990–98 (percentage of votes for parties elected in 1998)

Party	1998	1995	1990
IMRO – Democratic Party	28.1	–	31.7 (seats)
Social Democratic Union of Macedonia	25.2	48.3	–
former League of Communists			45
Albanian coalition	19.3	–	–
Party for Democratic Prosperity	–	8.3	15
People's Democratic Party	–	3.3	5.8
Democratic Alternative	10.1	–	–
Liberal Democratic Party	7.0	24.2	–
Socialist Party	4.7	7.5	–

Table 3.1c continued

Montenegro 1993–98 (percentage of vote for major parties)

Party	1998	1996	1993
For a Better Life coalition	48.9	–	–
Democratic Socialist Party (supporting new president Djukanovic)		63 (original party under Bulatovic)	54
People's Party		20	16
Social Democratic Party		–	5
Socialist National Party (ex-DSP Bulatovic supporters)	35.6	–	–
Liberal Union of Montenegro	6.2	18	15
Serb People's Party	1.9	–	–
Democratic Union (Albanian)	1.6	–	–

Serbia 1990–97 (percentage of seats for major parties)

Party	1997	1993	1992	1990
Joint list	44	–	–	–
Socialist Party of Serbia		49	40	78
Yugoslav United Left				
New Democracy				
Serbian Radical Party	33	16	29	–
Serbian Renewal Movement	18	–	–	–
Democratic Movement of Serbia	–	18	20	–
Democratic Party	–	12	3	3
Democratic Party of Serbia	–	3	–	–

Bosnia and Herzegovina 1996–98 (percentage of seats in House of Representatives)

Party	1998	1996
Coalition for Single and Democratic Bosnia – Party of Democratic Action (Muslim)	40.0	38.0
Croation Democratic Union	14.0	17.0
Sloga (Unity) Coalition	10.0	
Serb Democratic Party	10.0	21.0

singled out for early criticism. Unacceptable activities have also been identified in Croatia (1993) and Ukraine (1994).[5] President Lukashenka's increasing drive for a power monopoly in Belarus was too, at the very least, linked with increasing pressure on parliamentary candidates in 1995 and their denial of financial resources and most media facilities. His evident contempt for party politics and the parliamentary vote was, to judge from the number of spoilt ballot papers, nevertheless frequently shared by members of the electorate.[6] The democratic

Table 3.1d Election results in the former Soviet Republics

Moldova 1994–98 (percentage of vote for major parties)

Party	1998	1994
Communist Party of Moldova	30.1	–
Democratic Convention of Moldova	19.2	–
Christian Democratic People's Front		
Bloc for Democratic and Prosperous Moldova	18.2	–
Party of Democratic Forces	8.8	–
Congress of Intellectuals, Free Farmers, National Liberals		9.2

Ukraine 1994–98 (percentage of vote for major parties)

Party	1998	1994
Communist Party of Ukraine	24.7	12.7
Rukh	9.4	5.2
Socialist and Peasant Bloc	8.5	
Socialist Party		3.1
Peasant Party		2.7
Green Party of Ukraine	5.5	–
Ukrainian National-Democratic Party	5.0	–
Hromada	4.7	–
Social Democratic Party of Ukraine	4.0	0.4
Progressive Socialist Party	4.0	–
Total vote for parties (per cent):	–	33.5
Percentage of seats for parties:	74.2	–

Belarus 1995 (percentage of seats for parties and independents)

Communist Party of Belarus	21.2
Belarusian Agrarian Party	16.7
Belarusian United Civic Party	4.5
Party of National Accord	4.0
Party of All-Belarusian Unity and Accord	1.0
Belarusian Social Democratic Grammada	1.0
Independents	48.0
(Seats unfilled after third round	31.3)

impulse, it should be noted, has not only to be tolerated and allowed to express itself in the absence of government coercion but often – particularly in new democracies with little or no experience of uncoerced participation – actually requires real encouragement from the authorities if it is to thrive.

Particularly strong criticism of government activity during the 1996 Albanian election was expressed, a situation that undoubtedly contributed to the resentment against the regime that finally erupted the following year after the uncovering of government-sponsored corruption and the collapse of an extensive pyramid scheme. Monitors from the Organization of Security and Co-operation in Europe (OSCE) were denied accreditation by the Albanian foreign ministry while, confusingly, representatives of the Council of Europe were allowed to oversee electoral procedures and decided to validate the outcome.[7] Most elections in eastern Europe have indeed been broadly endorsed by the monitoring organizations, but there are notable exceptions. The process leading up to the 1997 parliamentary elections in Serbia was condemned for its flaws by the OSCE, with media bias in favour of the ruling coalition being singled out for criticism. A similar lack of balance in the performance of Public Television in Slovakia was noted the following year.[8] A foreshadowing of later developments could be seen in the fundamental flaws detected in the Serbian presidential elections in December 1997 and the particularly serious doubts cast on the electoral process in Kosovo, where near-100 per cent turnout and votes for Milošević's candidate were recorded in constituencies where polling booths did not even open.[9]

The role of international agents and the influence they exert over elections is itself a complex, and sometimes contentious, issue. Official representatives of the United States have been particularly criticized for intervening in the developing east European democratic process. This was initially apparent in the case of US embassy staff present during the 1990 election in Bulgaria, where the recently transformed communist party was particularly well placed to dominate the electoral process. According to M. Glenny, the role of US representatives in this context 'was an absolute disgrace' and their support for the opposition Union of Democratic Forces judged counter-productive because of its clumsiness and blatant character.[10] Elsewhere in the Balkans, US ambassador Ryerson was reported to have developed (perhaps on the basis of his extensive experience in Latin America and democratization in that region) a 'strong emotional commitment to Albania and to the Democratic Party', which appeared to strengthen the resolve of President Berisha as well as a current of pronounced intolerance in the president's treatment of political opponents.[11]

Broadly speaking, though, most east European elections seem to have been reasonably well conducted and their results accepted as being largely authentic. The exceptions are not difficult to identify in terms of clear examples of authoritarian behaviour such as that of Lukashenka steering Belarus through a rapid return to authoritarian rule, the corruption of the Democratic Party regime in Albania leading the country into a state of popular revolt and virtual civil war, and Milošević riding rough-shod over all obstacles to his vision of Serbian nationalism and continuing personal rule.

Further factors determine the effectiveness of elections in facilitating party development and clarifying the pattern of political competition. Third, elections must be reasonably inclusive and involve a major part of the population. Although electoral participation both at the individual and group level must be free and uncoerced in a liberal democracy, the involvement both of a significant proportion of the population and of a sufficiently wide range of parties is necessary for competition to be meaningful and elections to be regarded as valid and authoritative. In terms of individual participation the countries of eastern Europe have shown considerable variation, and high levels of electoral turnout are by no means clearly associated with effective democratization or party development (see Table 3.2). They are, on average, not greatly different from those noted in western Europe and are nearly all higher than the 49 per cent registered for the US election of 1996.

The most striking levels of abstention from east European elections were seen in Poland, where turnout during the 1991 election was particularly low. Abstention and political passivity during the 1989–91 period in Poland were found to be associated with a low level of education, low wages and income, but also with less frequent religious practice and general indifference towards religion. In terms of socio-economic background at least, the Polish non-voter was very similar to his western counterpart.[12] The low ranking of Poland noted in the previous chapter in terms of popular trust in parties and public confidence in them (Table 2.3) is amply confirmed by such patterns of behaviour. Another study of participation in the 1991 Polish election showed turnout to be positively associated with the influence of the Church and negatively affected by unemployment.[13] But while the religious factor may well have been a characteristic feature of electoral participation and party development in Poland, it did not

Table 3.2 Electoral turnout (per cent)

	1989	1990	1991	1992	1993	1994	1995	1996	1997	1998	1999/ 2000
Czech Republic		(97)		(85)				76		74	
Hungary		63				69				57	
Poland	62	61	43		52		68		48		
Slovakia		(95)		(84)		76				84	
Slovenia		80		75				74			
Estonia				67			69				57
Latvia					90		72			73	
Lithuania				75				53			
Albania			99	90				80			
Bosnia										78	
Bulgaria		90	80	75		74		63	58		
Croatia		85		75			69				78
Macedonia		85				78					
Montenegro		75						67			
Romania		86		75				70			
Serbia		72		69	62				62		
Moldova										67	
Ukraine										70	74
Belarus							65		85		

West European average: 76.4 (*Governing the New Europe* (eds J. Hayward and E.C. Page), Cambridge, Polity, 1995).

prevent the electoral victory of more secular social democratic forces in 1993. The link between low status and non-voting was confirmed in later polls, and all forms of associative behaviour (political and trade union as well as religious) were found to be strong contributing factors to the formation of participatory patterns of voting behaviour (with the under-25s now emerging as a distinctive group of non-voters).[14]

Fourth, the availability of a sufficiently wide range of parties or organized groups for the voter to choose from is a further condition for effective competitive elections. Lack of material resources or organizational capacity prevent many of the smaller parties from presenting themselves to a mass electorate, whereas electoral legislation may impose further costs and require an organization to pay a deposit or present a large number of signatures before even being allowed to present candidates for election. It should be acknowledged at the outset in any case, though, that the high number of formally registered parties in most new democracies has had little connection with the real extent of active and politically relevant organizations. The proliferation of parties in Poland was well documented, with as many as 370 being registered before new legislation in this area was passed in 1997. But even of those registered in 1991 only around a third took part in that year's election.[15] Of the eighty-six parties registered in the Czech Republic at the beginning of 1997, thirteen were reported to be inactive.[16] The vagaries of political life in the new democracies already introduced an extensive sifting mechanism well before the impact of competitive multi-party elections, the restrictive effect of the particular regulations under which they were held and the nature of the mechanism by means of which the vote was turned into a concrete parliamentary outcome.

Registration procedures have in some cases imposed considerable obstacles to entry into the formal political arena and participation in the electoral process. Ukraine had particularly stringent registration procedures for party candidates, particularly in the early years of the state's independence. While independent candidates presenting in 1994 only needed the support of 300 citizens in a district, those standing on a party base had to be approved both by national and local organs while the registration of the parties themselves required the formal permission of a host of different ministries as well as local authority organs. Such barriers to party representation were clearly reflected in the high proportion of independent candidates returned in the 1994 election. Party registration rules could, therefore, be used to achieve a range of political objectives. In Belarus, President Lukashenka fought an increasingly aggressive campaign against opposition forces and attempts to restore the authority of parliament in the face of his continuing drive for dictatorial power. In this context, the decree he issued in January 1999 ordering all parties to re-register and raising the minimum membership required from 500 to 1000 people (twice the number required for trade unions and other public organizations) was a direct attack on the democratic opposition, particularly as the twenty-eight Belarussian parties currently registered were mostly thought to be quite unable to enrol so many members.[17]

Measures taken to restrict the number of parties represented in the Estonian parliament, on the other hand, were largely intended to reduce the extent of fragmentation and provide conditions for the establishment of more stable governing coalitions. Several steps in this area were taken to strengthen party democracy by restricting the number of organized participants. The minimum membership for party registration was similarly raised to 1000 before the 1999 elections, and parties were only to be allowed to remain in existence if they gained representation in two consecutive parliaments.[18] Further measures to limit the formation of party alliances intended purely to overcome the electoral threshold were also introduced just before the election.

Finally, one further method of party exclusion from east European elections has been that resulting from decisions taken by the parties themselves and the particularly high-risk strategies sometimes adopted by a political opposition. Faced with unfavourable conditions for political organization, access to the media and the mobilization of support against Milošević's ruling Socialist Party the democratic opposition in Serbia mounted a boycott of the 1997 election – a move that, perhaps not surprisingly, misfired and left it wholly excluded from the new parliament. The hope of undermining a particular electoral contest by forcing an authoritarian incumbent to observe official turnout requirements reflects a rather unrealistic political approach. The Internal Macedonian Revolutionary Organization had adopted similar tactics in the second round of the 1995 elections and similarly found themselves politically marginalized, only returning to power in 1998.

Electoral laws, and the precise mechanism by which votes are turned into a particular form of party representation, are a fifth and final aspect of the electoral process. They represent a different form of regulation both from that imposed by the initial registration of the political organization and that imposed on the candidate inscribing his name on party lists. Few electoral systems have directly reflected the wishes of the electorate in terms of translating the initial distribution of votes into equivalent numbers of parliamentary deputies – and where this has been attempted the results have not been encouraging. New democracies have had to take some fundamental decisions about these issues at the very outset. The rules operate at several levels. The basic matter to be resolved concerned the overall balance between governability and the representation of minority views.[19] This involves early choices between:

- proportional representation or winner-takes-all contests;
- one-round or two-round contests (the latter giving a further choice between stronger candidates emerging from the initial vote); and
- whether or not to impose a threshold in cases of proportional representation to exclude extreme minorities and facilitate the emergence of a viable majority for government.

The outcome in terms of electoral system adopted has been a varied one between the countries of eastern Europe, as different elements have been combined to produce a final outcome. Electoral systems have also changed over time as the drawbacks of the first system adopted often became apparent after initial experience. The great majority of east European regimes use some form of proportional representation, and impose a threshold for parliamentary entry in terms of specifying the percentage of the vote a party needs to attract overall before any of its candidates can be deemed to have won a parliamentary seat. The outcome of the 1991 election in Poland, the first fully competitive contest in that country, provided a valuable lesson in this respect and warned against the dangers of not imposing any threshold at all. Having begun the process of post-communist democratization at an early stage when the semi-free election of 1989 led to the collapse of the communist system, conflicting political interests were already well entrenched as the lengthy process of preparing the legislation under which the first fully competitive elections were to be held got under way. Influential groups feared exclusion from the legislature if any threshold at all was applied and, after heated debate, an open system of proportional representation was adopted.[20] In consequence, twenty-nine different groups were represented in the new parliament (by no means all parties), no 'natural' majority was present for a government to be based on and the formation of any viable government coalition at all was extremely difficult.

Similar procedures were only followed in a few other cases such as the early elections in Albania and Romania, where political differentiation and development overall was far less advanced and the consequences of that particular electoral mechanism correspondingly less pronounced. The question of when the critical first election was held therefore proved to be particularly important: if civil society was already advanced in terms of pluralization and the process of party formation when this occurred the dangers of fragmentation were considerable. If, on the other hand, elections were held quickly (and, in terms of democratization and institutional pluralism, prematurely) established political forces were in a strong position to perpetuate their rule and exert a restraining influence over processes of political change (as indeed happened throughout most of the Balkan area).[21]

Questions of timing and context were, therefore, just as important in terms of the broader political outcome as the electoral mechanism adopted. Poland subsequently applied a five per cent threshold and from 1993 has seen far less fragmented parliaments and more stable government. It is now general throughout eastern Europe to apply a threshold of between three and five per cent for single parties and a higher level for coalitions – which may, further, be on a sliding scale according to the number of parties involved (one as high as 11 per cent has been seen in the Czech Republic).[22] By this method many countries seek to achieve stable parliamentary government by excluding parties with a small following and avoiding some of the more extreme problems of coalition government. Others have eliminated small parties and endeavour to create a viable parliamentary majority by employing a two-round system similar to that used in France, where voters in the second round of elections choose from the two leaders identified in the first (a system originally used in Albania, Latvia, Lithuania and Macedonia but since changed or amended).

The picture in eastern Europe is a diverse one, and one country may combine elements of different systems in a varied pattern. Individual cases have features both of majority and proportional systems, and some cases achieve high levels of complexity. Mixed systems have increasingly been adopted. The Hungarian system is one of the best known in this respect and uses three different methods simultaneously to select its deputies, although the voter only casts two votes (following the German model) – one for the local constituency and one for a multi-member county list.[23] The emergence of a well-defined party system and the formation of stable government coalitions in that country suggest that the Hungarian procedure works rather well, although the fairly low turnout for elections may also be linked with their complexity and the complicated method of arriving at the final outcome having a certain alienating effect on the electorate.

Some countries have carried the exclusionary effect of electoral arrangements to an extreme level and generally held back the process of democratization as a whole. In particular cases it has had the effect less of producing a few relatively strong parties than of obstructing the parliamentary entry of parties overall and slowing down the whole process of party development. This has been seen in the post-Soviet republics, and particularly Ukraine, where parties did not face a general threshold but originally had to achieve an overall majority in their constituency as well as having onerous registration procedures imposed on them. Particularly testing was the requirement that candidates secure the support of 50 per cent of the electorate in a given district before they could enter parliament (a direct legacy of the Soviet period).[24] Such regulations militated against the overall development of parties as agencies of representation as well as favouring the interests of incumbent office-holders and local power-brokers. The weakness of party development under such conditions was not just a function of poorly defined public preferences and problems of organizational capacity but also – and in this case primarily – the consequence of weak elite commitment to the very notion of party politics and early resistance to democratization more generally. The main aspect of constitutional reform that accompanied the move towards Ukrainian independence was the establishment of a presidential system in July 1991. As in some other post-Soviet countries, such as Belarus and Russia itself, this tended to hold back rather than facilitate broad processes of democratization and institutional change.

The situation in Ukraine evolved, however, and changes in the direction of a more proportional system were made in 1997 prior to the 1998 election, with half the deputies now being elected by simple majority and the other half by a proportional system. While the changes introduced had some positive effect and the proportional representation element helped reduce tendencies to fragmentation, nevertheless, 'in neither its mechanical nor its psychological aspects did the single-member component of the system enhance party system consolidation'.[25]

A pronounced authoritarian and anti-parliament stance on the part of President Lukashenka remained apparent in Belarus, where a strongly majoritarian system was also in place. After a first round of elections on 14 May 1996, it took several more goes just to produce a quorate Supreme Council by December.[26]

Lukashenka's stance was as much dictatorial and anti-parliamentarian as anti-party *per se*, although the implications for party development were far from positive either. His attitude to party activity was made more clear in 1999, when the rules for party registration were made even more demanding. In Ukraine, the position of the elite was fundamentally conservative and anti-democratic, if less antithetic to the idea of parliamentary rule itself. But it remained notably unsympathetic to the growth of party opposition, and parties continued to provide less of the basic organizational framework for the operation of parliament than they do in most other countries. Majoritarian electoral systems of this sort led to the promotion of local personalities rather than party candidates, as well as a strongly polarized parliament.

The post-Soviet cases exemplify if only in a negative way the strong association that exists between democratization and party development, as well as the tendency in the post-communist context for competitive politics in weak democracies to focus on the presidential arena. They demonstrate both the weak roots that democracy has in this part of the region overall, and the stronger basis for party-led democratization provided by countries with an established civil society and a legacy of organized opposition to communist rule. No particular electoral system would be sufficient to overcome these problems, and a whole range of factors determined the way in which elections influenced processes of party development. We now turn to an overview of how the electoral process itself developed in eastern Europe.

The sequence of post-communist elections

During the nine years that followed the first democratic multi-party election of post-communist eastern Europe, held in Hungary during March 1990, most other countries held three or more reasonably free competitively organized elections too. The main exceptions have been the countries of the former Soviet Union, where the early elections were decidedly pre-transitional and the population's experience of competitive party politics has been decidedly more limited.[27] Their sparser electoral record is certainly reflected in a lower level of pluralist party development and the general absence of anything like a stable party system. But party development has also been limited in some of the other countries of eastern Europe, and particularly the Balkans, not least because formally organized groups were not always prominent in the competitive political process and ruling cliques based on the old establishment were quite successful in holding on to power in some countries. Party development has clearly been more robust in countries with stronger political rights and greater civil liberties, and which score higher on a general 'freedom ranking' (Table 1.1). Competitive parties develop better in a pluralist context, and the broader political environment has a strong influence both on how successfully parties are able to organize and the overall significance of the electoral process. Numerous competitive elections were held in eastern Europe during the first post-communist decade, and they may be separated into four distinct stages.

With the exception of Hungary, initial elections (as outlined in Chapter 2) hinged on the contest between communist forces and the anti-communist opposition as representatives of different systems rather than as expressions of discrete interests or conflict between actual parties. In 1990 independence movements or anti-communist coalitions prevailed in Czechoslovakia, Lithuania, Latvia, Slovenia and Croatia, and made a strong showing (and thus exercised a determinant influence on the political outcome) in Estonia and Moldova. The nationalist Internal Macedonian Revolutionary Organization achieved a similar victory in its homeland, while an equivalent ethnic-based outcome was reached in Bosnia. The same year the existing establishment won some kind of popular mandate in Ukraine, Belarus, Montenegro and Serbia (with a second round in January 1991), while rapidly recast communist forces were victorious in Bulgaria, Albania (in March/April 1991) and (in the ambiguous guise of the National Salvation Front) Romania as well. These were the dominant forms of conflict during the early post-communist elections.

Phase One thus saw generalized forms of political conflict or the reconsolidation of establishment power on quasi-democratic grounds, neither variant showing as yet much development towards organized party politics. In the early post-communist period only Hungary saw an electoral contest between major independent political parties and one that, moreover, produced a relatively stable and effective form of party government that lasted its full constitutional term of four years. Reference in the general literature on democratic transition is often made to the early formal contests in the post-authoritarian countries as 'founding' elections that set the scene for subsequent development of a pluralist order and broadly identified the main players in the newly liberated political arena. In eastern Europe, however, the idea of such founding elections needs rather to be extended to encompass second, third or even subsequent ballots as the complex process of post-totalitarian pluralization and institutional development slowly progressed.[28]

The multiplicity of elections certainly contributed to the unfolding process of democratization. A second wave of elections, some in 1991 (Poland and Bulgaria) but most in 1992 (Czechoslovakia, Romania, Albania, Slovenia, Croatia, Serbia, Estonia and Lithuania) followed the early contests. In some cases they pointed to a new direction of political development, in others they confirmed the line already taken. New elections were held just 1 year after the initial ballot in Bulgaria (in October 1991) and Albania (March/April 1992) that reflected a shift to right-wing, anti-communist forces (see Table 3.1). In 1992 further elections were held in the now independent states of Slovenia and Croatia, which confirmed respectively the essentially pluralist and national populist regimes in the two countries. A nationalist victory was also secured in Latvia during 1992, while in Lithuania a post-communist Democratic Labour Party was propelled to power by popular dissatisfaction with declining living standards and social upheaval that characterized the early transition period. Strong socialist majorities were again confirmed in Serbia and Montenegro, and an equivalent victory obtained for President Iliesu's portion of the NSF in Romania.

Further elections were also held in Czechoslovakia, as provided for in the

1990 agreement, and produced a decisively right-wing oriented government in the Czech lands and a more ambiguous form of post-communist nationalist domination in Slovakia – an outcome that led directly to the break-up of the federal state at the end of the year. At the close of 1992 considerable diversity was evident throughout the region and different kinds of parties were clearly emerging – and indeed, a large number of them. This was the major outcome of the second stage of the electoral process. Whether Olson's observation that this period represented the 'freezing moment' of the new, post-communist party systems may be questioned, but his statement that the typical result of the second elections was a fragmented party system was certainly close to the mark.[29]

Phase Two of the electoral process was characterized by the dissolution of the broad anti-communist movements and the erosion of the power of most ruling groups surviving from the former communist period. In 1990 the 25 per cent of the vote taken by the Hungarian Democratic Forum appeared rather a modest accomplishment beside the 46 per cent cast for Civic Forum and Public Against Violence in Czechoslovakia and 55 per cent of DEMOS in Slovenia, let alone the 78 per cent of the relatively unreconstructed Socialist Party of Serbia and the other communist parties of Ukraine, Belarus, Albania and Montenegro whose position was so far relatively untouched by the ongoing regional regime transformation. The political supremacy implied by these high totals turned out to be of strictly limited duration.

By 1992 Civic Forum and Public Against Violence in Czechoslovakia, Solidarity in Poland, DEMOS in Slovenia and the Popular Front of Estonia had already fragmented and largely passed from the scene. The ambiguous National Salvation Front had also split in Romania. The proportion of votes or seats now taken by virtually all parties or groups at the top of the electoral lists – anti-communist and post-communist alike – was considerably lower than that gained in the first election. Fragmentation was most pronounced in Poland following the election of 1991 conducted without a threshold, where the largest parliamentary group was the Democratic Union with only 12.3 per cent of the vote. Even the conservative regimes of Serbia and Montenegro saw a decline in their previous dominance. The results also showed considerable fluidity: a strong majority for Albania's post-communists being transformed into a right-wing victory in 1992, while – foreshadowing later developments in Poland and Hungary – Lithuania's nationalists lost heavily to post-communist socialist forces.

By the end of 1992, too, the state system of the region itself was showing signs of fragmentation and growing diversity. The Soviet Union was no longer in existence and while some of its constituent republics were, such as the Baltic states, ruled by democratic nationalist groupings others (particularly Ukraine and Belarus) were ruled by elites not greatly different from those of the old communist establishment. Most of the Yugoslav federation had also broken up and four of its components, Bosnia, Croatia, Serbia and Montenegro, were involved to a greater or lesser extent in armed conflict. Only Slovenia had escaped the nationalist imbroglio and was successfully developing as a pluralist democracy. While the other states of east-central Europe were making considerable political progress, they nevertheless saw growing diversity and showed signs of considerable political instability with a feuding parliament in Poland and the Czechoslovak federation on the verge of division. In the Balkans right-wing western-oriented governments were now installed in Bulgaria and Albania but there were few signs that effective democratization was making much progress.

Although the situation was fluid and highly differentiated there were signs that a new pattern of party forces was emerging. Indications of a new constellation of political forces became more prominent in 1993. Parties of a recognizable liberal or conservative character that bore a resemblance to those in the west could be identified on the right wing of the party spectrum in some countries and were becoming more influential in the pluralist states of east-central Europe. Elsewhere, parties that sprang directly from the communist establishment were prominent. In some countries, particularly those of the former Soviet Union and the residue of the old Yugoslav federation, their direct successors still ruled. In others, former communist organizations had been taken over by reformist groups and were being reconstructed along authentically social democratic lines to provide the kind of left-wing alternative prevalent in western Europe. This was most obviously the case where the former communists had lost power and had to win back power in a multi-party election, as happened in Lithuania and was soon to be the case in Poland and Hungary. It was, too, becoming apparent that the revived 'historical' parties had little prospect of becoming a dominant force, playing at best a marginal role in the new democracies. The bigger players were increasingly either new parties or different kinds of ex- or post-communist party.[30] The precise nature of the parties was open to considerable doubt, though. The degree to which communist parties had indeed reformed was a matter of some controversy, while the nature of the growing range of right-wing parties was also diverse.

Phase Three of political change in the electoral context thus saw new forces taking shape and the emergence of firmer structures of party competition in which the successors of former communists increasingly found a distinctive place. After further elections in 1993 and 1994 the number of east European governments formed by parties deriving from the former communist establishment rose yet further. Social democrats and socialists returned to power in Poland and Hungary respectively, while ex-communists of a less definitively reformed character took office in Bulgaria and Macedonia. By the end of 1994 (and leaving to one side Bosnia, where all normal political life was now engulfed by fierce warfare) the decided majority of 'post-communist' states were actually governed by communist-successor parties – eleven were ruled by various forms of socialist or communist administration, and seven by various forms of liberal or nationalist party.

This was the major development during the third stage of the post-communist elections. In some cases this simply reflected the slow pace of political change and the reluctance of influential groups to move away from earlier patterns of authoritarianism. In others, though, it represented a shift away from the dominance of the early anti-communist movements and the relative weakening of the largely right-wing parties they had formed. Different explanations have been offered for this distinctive tendency during the early years of political change in eastern Europe. Factors held responsible by various analysts include the influence of forces generated by the major process of economic transition and the systemic transformation seen to some extent in all countries;[31] disillusion after early post-communist euphoria and the continuing strength of a socialist value system;[32] the overall dynamics of the transition period in junction with the differing capacity of parties to adapt to a changing environment;[33] varying levels of organizational strength and contrasting leadership skills;[34] and the capacity of parties to strike a politically rewarding balance between the benefits of transition and the costs voters have to pay.[35]

Phase Four of this sequence reflected the consolidation of this tendency in a number of east European countries, though by no means all. It saw the emergence of a more distinctive structure of party competition, particularly in the increasingly democratized countries of east-central Europe. By the time three or so reasonably competitive elections had taken place in most countries of eastern Europe, a process mostly completed by the end of 1998, a range of identifiable parties or parliamentary blocs not wholly dissimilar from their western counterparts could be detected. Something like a party system or relatively stable pattern of party relations seemed to be emerging. In the more developed countries of east-central Europe and Lithuania there were clear signs of a two-party, or two-bloc, system coming into existence. Of course, it takes more than that for a fully-fledged party system to be identified, and the attributes of 'systemness' in this context will be examined in more detail in Chapter 5 in association with the characteristics of the different kinds of party relations seen in eastern Europe. But by the end of the first decade of post-communist rule in eastern Europe early forms of party system in some countries gave an indication of the progress made in terms of the establishment of party democracy, and signs of the establishment of a solid institutional basis for party development.

Varieties of electoral party in post-communist Europe

The above account provides a broad guide to the kinds of party that have emerged after four electoral phases and a decade of political change since 1989. It is nevertheless general and rather loose in its definition of the parties that have come to prevail at this stage of the east European electoral process and combines two different kinds of classification. One refers to the origins of parties – whether their roots lie (directly or indirectly) in the former communist establishment or whether the institutions are new creations formed during or after the transition to democracy. Another aspect is programmatic and based on definitions of ideological affiliation – whether parties tend to be left- or right-wing in orientation. The two dimensions tend to coincide in contemporary eastern Europe in that the left of the political spectrum is dominated by parties derived from the ruling organizations of the former communist regime (although the fit is by no means perfect and does not cover, for example, the Czech Social Democrats). This pragmatic conception of the modern party spectrum actually encompasses contemporary east European conditions, as discussed in Chapter 2, quite well.

But these aspects of party difference by no means exhaust all dimensions of party identity. H. Kitschelt, for example, identifies three 'pure types' of party that include, apart from programmatic or ideologically defined organizations, charismatic and clientilistic parties.[36] Differentiation by origin, it should be noted, does not identify a 'pure type' but involves another dimension of party identity. Charismatic parties tend to be short-lived and are characteristic of a particular stage of organizational development. They are oriented to the leadership style of a particular individual and their members are largely under the sway of his or her personality. The authority such parties – or individuals – exercise is generally short-lived, needing to be 'routinized' (as German sociologist Max Weber formulated it) and transformed into a programmatic or patronage-based, clientelistic form. Modern parties that survive for any length of time thus tend to be predominantly programmatic or clientelist in nature. In practice, the character of contemporary east European parties is quite mixed in terms of such types, as well as showing considerable diversity in terms of their origin.

In any specific context the sources of party identity are quite diverse and the balance of particular factors in party development not easy to pin down. New right-wing forces have contained a wide range of liberal, conservative and national tendencies often merged with one another, as noted in Chapter 2. The evolution of former communist organizations has been equally differentiated. The clarity of Kitschelt's early discussion of the formation of party systems that foresaw either the turn of the old communist left towards authoritarian nationalism or the embrace of full market liberalism if it was to survive in any viable form was based on deductive arguments that downplayed the inconsistencies and diversity of influences on real party politics.[37]

In practice, as Polish and Hungarian developments were to show, some post-communist parties were highly successful in embracing both economic and social liberalism whilst maintaining a left-wing identity and avoiding the emergence of any significant electoral challenge from alternative forces on the left. Unlike other former communist parties, both emphatically left the area of nationalism and ethnic populism to right-wing forces. Faced with far stronger and more effective right-wing parties and levels of anti-communist opposition than was seen in the Balkans and former Soviet Union, the east-central European post-communists thus succeeded in developing a broad and more diverse electoral appeal.[38] This was strengthened and maintained by well-honed leadership skills and public relations techniques, not dissimilar from those characteristic of what might be termed the contemporary centre-left in Great Britain and the United States. But this path was not followed by all former ruling parties. While old communist parties in Hungary and Poland became quite effective vehicles for social democracies, those in some of the former Soviet republics have moved only a limited distance in this direction and tended to promote nationalist values, a transformation also carried to the limit by President Milošević in Serbia.

The former communist parties were not the only organizations to adapt to changing conditions in this way. An existing satellite organization such as the United Peasant Party in Poland also performed well politically in the post-communist period and was in government from 1993 to 1997, although the Democratic Party – its establishment partner until 1989 – survived and developed to some extent but remained a very minor political player. Former communist allies have not in fact generally fared very well – it was, for example, not the allied Czech Socialist Party but its social democratic rival (the CSDP) that rose to prominence after the 1992 elections and formed a government in 1998. The Liberal Democracy of Slovenia (LDS), which has been the central pillar of the post-communist democratic state, had somewhat different origins and grew out of the former League of Socialist Youth to form a successful competitive party. Although different in terms of institutional origin, the LDS shares direct roots in a youth movement with another of the dominant parties of the stronger democracies of east-central Europe, the highly successful FIDESZ in Hungary.

Legacies of political activity and roles performed under the old regime have also continued to influence the identities of parties in the centre and right wing of the Polish party spectrum, and common origins have played a particularly influential role in relations between the diverse offspring of the Solidarity movement. Shared anti-communism and strong antagonism to the modern Social Democracy, for example, helped overcome the differences in economic policy and contrasting levels of commitment to liberal principles on the part of Solidarity Electoral Action and the Freedom Union following the 1997 elections.

The strength of the historically derived identities of the main east European parties in terms of their links with the former communist regimes has in some ways been surprisingly strong, but it is their capacity to meet the requirements of the modern governmental and electoral environment that now determines their political status. Continuity has been strong in terms of organization, property and leadership role but far less in terms of ideology and policy – particularly to the extent that the individual country has moved further along the democratic road.[39] Links with the former regime and a party's historical record are of considerable importance in some cases, but they provide no sure guide to the party's capacity to respond to contemporary electoral challenges and secure a place in the post-communist political spectrum.

Of the different types of modern party it is increasingly the programmatic party that tends to dominate, although elements of clientilism also help define their character and the strength of the position they occupy in any emerging party system. An early model of emerging party cleavages suggested that it was not possible to generalize about the extent of programmatic party competition that was likely to emerge in eastern Europe as whole, but that different national conditions and different configurations of players would lead to divergent political outcomes.[40] Although the structure of the model proposed was quite complex, the likelihood of programme-based party formation was in fact closely associated with levels of socio-economic and ranking in terms of national wealth as seen in Table 1.1. Both Slovakia and Croatia emerge with relatively high expectations of programmatic party development, therefore, although their modest achievements in terms of democratization may equally suggest that their development in this area of political differentiation has been similarly limited.

Preliminary analysis indeed confirmed that relatively developed, democratically advanced eastern European countries were more likely to have programmatically defined party systems. Comparison of Hungary, Poland, the Czech Republic and Bulgaria showed that it was the latter that had a 'classic form of unconsolidated democracy whose party system had the lowest level of programmatic structuring'.[41] But there were also some surprises, not least in terms of the relatively strong degree of party system structuring in Poland, most probably caused by that country's particular experience of communist rule. Programmatic distinctions between parties only provide a limited guide to a country's political geography, and attempts to apply the established left/right-wing continuum in the new democracies have been particularly difficult. A complicating factor of some importance in the east European context has been the prominence of nationalist tendencies in many parties, which, with an emphasis on values of community and cultural tradition, place them unambiguously on the right (as east European surveys quite strongly confirm). But nationalism also implies forms of economic protectionism and defence of popular economic interests that overlaps with currents on the left, and this contributes to a blurring of the political stance taken by many of the new parties.

Public opinion surveys nevertheless show quite well-developed ideological identities, particularly, once more, in the developed east-central European countries. Considerably more Czechs and Slovaks than Hungarians, and more Hungarians than Poles, could identify one or more parties as the 'owner' of a particular issue.[42] Differences in the social basis of some parties corresponded relatively directly with their political profile, although this was more obviously true of parties that made an appeal to a specific constituency – such as ethnic organizations, peasant parties and clerical associations.[43] Somewhat less guidance to the ideological identity of different parties could be derived from actual electoral behaviour, though. The only general weighting of preferences that could be identified for parties based on the old communist organizations, for example, was to be found amongst older voters.[44] In Poland, as elsewhere in eastern Europe, it was pensioners (as well as white-collar workers) who originally tended to vote for the post-communist Democratic Left Alliance. Even this identification weakened during the 1993 elections, however.[45] In 1997 Polish workers voted slightly more frequently for the mainstream right-wing Solidarity Electoral Action, but the only striking class affiliation that could be seen was the farmers' vote for the Peasant Party, which overall performed very badly in the election and found itself marginalized in the new parliament.[46]

Outside the more developed post-communist democracies ideological identities have been even more difficult to establish. Mečiar's Movement for Democratic Slovakia derived from Public Against Violence as the country's prime anti-communist movement, but included strong features of nationalism and the economic protectionism characteristic of left-wing organizations. The nature of its political identity was particularly problematic in view of the party's dominant national status, as it was very much the main institutional player in Slovakia's political life after the 1992 elections until the party's electoral defeat in 1998. The marked ambiguities of the MDS underpin the conception of 'non-standard' parties developed in Slovakia.[47] Many of the dominant parties in the less rapidly democratizing countries of eastern Europe were, indeed, not primarily programmatic in nature – a characteristic that helped strengthen the increasing diversity of the post-communist systems. Strong charismatic or leadership-oriented elements were apparent in Mečiar's MDS – as they are in many modern parties – and this was an element in the identity of the 'non-standard' party that influenced its development and activity far more that any formal programme. Like the charismatic leaders of other parties, Mečiar and the MDS made much of their nationalist outlook – the personal attraction of the leader combining well with the emotional appeals of political nationalism.

Strongly nationalist parties have indeed often been leader-dominated (Moczulski's Confederation for Independent Poland and Csurka's Life and Justice Party in Hungary are further examples), and this is often a factor responsible for their remaining quite small organizations relegated to the margins of parliamentary life – if indeed they achieve such electoral success. The Movement for the Reconstruction of Poland has been a similarly typical nationalist vehicle for former prime minister and presidential candidate Jan Olszewski, as a party that remained outside Solidarity Electoral Action and gained a handful of parliamentary seats in its own right in 1997. Small groups headed by Olszewski had come to grief in the past and, true to form, disputes over leadership rights within the Movement broke out within weeks of the election and led to a party split that further marginalized its parliamentary position. The political attractions of post-communist nationalism often compensate for the difficulties many new parties have experienced in developing as effective programmatic organizations, and the strength of direct nationalist appeals has helped sustain the position of ambitious leaders who have little in the way of party organization to support them.

Survival of the more successful leadership-dominated parties has often been facilitated by patronage and control over state resources, conditions that have again been more prevalent in the less democratized countries of eastern Europe. Elements of clientelism helped sustain the position of the Movement for Democratic Slovakia, and represented one way for it to perpetuate its authority as Mečiar's personal dominance encountered political challenge. To the extent that the orientation of the MDS was predominantly nationalist, the idea of nation-building it involved was from one that involved 'the spinning of thick webs of politicized self-interest'.[48] Such features were far from lacking in dominant parties elsewhere, particularly in Croatia and other Balkan states; it was also an aspect of the MDS that linked it with the more unreconstructed communist successor parties and the support they commanded from local elites in Ukraine and Belarus.[49]

The relatively nationalist and clientelist path taken by the established dominant parties in the former Soviet republics distinguish them sharply from the more distinctively post-communist path of development taken by the old socialist and workers' parties in Hungary and Poland. Elements of corruption and financial abuse of office have not been absent in east-central Europe, but they have been marginal to the primary identity of the communist successor parties rather than the basic means of its survival in post-communist political life.[50] They are common pitfalls of party life in the new democracies of eastern Europe as elsewhere and proved to be surprisingly strongly entrenched in the Czech Republic on the right as well as the left of the political spectrum, helping to bring down the government of Václav Klaus in 1997. The restructuring of many areas of east European social life offers far-reaching possibilities for the extension of clientelist relations on the basis of party affiliation, a tendency that has been found to be surprisingly strong in unexpected areas such as Poland's reorganized health funding system.[51]

Overall, indeed, the party landscape of post-communist eastern Europe has been sufficiently complex and fluid to resist easy definition and effective analysis through the prism of any single classification system – although the post-communist half of Europe is nevertheless small enough to be divided into sub-regions whose characteristics give a good idea of the configuration of parties prevailing in each area at this relatively early stage. They comprise, firstly, the distinctively communist-influenced post-Soviet republics of Ukraine, Belarus and Moldova where opposition movements were largely absent, any transition process dominated (or at least strongly influenced) by the local communist parties, and alternative parties weak and still of marginal importance – with nationalist tendencies and parties neutralized or absorbed by the dominant leftists. East-central Europe, on the other hand, showed rapid evolution away from the Soviet model with party systems reflecting an increasingly distinctive arena of left-right competition – although with the strong dominance of a politically ambiguous party in Slovakia until 1998.

Third, the Balkans lay between the two and saw either the lengthy dominance of partially reformed communist establishment with a relatively weak opposition or the rule of rather authoritarian right-wing governments whose democratic credentials were little more convincing than those of their immediate neighbours. The states of most of the former Yugoslavia fall easily into the first category, while Slovenia was well on the way to abandoning its 'Balkan' history and merging with the more positive current of change in east-central Europe. Fourth, in the Baltic states a shorter period of communist rule and stronger nationalist opposition helped provide conditions to overcame the communist supremacy more successfully than in the other former Soviet republics and promoted the more rapid democratization of the three small states.

Electoral volatility

The emergence of broad patterns of party representation is by no means the only way in which the political impact of successive elections can be assessed. The extent to which parties survive a sequence of electoral tests, carry a large body of their supporters with them through their political careers and succeed in carving out an identifiable space in the electoral landscape provides another important measure of party development. Measures of electoral 'volatility' (which reflects the fluidity of voting patterns and the extent to which parties command a steady level of voting support) and estimates of the number of 'effective' parties (those that can reasonably be expected to form a stable government and escape the weaknesses associated with excessive parliamentary fragmentation) are also measures of political maturity used widely to gauge the formation of stable patterns of democratic political life and pluralist party development.

Calculation for parties with parliamentary representation in 1996–98 is shown in Table 3.1, with addition of parties represented in earlier parliaments (Civic Democratic Alliance, Association for the Republic, Moravian Silesian Movement, Liberal Social Union in Czech Republic; Christian Democratic People's Party in Hungary, etc.).

The index of volatility measures the extent to which party strengths change from one election to the next, and represents the sum of the differences between each party's share of the vote in two successive elections presented on a percentage basis (Table 3.3). Comparison of a number of calculations of east European electoral volatility suggests two general conclusions. Firstly, that electoral volatility in eastern Europe has been far higher than that seen in stable western democracies. In British terms, even the landslide election victory of the Labour Party in 1997 only yielded an index of 12.5, which was nevertheless far higher than that of 5 in 1992. In the United States, the intervention of Ross Perot in the presidential election of 1992 produced a relatively high index of 18, while that seen in 1996 was down to 10.5 points.[52] Elections in eastern Europe have produced far greater volatility indices and reflected considerably higher levels of political flux, approaching an index of 90 even in the more developed states of east-central Europe according to some calculations (see Table 3.3). East European volatility has also been higher than that in the countries of southern Europe and post-war Germany at an equivalent stage of early democratization.

Although this much is clear about the east European situation, the statistics are open to rather different interpretations. In one account high volatility reflects the fragmentation of the original anti-communist movements, uncertainties of the overall process of party formation, and the learning process in which a multitude of politicians and organizations test their appeals against the preferences of a newly liberated and inexperienced electorate. From this perspective volatility indices could be expected to decline quite rapidly as the political systems matured, as they did after the establishment of new democracies in western Europe, and this indeed is the view expressed by David Olson.[53]

Others, however, conclude that volatility in eastern Europe has actually risen during the course of successive elections through the 1990s and generally been significantly higher than the volatility seen during the early years of most new democracies in western Europe after World War II. Either, therefore, political processes have been different in the east from those in the west even at equivalent stages of democratization and party development, or the political climate of the late twentieth century is significantly different from that of the 1940s or 1970s.[54] Further analyses, equally, stress not just the higher level of volatility in

Table 3.3a Electoral volatility in eastern Europe – review

		Mair	*Rose et al.*	*Cotta*	*Olson*	*Pettai, Kreuzer*
Czech Republic	1990–92	19.9	9.5	28+	89	–
	1992–96		19		29	
Hungary	1990–94	25	24	23	26	–
Poland	1991–93	27.6	28	70?		–
	1993–97		29.5	25+	26.5	
Slovakia	1990–92	25.9	13	41+	80	–
	1992–94	(combined)	7		28.5	
Slovenia	1990–92	–	18	–	–	–
	1992–96		25			
Estonia	1992–95	–	26.5	–	–	24
Latvia	1993–95	–	32.5	–	–	35
Lithuania	1992–96	–	28	–	–	27.8
Bulgaria	1990–91	–	13.5	20	22	–
	1991–94		15.5			
	1994–97		24.5			
Romania	1990–92	–	4.5	30+	63	–
	1992–96		11			

Sources: P. Mair, *Party System Change: Approaches and Interpretations*, Oxford, Clarendon Press, 1997, p. 182; R. Rose et al., p. 119; M. Cotta, 'Structuring the new party systems after the dictatorship', in Pridham and Lewis, *Stabilising Fragile Democracies*, p. 71; Olson, 'Party formation', p. 460; V. Pettai and M. Kreuzer, 'Party politics in the Baltic states: social bases and institutional context', *East European Politics and Societies*, 1999, **13**: 9.

Table 3.3b Estimated electoral volatility over last three elections

	1990–96	*1992–98*
Czech Republic	19	15
Hungary	22	28
Poland	28	30
Slovakia	29	34
Slovenia	18	25
Estonia	53	26
Latvia	49	40
Lithuania	42	28
Bulgaria	22	16
Romania	63	27

eastern Europe compared with that in the west, but also the relative fluidity and greater volatility of eastern Europe when set against the experience of new democracies in Latin America.[55]

Secondly, the review of different sources presented in Table 3.3 shows surprisingly large differences between the measures of volatility that different analysts have calculated. There are clearly major differences both in the way in which the statistics are interpreted and in the status of the indices themselves. Technical differences exert a major effect on the outcome, and sheer error is also by no means excluded. Some of the original tables, it appears, were not presented on a percentage basis (which could be recognized from references to agreed statistics on early post-war cases of democratization), and have been standardized for Table 3.3. There is, too, a broad measure of agreement on volatility in Hungary between 1990 and 1994, which is the simplest of all cases to present because of the unusually stable pattern of party representation in that country. Institutional fluidity was far more apparent in all other countries, and measures of volatility were themselves correspondingly more uncertain and subject to the vagaries of individual judgement.

A considerable measure of arbitrariness is thus involved in judging whether a party that presents for election on one occasion is wholly the same or different from that in the next. It was not clear, for example, what was to be made of the division of the National Salvation Front between Romania's first two elections and how 'new' in this respect was Iliescu's Democratic National Salvation Front formed in response to former prime minister Petre Roman's departure from the original Front to form a Democratic Party (NSF). Only consideration of the context of political change and evaluation of later developments can really help in such cases (as, for example, it turned out that the DNSF was very much the continuation of the former organization). Major problems are inherent in such judgements and the volatility calculations that are based on them, and the way in which they are handled can change any broad conclusions that are reached. The table of recalculated electoral volatility is probably more accurate than some of the earlier offerings in that it draws on the results of later elections where the party spectrum has become more stable and thus less subject to subjective interpretation. It suggests that volatility is on the whole declining, but that the trend is by no means unambiguous. But it is also just a statistical guide to a changing situation rather than an unambiguous representation of electoral outcomes.

More differentiated treatment of these issues has been conducted in the context of individual countries, and this has presented a more nuanced picture. One approach thus separates general aggregate volatility (which disregards parties under specific names as they are formed and go out of business) and citizens' volatility (which does take account of the specific vehicle used by elite groups as they present themselves to the public). A particular problem in Polish terms was, further, the character of Solidarity Electoral Action whose formation was indeed a novelty on the electoral scene and had a strong impact on the outcome of the 1997 elections. Yet it was also clearly the direct heir of various Solidarity and right-wing organizations that brought an established electorate to the new organization. If such links and continuities were taken into account a more distinct learning process can be identified as stable constituencies emerge in the new party environment, with Polish volatility in this context declining in general aggregate terms to 22 per cent between 1993 and 1997 and citizens' volatility to 15 per cent.[56] Despite the problems involved in interpreting particular cases, then, it may well be the case that electoral volatility and party instability in eastern Europe is considerably less than some interpretations suggest. More detailed analysis thus strengthens Olson's argument rather than confirming conclusions about the uniquely high level of electoral volatility in eastern Europe.

'Effective' parties and parliament fragmentation

A further measure of political development and institutionalization based on the outcome of successive elections is derived by calculating the number of 'effective' parties in each parliament. Party government in less fragmented parliaments is understood to be more successful than in those with many small parties. Discussion of 'effective' parties therefore refers to bodies of sufficient size and parliamentary weight to be relevant for viable coalition-building and government formation in the parliamentary body, and is generally based on a statistical calculation of effectiveness based on the relative level of parliamentary representation formulated by R. Taagepera and M. Sobert.[57] By the end of 1992 two elections had been held in most of the former satellite countries of eastern Europe (Albania, Bulgaria, Czechoslovakia, Poland and Romania) and a relatively small number of leading parties identified (as had already been possible after the single Hungarian election of 1990). On this basis an early measure of 'effectiveness' in terms of the spread of key parties in eastern Europe was constructed (Table 3.4).

In this calculation the fragmentation of the Polish parliament elected in 1991 was clearly reflected, whereas the situation in all other countries appeared to be considerably less critical. In terms of fragmentation and prospects for the formation of stable government, though, Romania also emerges as politically critical because of the relative size of parliamentary groupings, while both Romania and Bulgaria had major problems of government stability because parliament was dominated by electoral coalitions rather than proper parties. Hungary, Slovakia and the Czech Republic were not so seriously affected in either respect. Only Albania, however, emerged as having something such as a 'two-party system', which soon turned out to be no guarantee of stability or government effectiveness either. The latter finding in particular warns that not too much should be read into this index as a measure of democratization, party development or the crystallization of stable party systems. It is a purely statistical indicator that ignores political factors and the broader context of party representation.[58] Latin America provides a number of comparable cases of party and parliamentary development that readily confirm that a small number of political parties offers no guarantee of stability.[59]

The measure of 'effective' parties in the former satellite countries of eastern Europe nevertheless gave an early indication of the way in which the electoral process promoted party development during the first phase of post-communist change. The sequence of elections helped distinguish relatively strong parties from those whose position was more marginal and that were less capable of making a significant contribution to government. The emergence of a smaller number of 'effective' parties represented a further stage of the winnowing effect involved in the electoral process and the steady evolution of party government,

Table 3.4a Party representation in parliamentary lower houses (1992)

	No. of parties in election	No. of parties in parliament	No. of effective parties	Percentage of unrepresented voters
Poland	67	18	10.9	10.3
Romania	74	7	4.8	20.0
Hungary	45	7	3.8	12.7
Czech Rep.	21	6	3.4	25.1
Slovakia	22	5	3.4	26.3
Albania	11	5	1.9	1.9
Bulgaria	37	3	2.4	24.9

Reproduced from McGregor, 'How electoral laws', p. 13. Single-seat party representation was excluded from the Polish total and those for national minorities in Romania.

Table 3.4b Party representation (of more than one seat) in east European parliaments, 1999

	No. of parties in parliament	No. of effective parties	Percentage of unrepresented voters
Czech Republic	5	3.7	11.4
Hungary	6	3.0	8.0
Poland	5	2.9	11.8
Slovakia	6	4.7	5.8
Slovenia	7	5.5	11.3
Estonia	7	5.0	10.5
Latvia	6	5.5	8.6
Lithuania	6	2.9	9.8
Albania	7	2.2	9.4
Bulgaria	5	2.5	7.6
Croatia	7	2.7	6.3
Romania	6	4.3	19.9

although such observations had to be qualified in many cases by the fact that elections were often fought by coalitions rather than individual parties. This created major problems in the conduct of stable and effective government. Nevertheless, the small parties seen early on disappeared from the scene. A large number of parties had indeed participated in the early elections, but this already excluded many registered parties that failed to present electoral lists either because of problems in meeting the financial or organizational requirements for electoral participation or because they had calculated the meagre chances they had of gaining parliamentary representation. Early elections saw the defeat of most potential competitors for parliamentary seats while, as the measure of effectiveness constructed in 1992 suggests, even representation in the legislature was not likely to assure a significant level of political influence or any close relation with government formation and control over national policy.

Few 'effective' parties likely to make a strong input to democratic party government had emerged at this early stage of the post-communist transition in eastern Europe. The early overview, moreover, did not encompass the newly independent countries of the former Soviet Union and Yugoslavia, where fragmentation may indeed have been avoided but where active oppositions were largely absent. In the former Yugoslavia, only Slovenia came close in 1992 to producing a counterweight to the majority party, with the Christian Democrats gaining 14.5 per cent of the vote as the second largest party after the Liberal Democrats. A precarious balance was also maintained for a time in Macedonia between nationalists and post-communist forces with their ethnic allies.

Elsewhere, in the newly independent republic of Croatia, an anti-communist party also gained a striking majority while the Social Liberal vote trailed a considerable way behind. The democratic credentials of Milošević's Socialist Party were equally unconvincing as it continued to maintain a firm grasp over the officially post-communist party system. In the Baltic states only Lithuania showed signs of developing a system with two effective parties following the path-breaking victory of the post-communist Labour Party in the September 1992 elections. In the more Russified states of Belarus, Ukraine and Moldova communist forces retaining strong links with the former Soviet establishment maintained their dominance, and there was far less progress towards the development of a plurality of effective parties and the establishment of a viable parliamentary democracy.

As democratization proceeded in the more developed countries the pattern of party representation stabilized and generally improved. The pronounced parliamentary fragmentation initially seen in Poland was drastically reduced with the introduction of a five per cent threshold for the 1993 elections. Other countries with a higher tally of effective parties (Hungary and Romania) saw their number decline, while others saw the total somewhat increased. In themselves, measures of the number of effective parties gave little indication of party system development or successful democratization. Countries such as Albania and Bulgaria, which had the lowest number of effective parties, were hardly the most convincing examples of post-communist democratization. The main factors sustaining party system development were not encapsulated by statistical indices of party representation. The Czech party system began to show signs of incipient collapse in 1997 as evidence of corruption and illegal forms of party funding emerged, whereas Slovak stability remaining largely dependent until 1998 on the dubious political virtues of Mečiar's leadership and the workings of the MDS party machine. Albania, Bulgaria and Romania also entered a period of major political change in late 1996 and early 1997, which had far-reaching changes in the content as well as the structure of party government, on grounds that were little related to the numerical pattern of party representation.

The party structure of the new parliaments reflected in such statistical terms was only one dimension of the development of multi-party democracy in post-communist eastern Europe. Developments in the Balkans, in particular, showed the restricted character of the conclusions that could be drawn from simple observation of party structures and calculation of the number of effective parties they contained. Although in purely statistical terms Albania showed the closest approximation to the two-party system characteristic of the most firmly established western democracies – with a count of 1.9 effective parties in parliament in 1992 it actually shared the mean party count of the United States between 1945 and 1980 (itself the lowest index of 22 democracies over this period)[60] – its implications for the development of a democratic system were quite another thing. The lengthy tenure of the Albanian Democratic Party in government, which indeed lasted its full four-year term until the ballot of May 1996, reflected its stabilization primarily as a clientelist party whose power was based on the distribution and control of scarce resources rather than as a programmatic party whose authority derived from the support of the electorate for its policies and the broad principles its government espoused. The type of party to which the 'effectiveness' index referred had then, not surprisingly, great significance for the actual practice and development of party government.

In general terms, nevertheless, there remains a definite relationship in established democracies between the number of effective parties a parliament contains and the durability of the governments it produces and maintains in power. Western experience since World War II shows, indeed, a clear correlation between party number and cabinet durability. The evidence from subsequent elections in eastern Europe is again broadly positive as, although the effective number of parties generally increased with the second election, it then decreased with the third.[61] This suggests that the number of effective parties in the east European parliaments remains at a relatively low level and that the trend in party representation is, in this sense, a broadly positive one. The variance between east European countries in terms of large numbers of effective parties in the early nineties, as well as the relatively high proportion of the electorate excluded from parliamentary representation, has been reduced, if not in all cases. The number of effective parties remains particularly high in Estonia and Latvia, where the party systems remain quite fluid and considerable obstacles in forming and maintaining government coalitions are still met. The relatively low number of effective parties in some of the Balkan countries shows that other problems are equally, if not more important, in democratization and the development of effective party government. There is also some evidence that the lower level of party system fragmentation is by no means always positively correlated, particularly in eastern Europe, with measures of system support and popular satisfaction with democratic rule.[62]

Party government and post-communist parliaments

After 10 years or so of democratization, the record of east European parliaments and the role of parties within them has been a mixed but largely successful one. Parliaments have been established on a democratic basis, grown organizationally and performed the necessary functions quite successfully, but remain underdeveloped in some areas and continue to face major problems of institutionalization.[63] Favourable conditions gave some post-communist parliaments a more positive start and contributed to a relative stabilization in Hungary, Poland and the Czech Republic, as well as in the Baltic states. Institutions in the first three countries also tended to be better placed for the exercise of dominant control over legislative processes relative to the head of state, the formation and recall of cabinets, and in terms of the fragmentation of their constituent groups and parties.[64] In terms of subsequent parliamentary development the record differs.

Somewhat contrasting views have been expressed about the role of parliaments in the different phases of the democratization process. Key negotiations and political decisions such as those concerning the removal from power of the communist party were generally taken outside the existing legislature and, according to Olson, it was only in the case of Hungary that the parliament itself was a major source of change, a development that constituted an exception to the general rule of parliament passivity.[65] Another view argues more for a 'centrality of parliament' thesis in which Hungarian, Polish and Slovenian parliaments all participated actively in demolishing the authoritarian system; from this perspective only in Czechoslovakia did parliament become a central site of political action after the obstacles to institutional reconstruction had been cleared.[66] The salience of parliaments then lessened during the process of post-communist change alongside consolidation of the democratic order as parliaments become just one actor among many. Parliaments thereby became less central to the pattern of change and early 'over-parliamentarization' of the post-communist order declined as a form of 'rational parliamentarism' emerged.[67]

In some ways, nevertheless, parliaments had a clear priority in the democratization process and played a critical role for party formation. They were prominent as the major site for the emergence of democratic parties and provided the context for the early definition of their identity. As with the early phase of party development in western Europe described by Maurice Duverger, most east-central European parties had 'internal' or parliamentary origins, which were likely to exert a distinct influence on their subsequent path of development. One important exception to this generalization might be emergence of the communist successor parties from the former establishment, but even here their experience as newly democratized parties in countries such as Hungary and Poland and full exposure to the forces of pluralist politics was crucial to the effectiveness of their transformation and reinvention as democratic socialist parties. The parliamentary conditions of party development soon changed, however. As parliaments were 'rationalized' electoral thresholds were raised, which, combined with the benefits of prior organization and early occupation of prime ideological sites in the political arena, gave many of the parties formed during the first phase greater political impetus, a higher level of resource and more staying power than late arrivals. The implications were in this area quite clear: parliamentary parties enjoy a definite comparative advantage.

To this extent the new parliaments of the region, still relatively underdeveloped and at an early stage of organizational evolution, also found their activities increasingly influenced both by a more experienced executive and by the growing strength of the political parties increasingly well rooted within them.[68]

The status both of parties and parliaments was also conditioned by the broader political context and the constitutional framework within which both operated. Most east European countries, with some exceptions in the former Yugoslavia and Soviet Union, adopted parliamentary rather than presidential systems of government. This was a decision generally positive for party development. Apart from having clear implications for the status of parliament, presidential systems also offer more limited opportunities for party development and fewer incentives for individual contenders and organized actors to stay with the overall political game if they fail to gain prime leadership positions.[69] Where presidential powers remain relatively weak to those of the legislature, the presidential contest has become increasingly structured by party relations and potential candidates are more identified with party interests.[70] But generalizations about such relationships are premature at this early stage of post-communist democratization, and much depends on the degree of institutionalization seen in the different political camps. The main effect of the second presidential contests in Poland, it was concluded, was more to accentuate the asymmetry between the dominant political camps than to exert any uniform influence on the party spectrum as a whole.[71]

There also continues to be something of a developmental paradox in terms of the relations between parties and parliament. Party strength might be identified as an obstacle to the development of parliamentary autonomy, but deficiencies of party organization within parliaments have also been a major weakness in the further institutionalization of post-communist legislatures. They continue to occupy an 'ambiguous status', while the nature of parliamentary party formation is still fluid and partial in character; they display a 'relative inability to control their own members', have weak discipline and form shifting alliances with other party groups.[72] Many implications of the measures of party effectiveness discussed above hinge on the political and organizational status in these terms of the groups involved.

Entities identified as parties in terms of forming parliamentary clubs or associations often owed their position in the legislature to having presented themselves to voters as electoral unions, and were actually composed of smaller groups or discrete 'parties' themselves. This, naturally enough, has had major consequences for the effectiveness of the larger group in forming coalitions and establishing governments with other parliamentary partners. The capacity to form workable coalitions has become increasingly critical both for democratic party government and for the survival of many formal 'parties' themselves. The relatively small number of effective parties in the 1997 Polish parliament was premised on the relatively fragile organizational status of the parties involved – Solidarity Electoral Action, for example, already lost fifteen members from its 201-strong parliamentary club in its first year of existence. Similarly severe problems of coalition-maintenance have been seen in the Slovak Democratic Coalition elected in 1998, which raise some questions about the country's capacity to follow the path of fast-track democratization.

Even though party groupings within the parliament gain importance, too, the process of faction institutionalization may be delayed and internal organization remains partial.[73] Parties are nevertheless depended on to raise the level of experience and skills of the parliamentary body, as well as the overall quality of their deputies.[74] The relationship between parties and parliaments as institutions thus remains an ambiguous one in the new democracies of eastern Europe. Continuing party weakness is one aspect of the underdevelopment of post-communist legislatures, but relative party strength may also be a challenge to the institutionalization of parliament's own practices.

As parties develop, too, they are increasingly likely to be able to draw on extra-parliamentary resources. Whereas national parliamentary elections naturally formed the major political arena for party development in the first stage of post-communist change, local elections have increasingly become an important area of activity and party growth as the new regimes take clearer shape. The expansion of party activity on an organized national basis has been a slow process, though, and has lagged well behind the development of established patterns of parliamentary party behaviour, gradual and chaotic as this process has often appeared. The difficult job of building nation-wide party organizations and the general lack of party resources has been a major factor in this (see Chapter 4), but local elections have by no means been of marginal importance. They were certainly regarded as major components of the first stages of post-communist change and the party affiliation of local leaders seems to be increasingly well defined.[75]

National and local areas of party activity were certainly little connected at the outset and, although parties and systems of some sort were coming into existence on both planes, the links between them were largely missing in the early years. In the context of early post-communist democratization the critical mediating functions of the modern party thus took some time to develop. Substantial differences between local and national politics were identified in the post-communist Czech Republic and the party affiliation of local politicians was not considered to be of great importance there in early elections.[76] It has taken several rounds of local elections for emerging patterns of party differentiation at national level to take shape locally, a process further complicated by the extensive local governmental reforms implemented in most post-communist countries.[77] The process of party development thus continues to be an uneven one, although elections have marked key stages of development both at national and local level.

4 Party organization and institutional development

East European politics and the modern party

The development of institutional structures and establishment of organizational linkages have been the weakest aspects of party development in eastern Europe. A range of parties have developed as effective electoral machines, and many have proved to be viable bases for government formation and the exercise of political power within the region's new democratic systems. Party systems have begun to establish themselves and an ideological spectrum has crystallized that helps to anchor many of the new groupings within a recognizable, if regionally distinctive, political landscape. But many of the stronger and more stable political formations in the early years were either relics of the old establishment (communist parties in Ukraine and Moldova, or Milošević's partially reformed socialist organization in Serbia) or their original antagonists that remained fixed in an early semi-authoritarian mode (Mečiar's Movement for a Democratic Slovakia – until 1998, and Tudjman's Croatian Democratic Union – until the end of 1999). Other newly established parties, of a more authentically pluralist nature, have generally been more unstable and less well developed in terms of organization.

Even in the more advanced democracies of east-central Europe many of the prominent parties formed in the first stage of transition showed little staying power and were unable to secure a stable place in the new parliamentary system. The Hungarian Democratic Forum, which secured 43 per cent of parliamentary seats in 1990 and established strong overall control of the new democratic government, saw its proportion of the vote decline from 25 per cent in 1990 to 12 in 1994, and less than five per cent in 1998. In the same country Fidesz, equally, captured nine per cent of the vote in 1990, seven per cent in 1994 but a striking 29 per cent in 1998. In Poland a number of groups deriving from Solidarity held office between 1989 and 1993, but none of them was able to create a strong right-wing party capable of standing up to the new Social Democracy or even muster a significant parliamentary presence. They remained marginalized until 1997, when a re-engineered Solidarity coalition again won the election and took government office. In some contrast to these developments, the Czech Civic Democratic Party dominated the political life of the new republic from 1992 to 1997, but then also threatened to dissolve amidst accusations of corruption and fraudulent financial dealings. It nevertheless recovered to perform surprisingly well in the elections of 1998 although not sufficiently to reform a government.

Shifting electoral preferences and performance in office obviously played a large part in such changes and instability in the position of leading political actors, but the organizational nature of the parties themselves was also relevant. Many of the parties had weakly developed structures and shallow social roots. Their membership basis was slender and they possessed a thinly developed network at regional and local level. Parties did not generally present themselves as an effective organizational link between the rarefied sphere of parliamentary politics and the mass public of modern democracy parties in the post-communist democracies. They have often seemed, as Hungarian analysts in particular pointed out, to 'hover over' society rather than representing its constituent social groups or embodying some organic link with it.

There are already several different kinds of party active in east European politics that can be distinguished, as seen in Chapters 2 and 3, in terms of origin, ideological orientation and general type. Whether they can usefully be differentiated in terms of organization is another matter. An early hypothesis formulated after the first few years of post-communist experience was that parties would continue to develop as formations with loose electoral constituencies, in which a relatively unimportant role is played by the party membership and the dominant influence exerted by party leaders.[1] On the basis of more general party organization theory it was difficult to predict any particular path of development – other than that they would not be mass parties. Several reasons as to why this should be the case and its implications for party organization in eastern Europe more generally have been advanced, but there is little doubt as to the overall position of the new parties in this respect.[2]

The importance of membership issues for the nature of party organization in east European parties has been confirmed by other writers. According to Attila Ágh three major tendencies have undermined the parties' organizational strength. They are the senescence of party memberships, in that it is mostly the elderly and senior citizens who have the interest, time and energy to devote to political activities; the 'law of small numbers', under which a large number of quite small parties tend to be dominated by a select number of enthusiasts and political extremists – which in turn reduces the parties' attractiveness to a broader public and wider range of political supporters; and, thirdly, the elitism and top-down construction of most of the parties, which further limits the significance of national organization and the broader membership.[3] There is often an implication in such observations that these characteristics of east European parties serve as clear distinguishing marks from the party models prominent in western democracies, although the issue is somewhat more complex than it might appear at first glance. The question is not just one of whether parties in the older democracies have more members than those in eastern Europe (although this is often more difficult to establish than one might think). It also involves ideas of what we expect a party to be and how it should develop.

It seems in many ways quite obvious that parties have not just to be organized in a basic sense but also require a reasonably high level of institutional development if they are to make any impact on the complex processes of contemporary political life. Precisely what party organization is actually for is not quite so obvious, though. Alan Ware sees modern party organizations engaging in three main kinds of activity: preparing for and assisting in the running of election campaigns; sustaining the party organization, membership and other resources; and devising new public policies and strategies for the party's elected representatives in public offices.[4] But it is clear that not all parties engage in these activities to anything like the same extent, and that the relative demands on parties have changed as the conditions of modern political life have also been transformed.

Some modern parties, particularly left-wing west European organizations, have been strongly organized groups with many members and an extensive bureaucracy, whereas others have been far smaller and more loosely organized. But the demands placed on the political party have now changed. Policy-making is rarely the function of the party organization as a whole, but is now almost exclusively the prerogative of the party in government (and thus its leadership) or of an elite with good prospects of assuming top power. Prior to taking office, too, parties are increasingly in the business primarily of maximizing influence or winning elections, and this requires large amounts of money (especially for media-related activities) to enable them to appeal directly to the voter. The party organization as a whole and the majority of its members have relatively little to offer in either of these areas.

Our understanding of the emergence of the modern party and its organization as a whole has, though, been closely bound up with the development of the traditional mass membership party. This linkage colours both judgements on the contemporary status of the political party and views of party development in post-communist eastern Europe. Opening his discussion of organizational levels of party activity in western democracies, Klaus von Beyme thus noted the development by liberals and conservatives in Great Britain during the nineteenth century of a modern mass party that had not previously existed elsewhere. It evolved throughout the century as the franchise was gradually extended, although the process of party organization really gained a lasting impetus following the third parliamentary reform of 1884/85.[5] Such institutions were the prototype for the kind of party that came to dominate the political life of developed states and the established democracies of the twentieth century.

What is particularly noticeable in this context is the way in which definition of the party form as both modern and mass hang naturally together. As one of the early analysts of the political party, French writer Maurice Duverger, observed in a book first published in 1951, the age of the individualist and decentralized cadre parties of the nineteenth century had clearly passed and that only the 'vast centralized and disciplined parties of today' suit the structure of contemporary societies. What is often overlooked in this observation, though, is that it was the centralized and disciplined character of the modern party rather than its vastness and size of membership that was most at issue.[6] The way in which a party was organized was generally more important than just the number of members it attracted.

Although a view of party development and contemporary forms of political organization that was highly influential Duverger's was never one that could be applied throughout the entire world of party democracies nor a conception that was universally accepted. The more loosely organized parties of the United States and their evident success in operating as key components of the world's most powerful democracy always posed a considerable obstacle to the general application of Duverger's view, and it was never fully accepted by American writers. It also began to appear problematic as signs of declining membership and the growing marginalization of the traditional party began to appear in western democracies during the 1960s. Much began to be written of the 'decline of party' as a key institution of western democracy as significant changes in its position were observed. The problem was, it was later concluded, that the decline of the mass party was treated as signifying the decline of party more generally. Earlier observations now seemed to embody a strong evaluative element, and the period of the mass party seemed to coincide with the image of a 'golden age' of parties, since which everything had gone downhill.[7]

As usual, with further analysis the picture turned out to be a more complex one. Much of the apparent decline in membership was relative, as national electorates had greatly expanded since the 1950s. In absolute terms the decline of party membership in western democracies was far less marked, although major falls did occur in Denmark, the UK and Netherlands. But six countries actually saw an absolute increase in levels of party membership from the early 1960s through the 1980s. The membership decline thesis was also more doubtful if a concept of membership broader than that of simple number was taken. In many cases, the rank-and-file membership became a less marginal component of the party as decision-making powers were devolved and individual members active in constituency branches became more influential.

The issue was also a conceptual one. For some time, following Duverger, parties were indeed differentiated by ideology or type (such as mass, cadre, or totalitarian) and were largely regarded as generic entities. The picture was sharpened and a firmer grasp of party change developed when distinctions were made between the party on the ground (the organization broadly defined by its membership), the party in public office (the organizations that appear in parliament and act in government), and the party in central office (the institution of party in its own right, with a distinct bureaucracy and its own pattern of operation). If a party was seen in terms of these distinct components, change could be analysed in terms of shifts between them and their relative importance, and the patterns of interaction that could be identified between them. From this perspective, the 'decline of party' (or even 'decline of mass membership party') so much discussed in the 1960s and 1970s could more be appropriately seen as the decline of the party on the ground. The party in central office and in public office had actually strengthened: this was primarily observable in terms of the growing wealth and increased numbers of party staff in many countries, and second in relation to the involvement of a higher proportion of significant parties in processes of government and access to the resources of the state.[8]

Party membership in eastern Europe

Estimates of the levels of party membership in some countries of east and west Europe are presented in Table 4.1. Figures in this area vary, and it is a general picture that is conveyed rather than a fully documented record. Apart from aspects of party secrecy and the bureaucratic obstacles to compiling accurate records the concept of party membership is a curiously ambiguous one and it is, suggests von Beyme, less easy to define a member of a political party than that of any other major organization.[9] The experience of long-established western parties shows this as well as the record of recently formed eastern ones. Aware of the organizational disunity that had underlaid the British Conservative Party's enormous defeat in the election of 1997, for example, party managers soon discovered not just that the number of those considered to be party members had fallen drastically (perhaps from 1.5 million in 1979 to 300,000 in 1997) but also that there were no national membership records at all and that, indeed, the party itself did not officially exist as a national body.[10]

It would hardly be sensible to expect practice to be better in many east European parties. When asked in 1995 by this writer about the number of members in the Polish Peasant Party, the national organization secretary expressed not just ignorance but also a general lack of interest in the question. What was important, he said, was the capacity to get a sufficiently large number of bodies on the street for a demonstration or parade. Analogous ambiguities could be seen in records of the (Polish) Democratic Union, where failure or inability to pay the necessary dues was not necessarily a reason for immediate removal from membership lists if the member was sufficiently active in the party organization. Party membership, particularly in recently established organizations, was by no means simply a matter of formal record but as much a reflection of a still evolving pattern of institutional norms.

Table 4.1 Party membership: east and west Europe

	As percentage of adult population	As percentage of electorate
Slovenia	9.6	–
Czech Republic	4	6.4
Hungary	2	2.5
Poland	1.3	1.5
Austria	16.4	21.8
Sweden	15.4	21.2
United Kingdom	2.5	3.3
Netherlands	2.1	2.5

Sources: S.P. Ramet, 'Democratization in Slovenia – the second stage', in K. Dawisha and B. Parrott (eds) *Politics, Power and the Struggle for Democracy*), Cambridge University Press, 1997; otherwise P. G. Lewis (ed.), *Party Structure and Organization in East-Central Europe*, Cheltenham, Edward Elgar,1996 (left-hand column); P. Mair, *Party System Change*, Oxford, Clarendon Press, 1997 (right-hand column).

Despite all these uncertainties, existing statistics do provide a useful indication of the contemporary situation. Indices for east and west Europe calculated both on the basis of party members as a proportion of the electorate and membership as a percentage of the adult population overall suggest that eastern levels in the countries where better figures are available are not just well below the levels of the western countries with high levels of party membership but also those of western democracies as a whole. But they are on average only just below those of the western democracies in which party membership was lowest and had declined most steeply after the 1950s. Not too much should be made of membership ratios in themselves, then, and the low levels generally seen in eastern Europe may simply be reflection of the new democracies having come into existence in an era of 'post-modern' politics.[11]

Statistics on the membership of individual parties give a fuller picture. Those for Poland between 1991 and 1995 show the situation with respect to the five parties and electoral blocs represented in parliament after the 1997 elections (Table 4.2). The picture it gives is in some ways limited as two organizations had been formed not long before and the process of tracing their antecedents would be unproductively complicated, but such organizational volatility has also been characteristic of east European politics as a whole. Such indications of developments during the early years of post-communist politics suggest that party membership was, firstly, not just low but also quite static, although significant progress in terms of FU organization and membership seems to have been made since the 1997 election.[12] Greater continuity was evident for other parties that had parliamentary representation between 1993 and 1995. The Confederation for Independent Poland had a membership of 21,000 in 1991 and one of 25,000 in 1995, although it did claim a peak in the election year of 1993. Ágh reports that party memberships throughout eastern Europe generally rose rapidly in the first phase of parliamentary activity, peaked in 1991–92 and declined slowly thereafter, but this was not clearly reflected in Polish experience.[13]

Table 4.2 Party membership in east-central Europe

Party membership in Poland, 1991–8

	1991	1992	1993	1995	1997	1998/99
Solidarity Electoral Action				2 million		
Social Movement				(union)		30,000
Social Democracy (SdRP)	60,000		65,000	60,000	60,000	
Demo. Left Alliance						80,000
Democratic/Freedom			15–			
Union	15,000	10,000	20,000	18,000	10,000	22,000
Peasant Party	180,000	200,000	200,000	190–	200,000	120,000
MRP				140,000	20,000	

Source: 1991 figures as reported in *Partie Polityczne w Polsce*, Warsaw, Polska Agencja Informacyjna, 1991; later figures from various press reports.

Table 4.2 continued

Membership of Hungarian parties (thousands)

	1990	1992	1995	1996
Hungarian Socialist Party	50	40	37	37
Alliance of Free Democrats	15	32	35	32
Hungarian Democratic Forum	21	30	23	25
Independent Smallholders' Party	40	60	70	60
Christian Democratic People's Party	3	18	26	27
Fidesz (Young Democrats)	5	13	10	15

Source: A Ágh, 'The end of the beginning: the partial consolidation of east-central European parties and party system', *Budapest Papers* (1996); G. Ilonszki, 'Representation deficit in a new democracy: theoretical considerations and the Hungarian case', *Communist and Post-Communist Studies*, 1998, **31**: 167.

Membership of Czech parties (thousands)

	1994	1998
Civil Democratic Party	22	22
Social Democratic Party	11.5	13
Communist Party	222	142
Association for the Republic	65	40
Christian Democratic Union	80	80
Civil Democratic Alliance	2.250	2.5

Source: A. Kroupa and T. Kostelecky, 'Party organization and structure in the Czech Republic', in Lewis (ed.) *Party Structure*; A. Ágh, *Emerging Democracies*, pp. 156–8.

One feature of party membership seen elsewhere in eastern Europe was the relatively high membership of the post-communist Social Democracy of Poland (superseded as a party by the Democratic Left Alliance), as well as that of the Peasant Party, which also derived largely from the former United Peasant Party. Allied to the main communist successor organization, it had enjoyed an official if politically emasculated existence before 1989. The relatively small Movement for the Reconstruction of Poland continued the traditions of the unstable and generally marginal right-wing formations from which it was formed, and showed signs of severe internal dissension soon after the 1997 election. In 1997, the largest Polish political formation appeared to be Solidarity Electoral Action, although the estimated two million membership of the trade union stood in an uncertain relationship with its small circle of national representatives and leaders of the 45 other groups and parties with whom they coalesced to form the SEA and win the September election.

It was certainly not a party with a multi-million membership. Its leaders registered a Social Movement of SEA as a new party in November 1997, but news of its further development was strikingly absent in the months that followed. In a far cry from the million-plus membership of the Solidarity union, the Social

Movement enrolled 30,000 members in its first year of existence rather than the 300,000 originally aimed for.[14] The Democratic Left Alliance also transformed itself from an electoral alliance into a formally constituted party in June 1999, a step it had little choice but to take as the new Constitution only permitted the lists of officially organized parties to be presented to the electorate.[15]

Patterns of party membership in Hungary are more similar to those of Poland than the Czech Republic. This is particularly true of the Socialist Party, whose membership level has been modest but reasonably strong in relation to other national forces. Electoral success in the early period seemed to have some association with the strength of party organization and a relatively robust level of membership. Equivalent membership figures for Czech parties show a comparable pattern. In similar fashion to the reasonably strong membership of the Polish Social Democracy and the Hungarian left, the extent of Communist Party membership in the Czech Republic, particularly in the early years, was very striking. But in this case the party retained its original identity and an unbroken organizational link with the communist period.

Also unlike the other east-central European cases, where the new social democrats are emphatically post-communist and have clearly transformed their political identity, the Czech communists have achieved limited electoral success despite their large membership. The CP and CDU, indeed, together accounted for 87 per cent of all party members in the Czech land, although they only attracted 20 per cent of the votes in 1992.[16] To the extent that votes rather than members are the primary asset that aspiring politicians seek to acquire, there have clearly been more direct ways of acquiring them than the arduous path of membership growth and organizational development. The Civic Democratic Party and Social Democrats emerged as the leading forces in the Czech Republic on the basis, for example, of a very modest membership base, as did the Hungarian Young Democrats who achieved such a surprising level of electoral success in 1998. The political fortunes of the Communist Party in the Czech Republic nevertheless began to show signs of improvement in the context of a shaky minority administration established by the Social Democrats in 1998. After nearly 10 years of testing post-communist transition, too, it also began to show a surprising capacity to attract young new members.[17]

The evidence from other countries tends to be more scanty and varies in reliability. A survey in Slovakia suggested that as many as 8 per cent of the population were members of political parties in 1994.[18] High as it seems, the figure was contrasted with the claim of 12 per cent belonging to a party in the Czech Republic. This is twice the level of reported figures, so the Slovak membership estimates might also be reasonably halved. Care clearly needs to be taken with estimates based on public surveys. Estimates based on reports of party membership totals in Slovenia have been similarly high, and reach levels in the area of 9.5 to 10 per cent of the adult population.[19] Such a degree of party activity might well be credible in the context of Slovenia's developed civil society, but later surveys have suggested a marked decline in organized participation. Surveys in other countries have also shown some suspiciously high levels of membership. 'Only' 5.1 per cent

Table 4.3 Membership of Ukrainian parties, 1994

Left:	Communist Party of Ukraine	123th
	Peasant Party of Ukraine	66
	Socialist Party of Ukraine	30
Liberal:	Christian Democratic Party of Ukraine	130
National Democratic:	Rukh	51
Nationalist:	Ukrainian National Assembly	14
	Ukrainian Republican Party	13

Source: I. Prizel, 'Ukraine between proto-democracy and "soft" authoritarianism', in K. Dawisha and B. Parrott (eds) *Democratic Changes and Authoritarian Reactions in Russia, Ukraine, Belarus, and Moldova*, Cambridge, Cambridge University Press, 1997.

of Ukrainians were described as professing any party affiliation, which in view of the state's large population would mean that 2.6 million were committed to this kind of party involvement.[20] Details of actual levels of party membership, however, showed a lower level of commitment (see Table 4.3).

Membership levels overall in Ukraine were not particularly low, especially compared with Poland, although for a country in which largely unreconstructed forces have retained such power even the left-wing forces do not have a very strong base. The numerical strength of the Communist Party hardly bears comparison with the 200,000-plus membership of the Czech organization, even though the population of the Ukraine is five time larger than that of the small central European country. The contrast bears out the strong anti-party sentiments prevalent in Ukraine and the organizational measures applied to hold back institutional development.

More fundamental disruption of the traditional power structure than that which has so far affected Ukraine has had a major impact on party organization and membership in Bulgaria. The Bulgarian Socialist Party, for example, was strongly hit by its removal from power in 1997. Having lost some 42,000 members nation-wide since 1994, the decline accelerated after its defeat in the 1997 election. Eleven thousand (over a quarter of the membership) left the party's branches in the capital alone. The party nevertheless remained the largest in Bulgaria, and the UDF simultaneously launched a drive to raise its membership to 80,000.[21] The negative effects of electoral defeat and membership loss on institutional development overall should not be exaggerated, though. It has been argued that change by defeat has generally been easier to deal with for reforming leftist parties and more productive than 'change by success'.[22] According to this account, it helps transform and 'purify' an established membership and discourages excessively career-minded people from joining. The overall impact of defeat can, therefore, in the long-run be positive for parties and their democratic credentials. Electoral success, or just entry to a governing coalition and access to central political resources, can provide a major boost to recruitment with consequences that are by no means always positive for democratization overall. Membership of the extreme nationalist Greater Romania Party thus rose from 20,000 in 1993 to 32,000 in 1995 when it joined the weakening post-communist government of Nicolae Vacaroiu and the party acquired a new capacity to 'distribute goods'.[23]

While the general idea of a party's membership simply refers to the people registered – with varying degrees of accuracy and according to various criteria – on a party's list, the role of members within a party as a whole can take very different forms. There is a general assumption that parties with more members are likely to achieve higher levels of electoral success, although this is by no means a general rule as the experience of the Czech Communist Party indicates. Apart from that, it is by no means clear what the role of members in the modern party actually is or should be. The way in which membership is structured and the organization of the party as a whole has considerable significance both for its political performance and for the implications of its members' behaviour. As Duverger pointed out in his original discussion, it was the nature of the modern party's organization as much as the size of its membership that gave it a special character.[24] The decline of the mass party therefore has distinctive implications for party organization and structure as well as for the number of its members.

Party structure

While the salience of the mass membership party declined in western democracies over recent years, in post-communist eastern Europe there was a distinct lack of enthusiasm for such forms of political organization from the outset. The communist experience left a distinct residue of anti-party sentiment in the population at large that has been widely recognized. Such sentiments often drew on deeply embedded feelings of suspicion and distaste for party political activity evident before World War II. For a number of reasons new political leaders of the post-communist countries were not necessarily eager either to establish formal parties or – when their necessity became accepted – to encourage people to join them. In Poland, for example, the group that was to found the Democratic Union in December 1990 agreed that the age of mass parties was over and that the attraction of members was not a major priority. The recruitment of even a select band of supporters proceeded, to say the least, in a highly relaxed manner.[25] It was accompanied by a similar relative neglect of organizational development in the early post-communist period.

The conditions of modern party activity, elitist attitudes on the part of many party leaders in eastern Europe, and the reluctance of the public to join them combined to give the members that parties have enrolled a relatively marginal role within the organization as a whole. This has also been reflected in the weak structural development of east European parties. In many cases there has simply not been any conception of what a rank-and-file party membership is for or how it could be most effectively organized. Their role as a confirmed pool of electoral support and assistance in promoting the party's cause at election time could be identified quite easily, but recognition of what members might do at other times was often lacking. The motivation for joining a party was weak. Supporters had no need to combine to press for the principle of representation, as had often been the case in many instances of party formation and structural growth in western democracies. Rapid social change, growing unemployment and intense pressure on living standards provided few incentives for party membership and give little promise of any direct payoff from such support. The attractions of organizational membership were few. Following the electoral success of Poland's Social Democracy in 1993, a spokesman for the party stated his opinion honestly (if perhaps cynically or just unimaginatively) that there was really little for local members and activists to do in the period between elections; they might attend meetings to be addressed by party leaders who were now ministers, but could hardly be expected to exert any influence over the behaviour at this level or do anything more positive for the party.[26]

Throughout eastern Europe, it seemed, questions of inner-party democracy were not just ignored but were rarely perceived to be an issue at all. Post-communist politics and the practice of liberal democracy was understood to operate at national level and within the narrow confines of the political elite – which might indeed be internally differentiated and in these terms pluralist, but that involved little conception of broader political participation or a more active form of mass democracy. It involved a very limited conception of the political party and provided few incentives for developing the party's organization or subnational structure.

In terms of the tri-partite model introduced earlier, it was very much the idea of the party in public office that prevailed in post-communist eastern Europe. If the party did succeed in achieving government office its own leadership became rapidly identified with the office-holders or particular clutch of ministries subject to its control. The weak institutionalization of the new democratic parties and absence of much in the way of any national organization readily sustained a situation of entrenched elitism. The picture was, of course, not an undifferentiated one. While the experience of Polish parties suggested the membership was often passive and that party structure offered little in terms of decision-making power and effective involvement in party affairs outside election times, Czech conceptions pointed in a different direction. There were indications from the early 1990s, for example, that local party organizations might develop as autonomous units and have the power to manage their own daily affairs, settle management and leadership issues on their own account, and control their own finances. Such 'stratarchic' relations between local party organs and national offices had been increasingly seen in western countries.[27] In Hungary it has been the resemblance of the new parties' structures to those of the former ruling communist party that has attracted attention, professionalization and bureaucratization leading to the emergence of a clearly restricted and elitist democracy.[28]

Empirical studies of east European party structure on a nation-wide basis and attempts to chart the extent of their local organization have been very limited. In Poland it was the Peasant Party (PPP) that has been identified as having the most extensive structure, which was not surprising in view of the fact that it was the best approximation to a mass party that the country had. It had an office with a full-time secretary in each of the forty-nine provinces and a central staff of about twenty.[29] The organizational network of the different parties varied in density throughout the country, but a representative sample of four Polish provinces in 1997 also suggested that the PPP scored highest in terms of territorial penetration and the possession of an organizational structure in 79 per cent of all communes (of which there were about 2480 nationally, indicating a national total of around 1950 circles).

The organizationally well-endowed post-communist Social Democracy came second with 65 per cent representation, while new parties such as the Freedom Union (FU) and Labour Union (LU) were represented in only 13 and 8 per cent respectively (which meant around 320 and 200 circles nationally). Even with the organizational superiority of the older established parties, the network of local party structures in Poland was very weak and in keeping with the low level of party membership nationally.[30] A survey conducted just previously suggested that the Christian National Union also had a restricted local network on lines similar to those of the FU and LU. The same investigation also turned up the interesting finding that most delegates to the main party conferences had an inaccurately optimistic view of their party's organizational network and had little conception of the significant differences of the parties in this respect.[31] Earlier reports had suggested an even greater discrepancy between the post-communist organizations and recently formed parties, with the Social Democracy having 2500 local circles in 1992 in contrast to 287 for the Democratic Union, 230 for the Christian National Union and just 31 for the Congress of Liberal Democrats.

A similar structural superiority for the post-communist socialist party was equally apparent in Hungary (see Table 4.4). Post-communist parties both in Poland and Hungary had origins in the former regime and a political legacy that gave them major advantages in terms of a residual (though comparatively now large) membership, a committed electorate, as well as major organizational advantages in terms of personnel and property. Once the initial phase of anti-communist enthusiasm had passed, and the Hungarian Democratic Forum and populist movements such as Solidarity and its political offspring lost much of their popularity, it was perhaps not surprising that it was the better organized

Table 4.4 Number of local party organizations in Hungary

	1990	1992	1994	1995
Hungarian Socialist Party	–	1844	2080	433
Christian Democratic People's Party	–	700	885	684
Hungarian Democratic Forum	327	824	820	719
Alliance of Free Democrats	320	900	759	737
Alliance of Young Democrats (Fidesz)	150	468	324	363
Independent Smallholders' Party	–	1630	–	2100

Source: Lomax, 'Structure and organisation', 1996; Ilonszki, 'Representation deficit', p. 167. To facilitate comparison, it should be noted that Hungary's population was only 27 per cent that of Poland and its area 30 per cent.

and more professionally staffed parties such as the Polish Social Democracy and Hungarian Socialists that came to dominate the electoral scene in 1993 and 1994. As well as being far better organized, however, they were also ideologically distinct from the early right-wing parties that formed governments in the early 1990s and represented quite different political values. It has, indeed, been argued that it was precisely their different political orientation and contrasting values that brought them to power rather than their superior organization. The relative influence of the different dimensions has been the subject of some debate, although the results of a recent empirical investigation conducted by Gábor Tóka suggest, indeed, that values are 'at least as effective as is the political mobilization of organizational networks' in sustaining party performance.[32]

Despite the prevalent view of the structural weakness of east European parties, it is evident from the limited evidence available that both the countries of the region and the parties within them are significantly differentiated in their organizational aspects. Alternative sources of strength may also impinge on relative party influence during successive phases of political change. Neither can any evaluation of party performance just be restricted to the electoral sphere. It has, indeed, been established that the electoral success of parties is a dimension less well explained by organizational conditions than is other aspects of party performance such as the legislative cohesion of party groups or the breadth of party activities. Nor are all parties alike in this respect. What have been termed 'doctrinaire' parties are highly centralized and have members with a high degree of involvement; such forms of organizational development sustain strong party cohesion in the legislature but relatively weak electoral performance. The achievements of differently organized 'mobilizing' parties reflect an alternative alignment of organization and performance.[33]

Party structures in eastern Europe may also be weak, but many of them are still young and have developed under difficult conditions. Some at least are likely to develop further in line with further democratization of the region. As the new parties were developing under less advantageous conditions than the long-established (if variously transformed) post-communist parties, so too were the less advanced democracies of the region developing party structures at a gradual pace. It was, for example, only after the Bulgarian elections of December 1994 that it became evident that the Union of Democratic Forces had passed a turning point in terms of its structural development and that a single political party was finally beginning to emerge from a range of ill-defined political tendencies and a clutch of competing proto-parties.[34] Despite the clear weakness of east European party organization, nevertheless, Ágh also traces a path of rapid development from early movement parties, through a process of rapid parliamentarization to the emergence of a dominant range of 'cartel' parties on the contemporary west European model.[35] Whether this recently advanced view of the gradually stabilized pattern of west European party systems is really applicable to the east is open to some doubt, but it does suggest the rapid pace at which some new party structures – despite their many imperfections – have actually developed.

Finance and party funding

One way in which the idea of the cartel party does point to important features of east European party development is the emphasis it places on parties' relations with the state and their growing dependence on state resources for their survival. The decline of the mass party and the reduced significance of the 'party on the ground' in relation to other aspects of party organization directs attention to a broad historical tendency in terms of the growing strength of links between party and the state that parallels the withering of ties between parties and civil society in western democracies. This accords well with the top-down development of east European parties and the parliament-based, generally elitist mode of functioning that has characterized their mode of operation, although other arguments for the validity of the cartel model are somewhat less convincing in the east European context.[36] Throughout the short history of east European post-communism the parties have not so much lost their organic links with civil society as failed to develop them in the first place, which is rather a different matter.[37]

The growing intimacy between party and state has been a major feature of developments in the west over past decades, a primary aspect of which has been rapidly increasing party dependence on the finance and other resources provided – or, more accurately, channelled – by the state and its diverse agencies. The growing trend since the 1950s towards direct financial subvention and state subsidies for parties has been the major sign of this dependence, a factor no less important than the support of party activity by parliamentary staff, the state regulation or direct provision of media outlets, dispensation (with varying degrees of legality) of public resources, and the growing significance of state regulation of political activity.[38] Access to funds is an important requirement for virtually any individual party, but as party structures begin to firm up in eastern Europe their absence can effectively bar a major portion of the political spectrum from effective representation – a weakness identified as contributing to the surprising failure of the radical Catholic right in the 1998 Polish local elections.[39]

Finance has been a critical dimension of party development. As in other countries, parties in eastern Europe tend to be secretive about the financial resources they control and the sources of their funds even if (as in Poland) parties are legally bound to make such details public. Such prescriptions are rarely observed in full and, where accounts are publicly registered (as in the Czech Republic), by no means all sources of funds are acknowledged. There is plenty of scope for financial scandal to erupt and undermine apparently stable processes of party government even in the more consolidated post-communist democracies – as happened with the resignation of Václav Klaus and the fall of the Czech government in 1997. There is, nevertheless, a fair amount of material available on party funding during the early post-communist years and some basic trends of development in this area have been established. The role of the state in the funding of party activity is one prominent feature (see Table 4.5).

In a situation where party membership is generally rather low, a major feature that emerges is the high level of state funding in comparison with the amount

Table 4.5 Party finances in east-central Europe

a) *Party funding in Czechoslovakia (1991, million crowns) and Hungary (1995, million forints)*

	CPBM	CM	CPP	CSP	HDF	HSP	Fidesz	AFD
Membership dues	41	0.062	2.5	0.8	9.7	19.5	0.7	3.1
State subsidy	9.5	14	8.5	1	135	302.7	97.7	198.1
Donations	49	1	2	9	9.9	43.1	0.8	9.4
Other	12.5	3	3	5	854.6	230.3	443.3	7.6
Total	112	18	16	16	1009	596	543	218

Source: P.G. Lewis, 'Party funding in post-communist east-central Europe', in P. Burnell and A. Ware (eds) *Funding Democratization*, Manchester University Press, 1998, pp. 138–9.

b) *State funding and allowances paid to wealthiest parties (million dollars)1995/96*

(Polish) Democratic Left Alliance	3.980
Polish Peasant Party	3.220
Hungarian Socialist Party	2.293
(Czech) Civic Democratic Party	2.275
Czech Social Democratic Party	2.018
(Polish) Freedom Union	1.522

Source: Lewis, 'Party funding', p. 147. Official allowances and salaries would need to be added to the Czech and Hungarian totals for fully comparative figures.

provided by members' subscriptions. This is particularly evident from the pattern of party funding reported for Hungary in 1995 ('other' sources of income were even higher in that year's accounts, but were well known to be derived from the sale of major property assets and hardly likely to appear as a regular item of party income). State funding also played a central part in supporting the Czechoslovak People's Party and Civic Movement in the same country. Even more striking there was the relative wealth of the Communist Party and the continuing capacity of a mass party to draw substantial funds from membership dues – although this did little to help its electoral fortunes. The strong showing of the Hungarian Socialist Party in the 1994 election similarly meant that it drew substantial funds from the state (more than half as much again as its closest rival) as well as taking more than any other party from the pockets of its members. In both Hungary and the Czech Republic, too, the share of party funding provided by the state rose steadily in the first half of the 1990s. Analysis of funding sources in Slovenia showed the state playing an equally large, and generally growing, role in the later 1990s.[40]

But not all of the new democratic states provided funds for party activity. Poland, for example, initially provided only a direct subsidy for party activity by reimbursing election expenses rather than offering a regular grant (although a new funding system was introduced in 1997). In the case of at least one small party (the Union of Labour) this was not just a major form of income in the election year itself but also provided an important source of funds in later years, as interest on the reimbursement continued to appear as a prominent feature in party accounts.[41] This suggests that close attention needs to be paid to the different channels for state funding. Various forms of state subvention were actually at issue in eastern Europe. They included:

1 direct state funding of parties;
2 reimbursement of election expenses;
3 provision of salaries, resources and payment of expenses to parliamentary deputies; and
4 diverse forms of support for party groups in parliament.

Provisions for state funding of parties in Hungary and the Czech Republic were quite generous, as well as providing for the reimbursement of election expenses at such a level that most Czech parties made a handsome profit from the 1996 election. The overall victor, the Civic Democratic Party, thus received the equivalent of $5.8 million and even the Civic Democratic Alliance (which formed the smallest group in the 1996 parliament) got $1.3 million. In distinction to Polish practice, in which it was only those gaining parliamentary representation whose expenses were reimbursed, electoral law in Hungary provided for each party to have its campaign financed in proportion to the number of candidates presented. By 1997, however, there was already resistance to underwriting the profligate activities of some candidates, and proposals emerged to set limits on personal and institutional contributions to campaign funds.

Despite their importance in supporting the activities of some parties, the payment of election expenses in Poland was not set at a particularly high level. Even the victor of the 1993 election, the Democratic Left Alliance (in which the Social Democrats played a decisively leading role), only received the equivalent of $1.4 million. The Non-Party Bloc for the Support of Reform, which became the smallest party in the new parliament, got $119,000 and thus recouped only 18 per cent of its election costs. Whilst Hungarians were discussing plans to cap election expenses and restrict the funds parties drew from the public purse, then, proposals were emerging in Poland for the regular funding of all parties that gained a minimum two or so per cent of the total vote.[42] Legislation passed in June 1997 finally set the floor for state funding at 3 per cent.

Party expenditure during the election campaign held in Ukraine during 1998 reached levels similar to those in Poland, and were well below those seen in the Czech Republic. The income of parties and electoral blocs mostly came from diverse social organizations (as legally constituted associations and 'individuals') and to a limited extent from separate parties or individuals (see Table 4.6).

But direct funding and the reimbursement of election expenses were by no means the only way in which parties could draw on state funds. The salaries and expenses of parliamentary deputies are formally, of course, quite a different thing from the funding of parties. But the two can be closely linked not just by the fact that deputies often tend to represent their party in the legislature more effectively

Table 4.6 Campaign expenditure in Ukraine 1998 by source ($ thousand)

	Parties	Associations	Individuals
Communist Party		1.246	11.222
Peasant and Socialist Bloc		10.000	43.484
Green Party		563.744	500
National-Democratic Party	500	957.468	
Hromada		95.666	
Social Democratic Party		46.950	
Progressive Socialists			5.535 (all sources)

Source: R. Gortat, *Ukraińskie wybory*, Warsaw, Fundacja Polska Praca, 1998, pp. 80–1. No return was made by the Ruch Popular Movement.

than they do their constituents (particularly when elected on a national party list), but also because some deputies were known to pass a portion of their salary directly to party headquarters. Although analytically quite distinct, in practice the party in public office could become very closely identified – and sometimes virtually indistinguishable – from the party in central office.

Together with state support from the party clubs most organizations formed within parliament, such financial provision emerged in Poland as a very substantial basis for party operations. There is little doubt that the local presence of a parliamentary deputy and the support of his office is a fundamental factor in the local strength of party organization and the party's capacity to mount an effective electoral campaign. Parliamentary staff and technical resources largely substituted for 'party' resources at this level.[43] While there was also payment of a salary and official expenses in Hungary they were set at a considerably lower level than those in Poland. Such differentials compensated substantially for the lack of direct state funding in Poland. Calculation of all expenses and allowances for party groups in the Polish parliament thus shows them, in the most generous cases, to be actually higher than the direct funding for major parties in Hungary and the Czech Republic (Table 4.5).

To the extent that questions of power and money are intertwined in the issue of party finances it is inevitable that the border line of legality is challenged and often crossed, while charges of corruption are rarely below the surface of political life. There is nothing very unusual about eastern Europe in this respect, although the specific characteristics of post-communist change do give it some particular features. One of these is the institutional legacy of communist rule, and the status of the organizational and financial inheritance passed on to the new social democracies and other kinds of post-communist party. Such issues rumbled on in Poland from the time of the first Solidarity government, with the pace of investigation and intensity of judicial review affected by the varying political colour of different governments (Solidarity-dominated until 1993, post-communist 1993–97, Solidarity Electoral Action from 1997) and presidents (communist Jaruzelski until late 1990, ex-Solidarity leader Wałęsa 1990–95, post-communist

Kwaśniewski from 1995), whose conflicting interests in the issue were quite apparent. The investigation tended to dig deeper when both parliament and president were dominated by the right and there was less reluctance to cover the matter up (from 1990 to 1993, therefore, with a post-communist government and social democratic president further slowing matters down between 1995 and 1997).

One issue concerned the receipt of 'Moscow gold', and the transfer to the former ruling party of more than a million dollars in January 1990. Some guilt was finally acknowledged, but the affair was put on ice by a post-communist minister in May 1995.[44] It also slowly became clear in Poland that both the Social Democracy and Peasant Party either inherited property and funds to which they were not entitled, or received them at too low a cost. This investigation also dragged on for some years, and resolution was not facilitated by the post-communists' refusal to disclose accounts and claim that they had no funds. In 1996 the debts of the Social Democracy were estimated at around $8 million, and agreement was slowly developing as to how the issues arising from the illegitimate inheritance were to be resolved. By the time the Social Democracy was dissolved and the Democratic Left Alliance replaced it as a formally registered party, agreement had been reached on such matters.

Such affairs, allegations and – sometimes – proof and admission of party corruption have by no means been restricted to Poland. Note has already been made of the enormous contribution made to the funds of some Hungarian parties by their inheritance of valuable property and its subsequent sale. Charges of collusion between former communist and opposition parties concerning the allocation and disposal of former communist party/state property were made that, in the light of the elitist and rather inward-looking nature of Hungarian party politics, rang only too true. Abuses of the privatization process for party purposes also came to light in 1996, when it appeared that funds were skimmed to produce a treasure-chest for left-wing parties during the 1998 election. Ministerial resignations followed when the charges were largely borne out.

In Czechoslovakia, on the other hand, most early problems arising from ambiguities concerning the status of communist assets were avoided by the speed with which the former regime collapsed. Anti-communist forces were able to take rapid action by confiscating all major communist assets before the party was able to initiate its own action and arrange for the transfer of whatever might be salvaged from its well-established holdings. Despite rumours of various affairs well before the 1996 elections, moreover, little evidence of corruption or financial misdemeanours actually came to light. It was only in 1997 that serious allegations saw the light of day. Accounts of dubious sources of party funding had been around for some time, but matters came to a head as dissatisfaction mounted within the Civic Democratic Party concerning Klaus's leadership of the party as well as his conduct of government, which fell in November 1997. Opponents within the party split off and formed a new party, the Freedom Union. The funding scandals spread to other parties and the Civic Democratic Alliance and Social Democrats were also affected by such allegations, some of which were soon substantiated. In terms of political consequences for the parties, though, perhaps most striking was Klaus's resilience and the relatively strong (though somewhat reduced) showing of the CDA in the 1998 election. The new FU, formed by 'clean' party dissidents, developed as just one more marginal right-wing force. Although, too, the Polish Social Democracy lost the 1997 election it actually increased its share of the vote, and it can hardly be concluded that corruption charges did much harm to its political chances.

Although such developments in the more consolidated democracies have received somewhat greater publicity and are better documented, indications of corrupt financial practices arise on occasion in most contexts. Major property deals, for example, were alleged amongst the membership of the ruling Movement for a Democratic Slovakia.[45] The lengthy tenure of Tudjman's Democratic Union in post-communist Croatia was also linked with pervasive patronage and the extensive use of privatization for political purposes. Elsewhere in the Balkans, the clientelist networks developed by the Bulgarian Socialist Party were a major factor in its hold on power until the economic and political collapse of 1997, when a virtual avalanche of corruption scandals contributed to major electoral defeat.[46] An OSCE report in 1999 identified a dense network of illegal links in Bosnia between political, business, criminal and police elites, and pointed to corruption as the life-blood of one-party rule in most parts of the republic.[47] Overall in the Balkans, the weakness of parliamentary development and the continuing prominence of personal rule provided scope for enormous corruption as new political and economic entrepreneurs emerged to benefit from presidential patronage and government-sponsored privatization.[48]

As in central Europe, other countries also require parties to make information about their sources of income public, but such prescriptions are often ignored. Thus major Lithuanian parties were found to have received not insignificant contributions in the region of $60,000 to $190,000 for the 1992 elections, but no information about sources was provided.[49] Although not all Latvian parties provided the necessary information on time, party officials in that country were relatively forthcoming on the issue and some corporate contributions were openly acknowledged (one of them being from a Russian businessman to the tune of one million dollars).[50] Individual contributions and membership fees were the major source of income, although only in rare cases did the dues paid by members provide the major portion. Once more the general pattern emerged of socialist organizations having a stronger membership base and greater financial autonomy, as the Socialists were one of only two parties in which members' dues provided the largest source of party income.

Relations with the media

Of all the changes in the broader social environment that have impinged on party organization in recent decades and generally undermined its role and significance in democratic political life, one of the most prominent has been the enormous expansion of the electronic media and the overwhelming impact of television. The time has long past when such fruits of technological development were restricted to the wealthier countries of the west. The use of modern media and electronics-based campaign techniques were critical in Latin American party politics during the 1980s where, as in contemporary eastern Europe, party change and organizational development occurred within a broad framework of regional democratization.[51] Television provides the means for candidates and national leaders to make direct appeals to large parts of the population and avoids the need for using the costly resources of party organization to get the message over to voters – even where such party organization exists in any developed form. In emerging democracies the existence of an established media network and opportunities for its less restricted development means that new parties can construct their identity and project it to the public without having to face the arduous task of party organizational development. The power of television showed itself at an early stage in Poland in the presidential campaign of 1990 when the émigré candidate Stanisław Tymiński emerged from nowhere to beat Prime Minister Mazowiecki into third place – and disappeared into virtual political obscurity soon after.

Exploitation of the media and the maintenance of a political monopoly on their use had, indeed, been of the characteristics of communist rule and was, in its time, one of the innovatory features of the communist approach to political life. This primarily concerned the printed media and use of the press, although a similar approach was adopted towards film, radio and the television as their use became widespread. The relative advantages of former communist parties over the new political formations soon disappeared in this respect. Although former communist newspapers often remained in existence their association with the party soon disappeared and survival increasingly depended on the maintenance of an independent political line, the ability to attract a popular readership and capacity to draw on new sources of capital (often from abroad).[52] Paradoxically, it was only after the end of communist rule that a mass membership began to figure more strongly as a political factor in communist party organization in this respect, as such assets remained largely unavailable to more recently established political formations.

Access to the media and skilled use of their resources were therefore particularly important for new parties, and this particularly concerned television. Press outlets were, however, a better known resource and generally more accessible to new parties at the beginning of their political career. By the mid-1990s the press in much of eastern Europe could be described as a pluralistic system of party-oriented newspapers.[53] The capacity of new parties to make effective use of the press was often limited, though, and they were not always able to hold on to media assets.

Much of the early pluralization of the press in Bulgaria was characterized by the proliferation of papers published by the resurrected or newly formed parties. But their circulation soon began to decline as prices rose, parties split and the novelty of press pluralism lost its early attraction for the public.[54] A similar tendency was seen in Slovakia after 1989 as parties established their own newspapers but then failed to maintain their circulation in the face of newsprint shortages, inadequate printing facilities and a weak distribution system (still, it should be noted, in state hands). A range of papers associated with the Christian Democratic Movement, various right-wing parties as well as the MDS had all closed by the mid-1990s.[55] In the Czech Republic the former communist party daily *Rudé Právo* succeeded in transforming itself into more of an independent publication attuned to the market and allied itself to the opposition Social Democratic Party. Other official organs of former establishment organizations lost circulation, were sold or closed down.

Party publications in Romania were also reported to have a limited readership and government-dominated media, in particular, were generally ill received by the public.[56] Neither was the political climate one that always encouraged the development of a free and diverse press. The end of communist rule did not necessarily mean the elimination of state interference, particularly when one party maintained a tight grip over its administrative structure and the course of government overall. Slovak independence did not start well in this respect when the editor of the largest independent daily was dismissed by the nation's government on its very first day.

The picture was, naturally enough, a differentiated one. But much of the early political diversity in eastern Europe, certainly so far as many of the new parties were concerned, did not survive the economic rigours of the newly established market place or, for that matter, the fickle preferences and increasing impoverishment of most of the consumers. By the time it was consolidated, for example, none of the privatized print media in Hungary clearly favoured the socialist government elected in 1994.[57] Private entrepreneurs and major foreign investors also became prominent on the east European print market, but often withdrew or sold back to the state as the industry did not prove to be particularly profitable on a long-term basis. The new owners could hardly complain that they had too little freedom. When the British speculator and press baron Robert Maxwell took over 40 per cent of the Hungarian government daily *Magyar Hírlap* he immediately demanded – and received – a new contractual agreement on powers of editorial appointment. Following his death it passed into Swiss hands, while many other publications also changed hands and often ended up back in state ownership, particularly because early expectations of good profits were just not realized.

Foreign and general entrepreneurial interest in the news media soon declined, while various kinds of consumer, leisure and technical publications survived as more profitable undertakings. But money, or the lack of it, was never the whole story. Milošević and his party retained their dominance over Serbian politics despite 'massive foreign aid' for the independent media, in particular the well-developed network of daily and weekly papers.[58] The party political impact of the newly liberalized print media thus often turned out to be limited in the long run. It was in any case radio and, particularly, TV that was more important – and it continued to remain more subject to state control.[59]

While the press and print media could be opened to new political groups and economic forces more easily (although with rather mixed results for the new parties in the long run), issues surrounding control over and access to the electronic media took considerably longer to resolve. Television in particular remained subject to state jurisdiction as new regulations were worked out – and often vehemently fought over, as in Hungary's 'media war', which flared up with particular ferocity in 1992. Control of state-owned radio and television was a major terrain of conflict between the new conservative government and socialist opposition, and the government's attempt to strengthen its influence by imposing controls over the media budget allocation provoked a furious response.

By the mid-1990s most countries in eastern Europe had introduced, but not yet necessarily implemented, legislation to introduce dual public–private broadcasting systems. The process was a lengthy one and bitterly fought over. New governing and opposition parties were both eager to maximize their own influence and deny it to competitors. For this, amongst other reasons, variants of the relatively politicized French model of regulation were adopted in preference to the more hands-off models of Britain and Germany. The dominant parties were very closely involved both in the reorganization and daily administration of the media. The outcome by the mid-1990s was that eastern Europe was far from having a pluralist framework in full operation. In 1996 Jakubowicz could make the broad statement that 'except in Poland, the Czech Republic, and Slovenia, electronic media are still direct extensions of the power structure, designed to function as mouthpieces'.[60]

Neither was it just a matter of opposition parties not having sufficient access to television and radio. Political culture and party attitudes towards this critical resource were the root of the problem. In consolidated democracies, on the basis of lengthy experience, governing parties are wary of making direct use of public controls over the media, as they are aware that such practices will all too quickly rebound on them in opposition. Such lessons have yet to be fully learnt in the east, whilst opposition parties tend to attack government manipulation only because they are not yet in a position to act in the same way. The idea of media autonomy with regard to party competition in a liberal democratic framework has yet to take full root. Parties have thus become particularly embroiled in tensions over the prime resource of television to the extent that they were in control of state resources or in a position to compete for such control.

The lengthy conflict in Hungary is a prime example, which even when politically resolved left such a complex arrangement that it was essentially unworkable. This was only one case among many. Mečiar's Movement for a Democratic Slovakia was anxious to consolidate its hold over television (as it was over other domains of public life), while Klaus's CDP in the Czech Republic placed numerous obstacles in the way of the effective privatization of segments of television that led to the launch of the highly successful TV Nova channel. In the end, the commercial channel was by no means unsympathetic to the interests of CDP and the government, both because of a strong market orientation on both sides and the TV owners' unwillingness to antagonize the government.

In countries like post-communist Croatia, where one-party government was as much the norm as during the communist period, governing-party dominance of the media has tended to strengthen monopoly control during the course of the 1990s.[61] But the alternation of parties in government has also created its own problems. Media diversity, such as political pluralism, has yet to become consolidated or fully rooted. The resolution of competing party interests in media regulation by building in a finely balanced representation of the different forces could hardly be permanent when subsequent elections were bound to change the balance of parties in parliament, if not the orientation of the government itself.

The rebirth of Solidarity as a major parliamentary force in the Polish elections of 1997 warned against any premature conclusion that the basic conflicts of 1989 had been fully superseded – in terms of the media as well as other spheres of politics. On taking over government with a strong parliamentary majority, the representatives of Solidarity Electoral Action again felt they were encountering an entrenched (and barely post-) communist establishment. Conflicts were further embittered by the pronouncement of the Supreme Administrative Court that the National Radio and TV Committee had not followed proper procedures in the allocation of private TV concessions. The media situation after privatization was further complicated by the emergence of autonomous media forces in their own right. At the end of the 1990s the possibility emerged in Poland of a media-based magnate becoming, following Berslusconi's example in Italy, a political force in his own right. Polsat owner, Zygmunt Solorz, was thus reported to have a solid parliamentary base of thirty deputies committed to his interests.[62] The group of deputies associated with the influential Catholic station Radio Maryja have also become an increasingly distinct political force. Such groups lend support to the observation that aspiring leaders of new parties could find novel sources of party strength and 'need not recapitulate the development sequences of western Europe, but can leapfrog directly into a mass communications video age'.[63] To the extent that votes rather than members are the primary value that aspiring politicians seek to acquire, there are more direct ways of achieving this than through the arduous path of organizational development.

Factionalism and party unity

The idea of faction is intimately linked with the concept of the modern party itself, and the line between the two is a particularly tenuous one during the early stages of party development.[64] Factionalism takes various forms and plays different roles in different countries and political cultures. In political discourse the term generally has a negative connotation and is often associated with disruption, weak party organization and narrow political interests. It has, however, played a relatively permanent role in Italian, Japanese and some French parties, and has generally become an accepted part of political life in those countries. The degree of party factionalism may be regarded as a standard aspect of organization broadly analogous to the less controversial dimension of coherence – although also one rather different in that, unlike indices of variation in this area (degrees of organizational complexity, centralization and membership involvement), leaders and the parties themselves have little power over its emergence or persistence.[65] In some contexts, too, the idea of faction has simply been identified with parliamentary clubs (sometimes then termed fractions) as the organization of a particular party's members in parliament.[66]

In view of these uncertainties and the rather diverse usage of the term, a distinction might be usefully made between faction as a distinct form of intra-party organization (which may often be surprisingly stable) and factionalism as a form of behaviour that creates, perpetuates or enhances instability and undermines processes of political institutionalization.[67] In broad terms factionalism tends to be particularly significant where party discipline is not well developed at parliamentary level and in systems where there are strong presidential powers, both features being quite prominent in parts of eastern Europe.[68] A distinct contrast may, indeed, be drawn between factional activity in a situation where parties are forming or are, for some other reason, in a state of flux and that seen within established parties.

The general context of party formation and organizational flux in eastern Europe created a significant overlap between the different categories. The imperatives of constructing a democratic competitive system provide an impetus for the party organizational development whereas other pressures create further internal diversity and heightened competition. Particular factors have been at work in eastern Europe in this respect. Factionalism was regarded as a particular sin in communist parties subject to strict Leninist discipline, although this by no means prevented its covert emergence in many countries of eastern Europe and the persistent inability of party leaders to eradicate it in countries such as Poland. After 1989, therefore, internal party factions could be seen as a healthy sign of democratic life.[69]

On this basis, and given the rapid development of political identities and weakness of party organization in the early years of post-communist development, the acceptance of factional activity could be a useful way of keeping the struggling new institutions together. It certainly seemed to make sense as large segments of the Solidarity movement emerged to take on a more tightly organized form and began to develop as parties. When the Democratic Union was founded in May 1991, then, the acceptance of factions was spelt out in party statutes to take account of the firm desire of the Democratic Right to retain its separate identity. Two other factions – the social-liberals and greens – were also formed.[70] But the political advantages were not permanent, and the continuing strength of factional tendencies contributed to growing uncertainty about the party's identity and problems in developing an effective political strategy.

Early factionalism developed in a context where the organizational control of party managers was particularly weak and could present further obstacles to institutionalization and organizational consolidation – a problem well recognized in the Polish Democratic Union over a lengthy period. The general restriction of party development in eastern Europe to the parliamentary arena and a prevalent elitism provided an atmosphere highly conducive to factional activity while, without a strong institutional network to act as a restraint, individualism and personal competition was allowed full rein. Factionalism has certainly been present in many east European parties, and their associated weakness and lack of coherence have been perceived as a common problem of democratic development and contributory factor to the fragmentation of party systems.

But factional tendencies have not always been seen in a negative light. The record of western parties, indeed, suggests that factionalism has not been a particularly strong influence on the political success or otherwise of a particular institution.[71] Hungarian experience, likewise, suggests that early factionalism had little effect on the overall political outcome. The major parties overcame early factional threats and almost all were able re-establish unity in time to fight the 1994 election. Those who split from the main parties were generally marginalized and gained little from such activity in the consolidating democratic system.[72] Although Csurka's Life and Justice Party made a far better showing in 1998 after its failure in the 1994 election, the radical decline of the Hungarian Democratic Forum was caused by the highly effective challenge presented by Fidesz and to a range of institutional weaknesses rather than to the prevalence of factional tendencies. While Czech parties (and particularly those on the right of the political spectrum) stabilized early, the split of the Civic Democratic Party and the fall of the Klaus government in 1997 showed that the political system even in a relatively well-consolidated new democracy was by no means impervious to such developments. In this case the party formed by the factional split, the Freedom Union, was soon marginalized and showed immediate prospects of political recovery.

The relationship between elections and factional developments within parties has also been an ambiguous one. The accretion of a distinctive faction around Csurka and his departure from the HDF led to the marginalization of the new party he led in the election of 1994. But it also left him in a position to take advantage of the growing support for extreme right-wing parties that emerged in many parts of Europe in the late 1990s. Somewhat surprisingly, though, the severance of their links with the Czech Civic Democratic Party by some of its leading figures in 1997 led not to the eclipse of Václav Klaus and the relegation of what was left of the party to the political sidelines but to quite the opposite outcome – the recovery by the CDP to win a very respectable 27.7 per cent of the vote (just down from 29.6 per cent in 1996) and a miserly 8.6 per cent for the Freedom Union of the former anti-Klaus faction.

While Waller and Gillespie suggest that the tendency of parties to be affected by factionalism is positively influenced by the electoral performances of individual parties, and to some extent by the capacity of victorious leaders to buy off internal opposition with the spoils of office, contrasting cases of sharp conflict within victorious electoral forces are not difficult to identify in eastern Europe.[73] After the elections of 1997 the Movement for the Reconstruction of Poland split within weeks of winning an admittedly modest level of parliamentary representation, while Solidarity Electoral Action (now in government and to some extent sustained by the benefits of public office) experienced a high level of internal conflict and faced the resignation of its deputy head (over an agreement with the left about the contentious issue of the reorganization of territorial structures) less than a year after taking office.[74] SEA on the other hand, it should be noted, remained very much an electoral bloc and not a party in its own right. Indeed, it contained several well-organized parties and coherent political groupings that were able to turn government office to their own distinct advantage.

Factionalism and the instability of party organization also remained a strong feature in the political life of other countries and was, for example, particularly prominent in Estonia and Latvia among the Baltic states. Weak institutionalization left the Baltic parties wide open to entrepreneurial newcomers, and established organizations remained highly vulnerable to the defection of parliamentary deputies and candidates.[75] Factionalism was closely linked with the fragmentation of the party structure in those countries' parliaments and the sequence of legislative measures taken to counteract such tendencies (see Chapter 3).

Although such flux and high levels of institutional change are generally seen as signs of political immaturity and obstacles to the emergence of more effective party systems, their role in eastern Europe can be seen as a broadly more positive one. In view of the rapidity of social change and the wide range of policy issues in relation to which parties and their diverse constituents must define their position, factionalism is a necessary process of organizational differentiation and a fundamental aspect of early party development.[76] The view firmly set within a historical context that factions are typically 'projections of individual ambitions in the context of personal and family rivalries and affiliations' and that politics within this framework tends to involve a 'small number of people competing with each other in a large number of weak, transitory alliances and groupings' certainly sums up some of the characteristics of east European politics but is by no means the whole story.[77]

Individual ambitions have been no less present in the east European party arena than in any other, and many alliances and groupings will no doubt turn out to be transitory in a situation where no institution has been in existence long enough to consolidate a new party identity and prove its durability. But with a political scene riven by a broad range of tendencies and orientations combined with the continual eruption of new issues and problems with regard to which positions have to be taken, it is hardly surprising that new lines of division run through existing parties and that new forms of interest aggregation often cross existing structures. Issue- and strategy-led factionalism can be seen to be as much a common element in modern party politics as are personal rivalry and competition on an individual basis within the newly opened political arena.

Organization and party institutionalization

While the contribution of such aspects of party structure as organizational growth and the moderation of early factionalism to institutional development should not be over-emphasized, they do nevertheless provide the necessary stability and important conditions for the development of parties overall. The achievement of at least relative stability and a pattern of steady development fosters the process of institutionalization that many writers see as intimately linked with the consolidation of post-communist democracy in eastern Europe. Although institutionalization does involve major organizational aspects it is by no means restricted to that aspect of party development. It is, according to Samuel Huntington, the process by which organizations acquire both stability and value, the acquisition of these attributes being reflected in an adaptability, complexity, coherence and autonomy.[78]

A more specifically party-oriented conception of the process developed by Angelo Panebianco places particular emphasis on such latter features and the organizational dimension more generally. It directs particular attention to the organization's autonomy and its level of 'systemness', involving the extent of interdependence between the party organization's different components.[79] By such means the party ceases to be just the means to some political end and becomes valued in and for itself, the goals to which its activities are directed becoming part of its existence and not something wholly external to its political being. It should be recognized in this context that all parties that have some staying power have been institutionalized to some extent; Panebianco took care to point out that the prime question is whether the institutionalization process produces strong or weak institutions. Put in slightly different terms, the point to be made about eastern Europe is not so much that its parties experience problems in becoming institutionalized at all, but that the process has generally produced weak institutions rather than strong ones.

Autonomy and coherence ('systemness') are the key measures of party strength and institutionalization within this conception, but the main determinants of the strength of these party attributes lie in the conditions of the organization's genesis and the precise way in which the party comes into existence – hence the importance in this view of what is known as the genetic model of party development. Critical factors in this situation are identified as (1) the territorial growth of party organization in terms of penetration or diffusion, (2) the presence or absence of an external institution that acts as a 'sponsor' to the party, and (3) involvement of a charismatic leader in the formation of the party.[80] Strong parties thus generally develop (1) through territorial penetration as founding elites maintain tight control of party organization, (2) on an independent domestic basis and avoid reliance on a sponsor in the immediate social environment – thus facilitating strong internal legitimation, and (3) without charismatic leaders whose personal standing would tend to obstruct organizational development. Organizational factors thus play a large part in this view of institutionalization, and the conception has been criticized for being cast at an excessively general level of analysis, for disregarding the importance of how parties behave in new electoral markets and placing too much emphasis on purely organizational constraints.[81]

An early analysis applied the model to party development in Poland, its insights helping to account for the higher level of institutionalization amongst communist-successor parties in contrast to those emerging from the Solidarity camp, and thus for their contrasting electoral performance in 1993.[82] But its overall relevance to the development of east European parties and their organizational characteristics may now be more limited. Panebianco's model is certainly helpful in directing attention to the absence of territorial penetration by the weaker parties in Poland, to the obstacles encountered by the post-Solidarity parties in disentangling their political prospects from the presidential ambitions of Lech Wałęsa and to the political ambiguities inherent in the charismatic attraction he held for much of the Polish electorate. This view is also useful in linking the low level of party institutionalization in eastern Europe as a whole with organizational weakness, low levels of structural articulation in terms of the establishment of local party networks, general lack of professionalism in party organization and technique,[83] financial dependence on the state, as well as the negative consequences for party development either of presidential systems in general or of close party involvement with the campaigns and ruling structures of individual presidents.

But Panebianco's model cast little light on subsequent developments in Poland and certainly did not provide any perspective within which the resurgence of a Solidarity coalition and its electoral victory in 1997 could be foreseen. While the Polish Social Democracy (although losing the 1997 election) maintained much of its institutional strength and political capacity the small Confederation for Independent Poland, which achieved a surprising degree of success in 1993 and seemed to fit the prescriptions of Panebianco's model, subsequently split and lost any individual importance. Most surprising from the point of view of the early organizational analysis was the founding of Solidarity Electoral Action in 1996 and its victory in the elections of the following year. Although ambiguous in terms of political identity and providing few clear pointers in areas of policy formation and government strategy, Solidarity's historical legacy proved its continuing strength as a political resource and symbol of national identity. It had indeed been observed after the defeat of the early Solidarity governments and the apparent fading of the Solidarity legend that the myth of Solidarity survived in far better condition than its actual organization.[84] Solidarity, like many other parties and political formations of contemporary eastern Europe, may well appear institutionally weak in terms of formal organization but continues to derive considerable strength from the values it embodies and its potential for representation in less tangible terms. As a political force in eastern Europe it is certainly unique in its character and historical record, but similar to a number of other institutions it finds other sources of strength to overcome its weakness in formal organizational terms.

The basis for one important determinant of party development lies outside the ambit of the individual nation altogether. International and pan-European influences on party development have been stronger on the new democratic parties of eastern Europe than they were in the case of the south European transitions.[85] The strong pull of western Europe and the attractions of EU membership provided a powerful model of party development and a range of resources to assist their construction once it became clear that the dynamics of democratic party government required the formation of relatively orthodox parties on west European lines. The ideological imprint of west European party families on the emerging east European party spectrum soon became apparent, and the acceptance of the new parties in one of the existing unions or internationals soon became an important differentiating factor in the success or otherwise of newly democratized socialist parties, aspiring Christian Democracies, and diverse liberal and conservative organizations.[86] International recognition was an important resource in its own right and a major basis of legitimacy in a diverse and highly competitive situation. It also carried the promise of significant material and organizational contributions to the diverse processes of party development. Europeanization and transnational party co-operation has therefore been a strong and multi-faceted factor in the institutionalization of east European parties.[87]

5 Party systems and structures of representation

Party systems and post-communist politics

Democratic parties and their institutional development are important not only –
or even primarily – in their own right but rather because of their relation to one
another. Their capacity to represent distinctive segments of society and pursue
the particular interests associated with them, and on this basis to seek power
through competitive elections, are the raison d'être of political parties in a democratic system. From this point of view, parties operating within a pluralist order
are fundamentally different from the monopolistic party that dominates under
communism. In the democratic context, too, it only makes sense to judge the
overall significance of a party in terms of its relations with others and its position
within the broader political framework. Parties are, in short, particularly interesting to the extent that they make up a party *system*. Party systems can be classified
by any number of principles, but four main classificatory schemes have been
used:

- the ideologies of the parties;
- the extent to which parties penetrate society;
- the stance of parties towards the legitimacy of the regime; and
- the number of parties in the system.[1]

One major recent study has sought to analyse post-communist party systems with
respect to the quality of the democratic process they sustain, primarily on the
basis of processes occurring in the electoral arena of party competition and voter
representation.[2] Aspects of the four dimensions identified above have been
explored quite fully in terms of different party families and the ideological programmes they espouse (Chapters 2 and 3), and the different kinds of party structure and their organizational penetration of east European society (Chapter 4).
Here we begin by looking more closely at the classification of party systems by
the number of parties they contain, the dominant way in which the study of
party systems has been approached – or at least in which much of the analysis
has started off.[3]

Study of the development of democratic party systems in eastern Europe
involves investigation of the emergence of political parties in relation to others

and the crystallization of a pattern of relations between them – primarily in the context of electoral competition and the democratic struggle for power. As Giovanni Sartori has emphasized, parties really only make a system when they are part of a whole: a party system is 'the system of interactions resulting from inter-party competition'.[4] Discussion of party systems directs attention to a different level of analysis from that of the individual party. Strictly speaking, the concept of system is meaningless unless it has properties that are distinct and separate from those of its constituent elements, and the system results solely from the patterned interactions of the parts that make it up. In practice, though, the individual party and the system formed by a number of them are often confused, and discussion of emerging party systems is often conducted in terms of the nature, organization and electoral clout of the few leading parties in a particular country.

Analysis of the parties themselves may equally direct attention primarily to the relative strength and characteristics of the organizations with respect to political competitors. Both aspects are very important and closely related in terms of overall post-communist political change, as they are in new unconsolidated party systems more generally.[5] It is nevertheless useful to maintain some idea of the difference between the two perspectives. Party development in contemporary eastern Europe may indeed have been limited and the institutions themselves relatively weak, but at least the organizations exist in recognizable form and they do serve as a basic structuring device in regularly held elections in most countries. The question of whether party systems have emerged is a different one, and it is far less certain that anything like a proper system of stable interactions has developed in any of the countries of the region.

Party systems and their stabilization nevertheless seem to play an important role in the consolidation of all new democracies.[6] Developments so far have not provided signs of major steps in that direction or much suggestion of stability in this area. Three reasonably standard elections have now been held in many parts of eastern Europe and, although levels of electoral volatility and party instability have been high, something like viable two-party systems have been identified (Chapter 3) in at least the more developed countries. But even this really concerns little more than the emergence of identifiable right- and left-wing blocs. Only in the Czech Republic have the leading contenders for power actually been the same parties in the last two elections, and after the unconvincing success of the Social Democrats in the 1998 elections inter-party relations here have shown strong corporatist tendencies and stimulated such public disillusion that support for the unreconstructed Communist Party reached 23 per cent in October 1999.

Elsewhere in east-central Europe the basic constituents of the systems – the parties themselves – showed a high degree of fluidity both in Poland and in Hungary. Solidarity Election Action only came into existence little more than a year before its election victory in 1997, whereas Fidesz became the dominant force in Hungary during 1998 and decisively replaced the Democratic Forum as the leading right-wing party. It is hardly possible to discuss party systems when the stable units out of which they might be constructed do not even exist. The outcome of the elections during 1997 and 1998 even in east-central Europe was not so much the emergence of party systems as such as the structuring of the political space into identifiable left- and right-wing segments that reasonably well organized parties could be expected to fill. Nevertheless, like most other observers, we shall continue to refer to party systems in the rather loose suggestive sense of political structuring and inter-party relations even though the formal conditions for 'systemness' do not yet exist.

In east-central Europe the political space was at least opened up by a clear break from the communist regime, generally in terms of one or more changes of government following fully competitive democratic elections. As much as the formation of governments by freely elected parties, this confirmed the importance of the emergence of effective oppositions for the development and stabilization of a democratic order.[7] Elsewhere in eastern Europe there have been less favourable conditions for the development of organized opposition and correspondingly fewer signs of party system emergence or even the proper structuring of a democratic political space.[8] The leadership-dominated parties that ruled in Serbia and Croatia in particular throughout the 1990s still lacked much of an organized or stable opposition and both stayed well in the train of the democratization process, whereas the breakthrough from a minimally reconstructed post-communism in Romania at the end of 1996 led to little more than an ineffective coalition government blocked both by a post-communist opposition and the conflicting demands of its own constituents.

The results of the 1998 elections in the Ukraine also showed few signs of the country moving much beyond the stage of tentative post-communist change as forces close to the former establishment retained much of their existing dominance, although greater prospects for change were apparent following the Moldovan vote the same month. It would not be realistic to expect very much in terms of a stable and clearly differentiated party system so soon after the collapse of the strongly entrenched form of authoritarian rule of the Soviet Union, but the signs of such patterns developing have been very limited indeed in some countries. Many deputies in Ukraine remain unaffiliated to any party, and the notion of an independent parliament in which parties could begin to develop a clear identity is currently still a distant prospect in Belarus. The establishment of a reasonably open democratic space is the basic pre-condition for the operation of the competitive processes that underlie the development of any party system, and these by no means exist everywhere in eastern Europe. Indeed, none of the former 'patrimonial' communist countries where much of the old political apparatus maintained much of its control could be described as an unambiguous democracy, a condition that characterized virtually the whole of the Balkans and the non-Baltic post-Soviet area.[9]

To the extent that even incipient party systems can be said to exist, it is by counting the number of relevant (generally parliamentary) parties that definition and initial classification generally begins. The number of parliamentary parties that appear to be viable contenders for government has long been used as the major principle of classification of party systems, and leads directly to the well-known and easily grasped identification of one-party, two-party and multi-party systems. But it is not just numbers that are at issue. Party systems can be seen primarily as structures of party competition and co-operation,[10] and it is the capacity of different sets of parties to perform these functions with a view to government formation and political rule that is particularly important.

Two-party systems, such as those in Great Britain and the United States, were originally thought to produce a particularly good basis for democracy in terms of the trade-off between stable government and adequacy of representation, and the contrast between two-party and multi-party systems was regarded as a critical differentiating factor. But effective democratic outcomes have now been recognized as quite likely to occur in certain kinds of multi-party system as well. The number of parties in a given system is indeed important, but so is the specification of which of them are politically relevant as well as their precise nature and the way in which they relate to one another. In one influential view the main question concerns not just the number of parties or the degree of pluralism but also its nature – and particularly whether the party system is characterized by moderate pluralism or the less favourable quality of 'polarized' pluralism, with extremist parties at either end of the political spectrum.

The presence of anti-system parties is of decisive importance, as these are organizations that reject the political order in which they operate and undermine the overall legitimacy of the regime they oppose. Polarization threatens the stability of the moderate centre, and therefore has strongly negative consequences for democracy.[11] But the application of such criteria implies evaluation of individual parties based on reasonably extensive knowledge and political experience of some duration, as well as the existence of states in which relatively distinct political structures have emerged. This may well limit the relevance of Sartori's more nuanced party system model to eastern Europe, which has such a short experience of pluralist party politics. Certainly no real progress was made, Sartori maintained, if western models were applied in the attempt to give 'premature shape to chaos' in areas such as much of sub-Saharan Africa, where a lack of political structure held back the development both of party systems and a democratic order more generally.[12]

In the context of the Third World and non-western political systems he nevertheless drew a distinction between states that had developed some kind of structure and formless states such as those common in Africa, where the political process was 'highly undifferentiated and diffuse' and many of its new states were represented by 'polities that are in a fluid state, in a highly volatile and initial stage of growth'. While Third World countries such as India and those of Latin America had also been subject to major regime change and were not necessarily modern, they were nevertheless sufficiently consolidated to have enough of an identity to be regarded as 'formed'. It did not, nevertheless, mean that they are fully structured or, in the case of Latin America, that their party systems had acquired the characteristics of structural consolidation – a good indicator of which was stated to be the presence of 'real mass parties'.[13]

All this points up the numerous problems involved in applying such models of party systems to eastern Europe. Far from showing any degree of structural consolidation, indeed, it may well be doubted if the countries of post-communist eastern Europe are even as 'formed' as those of Latin America. The prior entry of most of Latin America on to the path of democratic transition meant that they were likely to be more advanced in terms of party system development than eastern Europe. Their longer experience of democratization and the range of research carried out on its political processes and institutions thus makes the Latin American countries a valuable source of comparison for the developments in eastern Europe. Recent investigation in fact suggests that party system development in Latin America has been relatively limited. A comprehensive survey showed that only half its states had identifiable party systems, four being characterized by systems described as inchoate and two (Mexico and Paraguay) falling somewhere between the two categories.[14]

Latin American experience lends support to Sartori's argument for the significance of polarization as a primary aspect of party system differentiation. The three longest lasting democracies – Costa Rica, Venezuela and Colombia – have been marked by limited party polarization, whereas the countries with a large number of parties and a broad ideological spread between them tend to have less institutionalized party systems.[15] In terms of this conception, the institutionalization of party systems in Latin America has had four major aspects: first, the emergence of stability in the rules and nature of inter-party competition, with a fair degree of regularity in patterns of party competition; secondly, the development by major parties of reasonably stable roots in society, so that political preferences are seen to have some structure over time and there is a perceptible regularity in how people vote (this dimension also includes consistency in the relative ideological positions of major parties); third, major political actors show loyalty to the system, according legitimacy to the electoral process and the spectrum of parties as a whole; and four, party organizations are significant in their own right and have some autonomy distinct from the interests and actions of the leaders who are in charge of their activity overall.[16]

East Europe would not score highly on these criteria, either, with even the leading democratic countries showing little regularity in patterns of party competition. It is not difficult on this basis to see why east European party systems are likely to be less institutionalized than those of most Latin American countries. Despite major periods of authoritarian rule, the sheer length of time over which the various indicators of party development and meaningful electoral behaviour can be measured in Latin America testifies to possible levels of stability and institutionalization that are just not conceivable in eastern Europe. Historic parties, for one thing, have not been so prominent in post-communist Europe as in Latin America, where a number of parties have a lengthy pedigree – of the thirty-seven leading parties represented in Latin American parliaments in 1993, thirteen had been in existence for 25 years or more.

The major players in eastern Europe, on the other hand, are nearly all either wholly new parties or derive from institutions active in the communist era. Conditions overall have also been less favourable for the formation of party systems than in Latin America. The post-communist period has been too short for ideas of stability and regularity to carry much conviction, whereas the area has also seen major turbulence and extensive change in the architecture of the political space (with the break-up of the federal states) as well as in the basic rules of the political game (extensive and, in some cases, protracted constitutional change; the establishment of effective parliaments and development of democratic institutional procedures; new legislation on party organization and the electoral mechanism, and a whole sequence of changes and multiple reform in these areas in many cases). For such reasons, it has been argued, east European systems may also be considerably weaker and more fragile than those seen in other recently democratized regions of the world.

Patterns of democratization are different, Mair has suggested, the electorate is different, and both the context and pattern of party competition are different. At the present stage parties are unstable and their social roots quite shallow and, while political preferences do seem to be settling into more of a stable pattern, electoral volatility has understandably been at a high level. In the light of broad comparative estimates, the average electoral volatility in western Europe between 1960 and 1989 was 8.4 per cent (although under the different conditions prevailing between 1918 and 1930 it had stood at 12.3 per cent) whereas the equivalent value for the first elections in post-communist east-central Europe was 25 per cent.[17] The significance of such indicators should not be exaggerated though, and this degree of volatility was exceeded by five out of twelve Latin American countries in legislative elections held between 1978 and 1993.

Such experience strengthens the conclusion that the mere passage of time is by no means a sufficient condition for institutionalization and that electoral volatility can become a more or less permanent condition. Eastern Europe, it has been suggested, may well follow Latin America in developing such a pattern of instability and producing a situation of permanently low party system institutionalization.[18] Latin American experience also contains some parallels with eastern Europe in terms of particular models of transition and the evolution of certain types of authoritarian party. Mexico and Paraguay were, for example, ruled for decades by 'single parties fused with the state' in ways similar, though not identical, to those of communist Europe. On this basis the idea of 'hegemonic party systems in transition' emerges as one denoting structures that have not been fully institutionalized but are more developed than those classified as inchoate.

This type was by no means fully explored in the Latin American context, but it raises pertinent questions about the appropriateness of a uniform scale of institutionalization and the degree to which it can be identified with broader processes of democratic development. Because of their longevity and particular features it is indeed more accurate to refer to such hegemonic systems as part of a separate category rather than a point on some continuum of institutionalization.[19] They clearly belong in the indeterminate area between single-party regimes and liberal democracy proper that Sartori discusses, and problems of identifying relevant regimes and operationalizing this in-between concept have been raised in this context too.[20] Such problems loom even larger in the context of eastern Europe than in Latin America, and the status of communist successor parties has been a major source of controversy.

There is not necessarily a difficulty with the idea of communist successor parties within a pluralist party system *per se*, and the institutional transfer from one regime to another does not in itself cast doubt on the political credentials of new social democratic institutions in Poland, Lithuania and Hungary where the parties were voted into power and left office according to the rules when they lost a subsequent election. Complaints about their modus operandi, the bureaucratic mentality of their leading staff and continuing links with elements of the former establishment may not be irrelevant, but there is little serious doubt that the reconstituted parties now operate as part of a developing pluralist system. The same is broadly true of Bulgaria, although the early electoral victories of the socialists there were achieved in the face of a very weak opposition and in a barely developed democratic context.

More serious questions arise about other east European countries, where parties were renamed and reorganized as some elements of pluralist democracy were introduced around them while their communist leaders and their supporters never really lost power or had their dominant influence within the political system interrupted. A major aspect of the change was the introduction of competitive elections, whose impact and full systemic implications were nevertheless vitiated by the fact that former incumbents never left major offices of state and maintained control over much of the political – and indeed economic – infrastructure. Serbia and Ukraine thus provide equivalent examples to the 'hegemonic party systems in transition' identified by Mainwaring and Scully in the Latin American context. Less closely associated with the old political establishment but similarly distant from a full liberal democracy with a pluralist party system was the national populist semi-authoritarian polities of Slovakia and Croatia for much of the 1990s.

Outside the track of democratization and party development altogether lies the personal dictatorship of Aleksandr Lukashenka in Belarus who has shown a growing distaste for parties and all semblance of independent parliamentary activity in general. Classification of party systems by any criterion requires both conditions of relatively free political competition and a reasonable length of time for patterns to become apparent. Time has certainly been limited in this sense, although some kind of emerging multi-party pattern can at least be identified in the more developed countries of east-central Europe. Signs of any democratic party system are fewer elsewhere in eastern Europe where progress in the transition from authoritarian communist rule has been more limited.

Competitive politics and party systems in east-central Europe

Regional diversity has always been strong in eastern Europe, and has become yet more pronounced since the end of communist rule.[21] To some extent, as already suggested, the different parts of the region can be broadly identified with different types of party system. Only the countries of east-central Europe and the Baltic states possess anything like the competitive systems associated with modern liberal democracies, an association recognized by Charles Gati[22] and later affirmed more formally by the decision of the European Union in 1997 to intensify negotiations on integration with five of the more advanced post-communist states, all of them located in this region. But even in these cases it is only in an approximate sense that anything like a party system can be identified. In each of the five countries of east-central Europe three competitive elections had been held by the end of 1998.

Table 5.1 shows the range of parties represented in the parliaments over that period, and makes clear the fact that new parties were still gaining entry to parliament in the third sequence of elections. The smallest number of parliamentary parties overall was in Hungary, where only seven were elected during this period and six of these played a part in government in one or more of the three parliaments. They were therefore, in Sartori's terms, the 'relevant' parties in terms of his model and could be considered as components of what seemed to be the most viable party system in eastern Europe. But even in Hungary the Democratic Forum was almost completely replaced by Fidesz as the leading right-wing force between 1990 and 1998, and any 'system' that could be identified was not made up of quite the same components over this period. The presence of six relevant parties in the legislature for most of the time also placed Hungary in the high fragmentation pattern identified by Sartori, and denoted the polarized pluralism associated with unstable polities and weakly rooted democratic systems.[23]

Although no more than six relevant parties (or party groupings) were present in the parliaments of Poland and the Czech Republic between 1993 and 1998 at any one time, there was already more variation in the particular organizations involved overall in these countries during this period than in Hungary and thus even less 'systemness'. Nine parties gained parliamentary representation in the Czech Republic between 1992 and 1998 compared with seven in Hungary, while as many as twenty-four electoral committees (but hardly parties) were represented in the fragmented Polish parliament of 1991. Nevertheless, by 1998 something like a bipartisan legislature had developed in all three countries. This pattern was not followed in the two other countries of east-central Europe. The overall number of parties during the 1990s in Slovakia and Slovenia (ten and twelve respectively) was again higher than Hungary's, but their parliaments were nowhere near as fragmented as that in Poland between 1991 and 1993.

Slovenia also developed a rather different form of party government, in that new coalitions were formed after the elections of 1992 and 1996 with the Liberal Democracy continuing on both occasions as their central component. It had come to the fore after a change of prime minister in 1991, and the party continued as the main governing force for much of the 1990s. But Slovenia was far from showing signs of becoming what Sartori called a predominant party system, in which a given party was able to amass an absolute majority in three consecutive elections.[24] There was also a dominant party in Slovakia for most of the time between 1992 and 1998, but its authority was considerably less secure and the overall level of democracy in the country less advanced than in Slovenia.

Table 5.1 Party representation in successive east-central European parliaments

	First: 1990–92	Second: 1992–96	Third: 1996–98
Hungary	Hungarian Democratic Forum —————→		
	Hungarian Socialist Party —————→		
	FIDESZ —————→		
	Independent Party of Smallholders —————→		
	Alliance of Free Democrats —————→		
	Christian Democratic People's Party ——→		
			Hungarian Justice and Life Party
Czech Republic	Czech Social Democratic Party —————→		
	Civic Democratic Party —————→		
	Christian Democratic Union —————→		
	Communist Party —————→		
	Civic Democratic Alliance ——→		
	Association for the Republic ——→		
	Moravian Silesian Movement		
	Liberal Social Union		
			Freedom Union
Poland	Democratic Left Alliance —————→		
	Democratic/Freedom Union —————→		
	Polish Peasant Party —————→		
	Confederation for Independent Poland ——→		
	21 other committees represented		
		Union of Labour	
		Non-Party Bloc for Reform	
			Solidarity Electoral Action
			Movement for reconstruction of Poland
Slovenia	Liberal Democracy —————→		
	Slovene People's Party —————→		
	Social Democratic Party —————→		
	Slovene Christian Democrats—————→		
	Democratic Party ——→		
	Greens ——→		
	Party of Democratic Reform		
	Liberal Party		
	Socialist Party		
		Slovenian National Party —————→	
		United List of Social Democrats —————→	
			Democratic Party of Retired
Slovakia	Movement for Democratic Slovakia —————→		
	Hungarian Coalition —————→		
	Slovak National Party —————→		
	Party of Democratic Left (Common Choice) —————→		
	Christian Democratic Movement ——→		
		Democratic Union	
		Association of Workers	
			Democratic Coalition
			Party of Civic Understanding

Mečiar's Movement for Democratic Slovakia emerged as clearly dominant over all competing parties in both the 1992 and 1994 elections, with a lead of 22.5 per cent in terms of total vote over its nearest rival in 1992 and 25.3 in 1994.

This was far higher than the lead of any other victorious party in post-communist east-central Europe over its competitors. But the MDS was even further away than Slovenia's Liberal Democracy from developing as the institutional core of a predominant party system. The party lost overall parliamentary control in 1998, but had also found it difficult to preserve its dominant position in Slovakia's generally fragmented pattern of party relations at an earlier stage. In 1994 it failed to maintain relations with any viable coalition partner, lost control of the government and had to face a further election less than two years into the life of the independent Slovak republic. The MDS was dominant over other parties in terms of the number of parliamentary votes it controlled but able to find few partners with whom a governing coalition could be formed. It survived for the full life of the parliament elected in 1994 partly because other Slovak parties were also divided and did not form a coherent opposition, although one was finally put together to contest the 1998 elections that succeeded in defeating the MDS.

Elements of party competition finally prevailed, but for much of the 1990s Slovakia appeared to governed by something very much like the 'hegemonic party system in transition' identified in Latin America.[25] The major problem faced there in terms of democratic party system development, therefore, was less the lack of institutionalization commonly diagnosed in post-communist eastern Europe than the residual institutional strength of a transitional power structure based on the MDS with strong roots in the former regime. The main issue was once more less one of party system development but more the patchy nature of democratization and failure to develop the conditions for party competition. To the extent that we can talk at this stage of institutionalization and democratic consolidation in terms of party systems at all, then, it is the other countries of east-central Europe (Hungary, Poland, Slovenia, the Czech Republic) that best represent it.

Signs of similar patterns could also be seen in the Baltic states, although as a group their parliaments were more fragmented and saw even higher levels of party instability.[26] In some parliaments Lithuania and Latvia had parties that were dominant over other groups and scored particularly high electoral majorities. Both the Lithuanian Democratic Labour Party (in 1992) and Latvia's Way (in 1993) achieved a lead of 20 per cent or more over their closest competitor. In neither case, though, was the strong position of these parties permanent and – unlike the Movement for a Democratic Slovakia (whose lead actually increased between 1992 and 1994) – both parties lost their dominant lead in the following election. Less than a sign of even temporary party 'hegemony' the popularity achieved by various parties in the Baltic states was a symptom of political fluidity and early post-authoritarian turbulence (the Soviet Union having only finally disappeared, after all, at the end of 1991).

More striking than any signs of party domination by a single party has been the fragmentation of the party system overall in the Baltic states, although after the election of 1996 as few as five parties took 90 per cent of seats in the Lithuanian parliament. The situation in Latvia and Estonia was somewhat different. Following the 1995 election the Latvian parliament was made up of nine parties, all of which were relevant to the delicate business of coalition formation. Estonia had seven parties, not much higher than the average elsewhere in the region, but their nature and relative position was such that government formation and continuity was particularly difficult to achieve. Less than a reflection of Sartori's polarized pluralism or a fragmented party system, this was more a symptom of general fluidity and lack of structure overall. Three of Estonia's parliamentary parties were, indeed, established just before the 1995 election.

The country's party system was one only in a very restricted sense – a structure in which 'parties were a creation of the electoral system as much as they were representative of defined ideological or social constituencies'.[27] The situation in Latvia was not very different in terms of party development and coalition instability. The formation of a government after the 1995 elections was a protracted process, and a viable parliamentary majority was achieved under nonparty leadership on the basis of a coalition of six parliamentary groups that survived in that form only until May 1996. An important factor in Latvian politics (and one shared to some extent with Estonia) was the sensitive position of the large Russian minority, which had not been given full civic rights and whose position remained controversial and source of considerable international friction. The above discussion suggests that a broadly conceived post-communist east-central Europe (i.e. including the Baltic states) has produced party systems that are essentially pluralist – both relatively moderate and stable (after two or three elections) – in Hungary, Slovenia, Czech Republic and Lithuania, as well as patterns of party relations that are somewhat less stable in Poland and more fragmented in Estonia and Latvia. Slovakia's party system was also less stable and less pluralist in character.

The summary view taken here is also based on the number of parties contesting elections and gaining representation in parliament, processes that by no means determine the nature of party system dynamics once a legislature is constituted. The nature of Hungary's relative stability in the east European context, for example, is cast in a somewhat different light after further examination of relations within the parliament. In some contrast to the set of six parties that contested the 1990 and 1993 elections, for example, the Hungarian parliament in October 1993 contained as many as seventeen distinct political groupings.[28] Prior to the 1998 elections the Democratic Forum, the leading force in the 1990–94 parliament, had largely self-destructed as had the Christian Democrats.[29] Although the HDF survived to gain a small number of votes in the subsequent elections and became part of the government coalition, it achieved this solely by coming to an agreement with the victorious Fidesz. It therefore just counted as a 'relevant' party according to Sartori's classification.

Judgements on system structure and party institutionalization even in east-central Europe under these conditions must therefore be somewhat conjectural. But the notion of an emerging structure provides some perspective on party development in eastern Europe. It helps demarcate the more developed democracies from other post-communist countries, and defines the major characteristics of inter-party relations.

Democratic change and hegemonic party systems

Changes in some countries of eastern Europe involved conflicts that destroyed much of any existing state order or political community and negated the idea of institutionalization implied by the very notion of a party system. The protracted hostilities in Bosnia provide one clear example of conflicts which went far beyond the boundaries of any political process, whereas the collapse of the civil order in Albania in early 1997 showed the tenuous basis of the political community in that country as well.[30] Post-war Bosnia remained strongly segmented in ethnic terms and popular political support flowed automatically to the nationalist parties with minimal competition from the new pan-ethnic opposition. There was little of any civil society to support the opposition, and much of the influence it did have derived from the agencies of international support.[31] Macedonia, too, remained more intimately engaged with the problems of maintaining civic order and its integrity as a state than with developing a party system – as the assassination attempt on President Gligorov in October 1995 and the long-term presence of a United Nations peacekeeping force showed only too well. Instability throughout this area has been brought to a yet more critical level by the hostilities taking place in and around Kosovo. Serbia and Montenegro now also lie at the heart of this zone of intense uncertainty.

The political trajectory of Belarus also remains a singular one, with President Lukashenka having had considerable success in establishing a personal dictatorship in the face of opposition both from the parliament and virtually all the parties represented in it. Any discussion of party systems in countries with such levels of violent conflict and repression is largely beside the point. In the five remaining east European states (Ukraine, Moldova, Romania, Bulgaria and Croatia) violent conflict and overt repression have mostly been avoided, but the establishment of processes of party competition has been limited and notions of party systems remain very tenuous. To the extent that such systems have developed they often seemed to belong to the category of non-competitive politics. In most of these countries the role of established communist parties or their partially reformed successors has been particularly important, and the main question that often arises is whether their governing organizations should be more appropriately classified in terms of:

- either the hegemonic parties associated by Sartori and others with non-competitive systems; or
- the dominant parties that can emerge in contested elections; the 'predominant party' systems produced by dominant parties, as Sartori points out, stand at the edge of the competitive area but are nevertheless within it so long as alternation is not ruled out and the political system provides ample opportunity for open and effective dissent.[32]

The big question is, then, how solidly democratic institutions and processes have been entrenched in the post-authoritarian system. In concrete terms the line between democratic and not-yet (or still) democratic countries is indeed a difficult one to draw. Formal competitive elections are now held in most countries of eastern Europe but there are many grounds for doubt about the extent to which the provisions for effective party competition have been met. The continuity in office of considerable numbers of political and economic power-holders from the old regime raises particular questions in this context, and this points more to the strength of hegemonic elements in such countries than to conditions for authentically democratic party politics.

The weakness of party competition and absence of conditions for the emergence of democratic party systems are most clearly illustrated by developments in Ukraine. In both elections of the supposedly post-communist period the former ruling party maintained a strong lead over other organized forces, amongst whom independent parties played a very restricted role. Former communist party functionaries adroitly neutralized and assimilated the leadership of much of the limited organized political opposition that had developed. The authorities showed little tolerance of independent actors and made no pretence of encouraging the process of party development. Ukraine, apart from Belarus, remained 'the only country in Europe that denied political parties any explicit role in elections'.[33] The original election regulations explicitly favoured individual candidates over those standing on a party platform, and election required an absolute majority of voters.

Formal procedures were overseen by bodies with dubious democratic credentials. As an American CSCE report pointed out, the membership of the Central Electoral Commission was composed of representatives of the former nomenclature, more stringent regulation procedures were required of party candidates than from informal groups and labour collectives, whereas candidates with an existing power base were explicitly favoured. Violations of electoral procedures in 1994 were widely noted and violence was employed against political opponents, although the validity of the outcome overall was accepted by the CSCE Assembly and the British Helsinki group.[34] Under these conditions the electoral process could hardly be seen as democratic or its outcome one that reflected an authentic process of party competition. Any structure of party relations that could be identified was hegemonic rather than predominant in Sartori's terms, although there was extensive fragmentation and such a low profile of parties in the structure of power that reference to a hegemonic party system was largely beside the point in any case.[35]

The electoral regime and conditions for party politics in Ukraine were changed after 1994, but the outcome in the subsequent election was not very different. Regulations drawn up for the 1998 elections provided better conditions for party organization and closer party involvement in the electoral process. New parties were still being formed not long before the 1998 election, although the most successful organizations had a longer history and had all been participants in 1994. One result was actually a greater share of the vote for the communist party (from 13 to 25 per cent) and further complaints about electoral abuse and violations were heard.[36] A number of formally independent parties and individual candidates were in any case part of a broad pro-communist camp. Some elements of party system development could thus be seen and competitive features were probably enhanced in 1998, but any prospects of effective party pluralism in Ukraine remained distant.

Moldova has in some ways seen a similar pattern of developments – with, nevertheless, the dominance of communist forces being effectively reduced overall in 1998 and a non-communist coalition government formed by opposition parties after the election. Party development in Moldova was considerably less constrained than in Ukraine, and the constellation of party forces changed significantly as a number of new organizations were formed.[37] The Democratic Agrarian Party ('effectively the leadership of state and collective farms and the Moldovan equivalent of the economic nomenclature' elsewhere in former Soviet territories)[38] and the Yedinstvo/Socialist Bloc (a broad communist tendency distinguished by its recognition of the separatist Transdniestr Republic) together collected two-thirds of votes cast in 1994, but scored negligible totals in 1998. The Moldovan Communists, banned in the wake of the Soviet coup of August 1991 and re-formed soon after the elections of 1994, came top of the poll in 1998 but gained considerably fewer votes than the DAPM alone in 1994, ending up in an overall parliamentary minority when three right-wing parties combined to form a government. The dominance of communist parties in Ukraine and Moldova is to this extent not quite so significant as it might appear in either case – less in the case of Ukraine because of the weak development of party forces overall, and of limited importance in Moldova because of the strengthened position of competing parties.[39]

The post-communist order in Serbia was also characterized by a hegemonic party system with strong roots in the former regime. The rule, with various coalition partners, of the Socialist Party masked the continuing personal dictatorship of Slobodan Milošević, former leader of the League of Serbian Communists whose pursuit of national interests as vehicle for the enhancement of his own position led to the violent break-up of the former Yugoslavia. Manipulation of national sentiment under war conditions, together with a confused and disunited opposition, secured his continuing dominance and the rule of the Socialist Party. Elections in 1997 once more provided the Socialist coalition with a majority of parliamentary seats, but the victory also reflected the increasing problems faced by Milošević in retaining power. On this occasion it was achieved with a partial opposition boycott intended to bring the turnout-level below 50 per cent, which would (if successful) have invalidated the outcome. The result, however, was a twenty-nine-seat Socialist majority over the ultra-nationalist Radical Party, with whose quasi-fascist leader Milošević had in the past entered into a tactical alliance.

In recognition of the weakening Socialist position, Radical leader Vojislav Seselj became deputy premier in March 1998. There had in fact been a clear pattern of Milošević using the Radical Party and promoting its standing through the media when needed, and then marginalizing it when it became successful enough to pose a political threat. This use of the media was not a problem in view of the Socialists' control of the state and much of the economic infrastructure.[40] Such tactics recalled the behaviour of a classic hegemonic party such as Mexico's Institutional Revolutionary Party, which made similar use of 'second class, licensed parties' to maintain its position.[41] The progressive decline in Milošević's power was linked with parallel developments in neighbouring Montenegro, which made up a restored (though diminished Yugoslavia) with the Serbian republic. The dominance of the Democratic Socialist Party in neighbouring Montenegro became highly fragile towards the end of 1997 with the victory of Milo Djukanović as presidential candidate over Milošević's ally Momir Bulatović. The Montenegrin Socialist Party, as well as the orthodox communist-successor regime as a whole, was seriously split and critically weakened by these developments.[42]

A similar pattern of partial democratization, weak party development and hegemonic rule by survivors from the communist establishment was seen throughout the Balkans. For some years Romania and Bulgaria were governed by largely unreconstructed and relatively monolithic elites. In the early post-communist period they sustained what appeared to be a hegemonic party system similar to those of the more unreconstructed post-Soviet states, which distinguished them from the more differentiated east-central European societies that had developed pluralist party systems. The National Salvation Front that emerged in Romania as Ceausescu was overthrown developed as a body closely identified with the top leadership and central apparatus of the former communist party. Even when its unity was undermined by the divergent policy preferences of President Iliescu and Prime Minister Petre Roman, the NSF effectively perpetuated its dominance over Romania's political system under Iliescu's continuing presidency and through the Romanian Party of Social Democracy he later established.

Led by non-party independent Vacariou, the Romanian government's main parliamentary support from 1992 remained the RPSD and was joined for most of the time by the Greater Romania Party, the Party of Romanian National Unity and the small Socialist Labour Party. Although they had contrasting extreme right- and left-wing inclinations all had strong nationalist tendencies and a hostility to economic reform, with little commitment to liberal-democratic values. Even the right-wing parties openly expressed their approval of the former communist regime.[43] The radical right and major elements of the traditional left made common cause in supporting a power structure that was formally post-communist but certainly not liberal-democratic in character. To the extent that power was shared and elements of party pluralism could be identified it reflected the features of the polarized pluralist model outlined by Sartori, where the extreme wings of the party system are represented by anti-system parties whose activities threaten the prospects of future pluralism and democratic stability more generally. The strong traditions of right-wing extremism, at times emerging as outright fascism, seen in pre-war Romania and never fully disavowed by Ceausescu, were clearly present in the early post-communist period. The opposition meanwhile remained disunited and ineffective. Only in mid-1996 did it show a clear lead in local elections over the parties of the government coalition. In November this was translated into the removal of Iliescu from the presidency after more than six years, and electoral victory for the opposition Democratic Convention.

Significant changes in the nature of the Romanian and Bulgarian regimes in fact took place within a few months of one another at the end of 1996 and early 1997. Electoral outcomes and the party composition of successive governments had been different in Bulgaria, but the fluid character of party development and weak links with social constituencies also meant that much of the position and power of the former elite were preserved until that date. The Union of Democratic Forces won the 1991 election by a slender majority over the socialist bloc and joined with the largely Turkish Movement of Rights and Freedoms to form a government. Party discipline in the UDF was weak, and some members joined in an attack of the opposition Bulgarian Socialist Party on their coalition partner which allied with the BSP in October 1992 to bring down the government of UDF Chairman Filip Dimitrov. For the next 2 years, before a formal BSP election victory in 1994, the government was led by Liuben Berov, an historian and economist with no party affiliation but supported by the MRF and much of the BSP.

The period of UDF government had lasted slightly less than a full year. In marked contrast to the countries of east-central Europe, the programmatic crystallization of party appeals in Bulgaria was found to be weakly developed and the balance of parties' capacities for political governance generally unfavourable.[44] As major policy errors and incompetence on the part of the socialist government became apparent, signs of economic and political crisis grew. Conflict emerged within the governing party and opposition parties developed better relations. Victory of the UDF candidate in presidential elections held in October and November 1996 caused support for Zhan Videnov to plummet, and in December he resigned both the leadership of the Socialist Party and the prime ministership. Further elections in April 1997 produced a victory for the UDF and represented not only a change of power but also the end of the 'cultural parties' and 'sentimental voting' in which the BSP and UDF had been perceived more as political tribes than coalitions of interest groups.[45]

Bulgaria was, like Romania, thus ruled for much of the seven years that followed communist rule by groups derived from the former establishment and their democracy was at best partial. Both countries had during this period developed 'hegemonic party systems in transition' very much like those in some parts of Latin America. But the consequences of further democratization and the apparent new wave of Balkan pluralization that began in November 1996 have not been clear in terms of party system development. A period of at least some political stabilization followed in Bulgaria and was accompanied by measures of economic recovery and steady growth, at least until the conflict over Kosovo intensified. The new coalition formed in Romania by the DCR with the Social Democratic Union and the HDFR also promised a radical change of policy in terms of encouraging foreign investment, accelerating privatization and taking strong measures against corruption.[46]

But the new coalition government did not have much success in meeting these commitments and it became increasingly paralysed by internal conflicts. Tensions between parties deriving from the former establishment and the anti-communist opposition remained sufficiently strong to impede effective co-operation as coalition partners. Fragmentation and government paralysis seemed to be the initial outcome of the changing balance of political forces in Romania, with a change of prime minister in March 1998 representing a further attempt to establish effective democratic rule. In growing distinction to the tenor of political developments in Bulgaria, where president and government at least seem to making a concerted attempt at reform with a view to effective integration with western Europe, conflict within the Romanian elite resulted in a further change of prime minister in December 1999.[47] Neither were the changes or key conflict tendencies channelled by parties in ways that might have strengthened overall system development, as the struggle focused on tensions within the ruling National Peasant and Christian Democratic Party (the core of the electorally dominant Democratic Convention).

A hegemonic party system of a different sort was the original outcome in one more Balkan country. Croatia, like Slovakia, made a distinct break from communist rule but saw little pluralist development for a number of years. Franjo Tudjman's Croatian Democratic Union had a large electoral lead over rival organizations of 29 and 27 per cent of votes in the 1993 and 1995 elections. But unlike most other dominant parties in the Balkans in the early 1990s it was clearly anti-communist and operated, at least in the beginning, within more of a competitive system despite elements of authoritarianism and disregard for civic rights. Tudjman's party was also resolutely anti-Serbian, and it was conditions of regional conflict that provided the basis for CDU's persistence as a dominant ruling party and continued status as a 'pan-national "crisis" organization' or war-party rather than a more forward-looking modern political formation.[48]

In common with the staff of other hegemonic organizations, those associated with the Croatian party were open to extensive charges of corruption and various forms of abuse of office, tendencies enhanced by conditions of rapid economic changes and privatization. Factionalism and internal conflict weakened its effectiveness, and influential members left to join alternative political organizations. Such factors caused a decline in the party's electoral effectiveness, whereas worsening relations with the European Union were viewed with particular dissatisfaction by the electorate and encouraged unfavourable comparisons with neighbouring Slovenia, where the standard of living was twice that of Croatia. The seven largest opposition parties thus formed an alliance before the 1995 elections and scored gains that caused Tudjman serious political embarrassment, but they failed to maintain this level of support. Opposition weakness allowed Tudjman to maintain his position and the CDU did surprisingly well in local elections in April 1997. The hegemonic rule of the Croatian Community contained strong personal elements and survived for just as long as its elderly leader, who died in December 1999. Elections were held early in the new year and finally confirmed the supremacy of an opposition coalition led by Social Democrats and the Social Liberal Party. This certainly put an end to the dominance of Tudjman's original anti-communist organization and eliminated the hegemonic party system that had operated in Croatia throughout the 1990s.

What it meant for the future was less certain. An early phase of post-communist change had now finished and, as one observer put it, 'real politics have come to Croatia this year'.[49] The old Croatian Democratic Union split a matter of weeks after the election, and a wave of scandals broke that brought to public attention details of corruption under the old regime and the nature of privatization under the auspices of the formerly dominant party. The implications for party development were as yet unclear and, as developments in Slovakia after the electoral defeat of Mečiar by a coalition of opposition parties in 1998 suggested, the post-hegemonic phase of political change in eastern Europe was itself uncertain and provided no clear signs as to the contours of possible party system development.

Explaining party system emergence

Despite the problems involved in identifying party systems in the weakly structured politics of post-communist eastern Europe, as well as deciding whether democratization has progressed sufficiently to think of a competitive party system at all in the normal pluralist sense, many observers have not hesitated to outline developments and draw conclusions about outcomes in this area. It is interesting in this context how quickly references to new systems entered into discussions of party development in post-communist Europe. Against the background of party arrangements in established western democracies this is perhaps not surprising. The party system is not just a central feature of modern liberal democracy, it is also a relatively unchanging one whose characteristics tend to have a strikingly permanent character'.[50] Such stability was generally anticipated in eastern Europe at too early a stage.[51] Some early contributions discussed countries in which no parties apart from communist or communist-successor organizations were even in existence.[52] Other analyses were essentially deductive exercises concerning the dimensions of political cleavage that were thought likely to effect the shape of east European party systems, or extrapolations from the experience of the south European transition.[53] A few attempted some empirical generalization from the experiences of very early democratic transition.[54]

Later discussions drew more specific conclusions about existing party systems in terms of stability and degree of institutionalization,[55] identified a general but partial movement from party fragmentation to pluralist systems (without specifying a great deal about the nature of that pluralism),[56] or noted the beginnings of consolidation in terms of the declining number of 'effective' parties after early fragmentation.[57] Suggestions that critical steps have been taken towards the emergence of party systems have not been lacking[58] but the 10 years or so of post-communist politics have by no means produced clearly identifiable structures throughout the region. The most extensive and sophisticated empirical study made so far does indeed argue for the emergence of a 'structured diversity' and general non-randomness in the patterns of post-communist democratic politics, as well as the emergence of systematic patterns of party competition, but such clearly positive judgements are very much restricted to the developed countries of east-central Europe.[59]

In association with continuing fluidity and the general weakness of party structure or overall 'systemness', it is by no means easy to arrive at some explanation of how the degree of party system formation that does exist has come about. Accounts of why established party systems differ generally emphasize the importance of institutional factors, such as the electoral system and the structure of the state institutions within which the parties operate, or they take a more sociological approach and trace the structure of party systems to underlying social cleavages.[60]

In the context of post-communist eastern Europe another major approach directs attention to the impact of the pattern of transformation itself and the nature of the conflict between the authoritarian regime and the democratic opposition. The influence of the latter factor, however, is generally regarded as being of only temporary significance, particularly as democratization progresses and patterns of political competition become established.[61] One approach has counterposed 'legacies of the past' with the 'imperatives of liberalization' and suggests that, while the Leninist period expunged much of the legacy of an earlier past, structures of the communist period affected subsequent developments in a variety of ways and that the interaction of different factors was more important than the contribution of particular elements differentiated by time period.[62] The length of the communist period and its far-reaching social impact have also been considerably more important for emerging party systems than the particular mode of regime transition.[63]

It is difficult, too, to establish any direct relation between the electoral mechanism applied and the type of party system that has emerged. A plurality system, especially one based on simple electoral majorities, has generally been held to encourage the formation of a two-party system whereas proportional representation has been understood to favour the development of multi-partism. Nearly all east European states, however, have now adopted some form of proportional representation or a mixed system for the main parliamentary chamber, not least because it soon became apparent that there was no way in which two relatively well-balanced party antagonists could be expected to present themselves to the electorate at the beginning of the post-communist period.

Early cases where a majority system was applied (Albania, Macedonia) were hardly positive in terms of party development or the encouragement of democratic stability. Majority systems have generally been a part of the communist legacy that has quite rapidly been removed from the political scene. One country in which a plurality system was applied – Ukraine, where some (1998 elections) or all (1994) candidates had to gain 50 per cent of the vote – has been particularly unsuccessful in producing a balanced or effective party system. The requirement that successful candidates needed to gain the vote of half of all those entered on the electoral register in Belarus just made it extremely difficult to elect a quorate parliament at all – which was surely the objective underlying the regulation in any case. So the contrasts in party system that can be detected in contemporary eastern Europe are not just caused by major differences in the form of election. The poorly developed party system in some countries was as much caused by the incompleteness of the democratization process as by any single electoral mechanism.

Within a basic system of proportional representation there may also be variations in terms of whether two-stage elections are held (with the leading candidates in the first round proceeding to a run-off in the second as in France – which gives voters a chance to switch to a second choice), more complex systems in which multiple votes can be cast in different constituencies (for example at local and regional level), various mixtures of different systems to achieve elements both of proportionality and an effective majority, regulations of varying strictness on coalitions and election alliances (in which parties standing in an electoral coalition may be required to form a single party fraction in parliament if successful), and thresholds set at different levels (generally from three to five per cent) to exclude very small parties from the legislature. A threshold, generally of three to five per cent for individual parties, has been applied in most countries and has helped facilitate the emergence of moderate pluralism in terms of party systems.

Comparison of the 1991 election in Poland (when there was no barrier to parliamentary entry) with later ballots in 1993 and 1997 (where a five per cent threshold was imposed) certainly shows the importance of a threshold in having some effect in countering the fragmentation of the party system (twenty-four parliamentary groups were formed in 1991 compared with six parties in 1993 and five in 1997) and assisting the formation of stable government coalitions. The cost of achieving this degree of moderate pluralism was graphically shown in the 1993 election when much of the right wing (34 per cent of the electorate) failed to gain representation. Whatever the immediate effect in terms of exclusion from parliament, though, there was no doubt that the introduction of a threshold made a lasting impact on the process of party system formation. Changes in electoral institutions in the Baltic states have also prompted moves towards party system consolidation, and the abolition of electoral coalitions (or *apparentements*) in Estonia and Latvia has helped moderate fragmentation in those countries.[64]

A third approach to party system emergence is sociological, a particularly influential variant of which has been the model of multiple cleavages constructed by S.M. Lipset and S. Rokkan.[65] In this formulation modern party systems are seen as the product of several historic social conflicts and cleavages that developed over a number of centuries. The lines of cleavage comprise: one originating as far back as the Reformation and Counter-Reformation in the sixteenth and seventeenth centuries and focusing on conflicts of the centre and periphery, another stemming from the French Revolution and concerning state-church relations, and later cleavages originating in relations between forces deriving from land and industry or between the owner and industrial worker. This pattern of four major social cleavages has, it is argued, fed directly into the way in which political forces are organized in contemporary democracies and has determined the different form taken by party systems in modern industrial societies.

On this basis it was observed that the modern party systems of the 1960s were remarkably similar to those of the 1920s, and thus concluded that the lines of political cleavage that emerged in the 1920s became 'frozen' in a form that survived as the organizational template for the pattern of party relations in contemporary democracies. The validity of the 'freezing' hypothesis and its status some 30 years on is the topic of much debate and it remains a central point of reference for the understanding of modern democracies and their party systems.[66] But one of its major implications seems to be that established party systems have very deep social and historical roots indeed, and that new democracies might not have such good chances of replicating their experience.

The relation between social cleavage and patterns of political competition is, however, by no means a direct one and has been questioned on several counts. Lipset and Rokkan's notion of social cleavage has been criticized for failing to distinguish between the space of voter identification and that of party competition, whereas the fluid nature of post-communist politics in fact provides for a wide variety of such combinations.[67] Voters choose from a selection of parties that have come into existence for a whole range of reasons and subsequently decide to present themselves to the electorate on different grounds. Cleavages that might be significant within the society as a whole may or may not effect voting patterns, which, in turn, do not necessarily themselves determine the range of institutional choice available or thus shape the party system itself.

Such a perspective nevertheless raises the question of whether post-communist eastern Europe can develop anything resembling a fully structured party system at all. It is certainly clear that the 'frozen cleavage' hypothesis in its original form is not directly applicable to eastern Europe – although views differ on whether this is because the cleavages are different, because of their not freezing or freezing in ways that do not produce a clearly structured political space in which party systems can form, or because all of the east European regimes have been subject to more than one fundamental discontinuity and have just not produced the stable conditions under which 'freezing' can take place. Any freezing effect in eastern Europe has in fact been minimal; highly destructive warfare and the onslaught of diverse forms of totalitarianism not just destroyed earlier parties but also eliminated most of the cleavages they originally reflected and transformed the social structures in which they had been set.[68] Observers tend to agree that post-communism produces a relatively unstructured political field in which the conditions for party system formation are open rather than tightly constraining.

Early overviews of post-communist eastern Europe suggested that, of the three main cleavages that contributed to the emergence of party systems in western Europe, only that which produces autonomous or secessionist parties supported by national minorities was likely to appear with equivalent strength in the east. The socio-economic cleavage retained its importance but was likely to impinge in quite different ways on post-communist politics, whereas the resonance of religious cleavages appeared to be surprisingly muted.[69] The kind of party then developing also seemed to militate against the likelihood of such a freezing taking place. Durable party identifications were, in the views of some, unlikely to develop without mass parties – and it seemed as unlikely that they would become established in eastern Europe as they are to thrive in the contemporary west. With respect to prospects for stable party system development, indeed, eastern Europe can expect low levels of institutionalization precisely because its experience is now similar to that of the west.[70]

But it is certainly not the case that no traces of cleavages from earlier periods appear in contemporary alignments of party support. One sign was that Polish voting patterns in early post-communist elections reflected some of the pre-1914 divisions of the country's territory between Russia, Austria and Prussia.[71] More generally, though, east European regional variations at least in the perception of party stances were very limited and systems of party competition operated on a strongly nationalized basis.[72] Patterns deriving from different historical experience have by no means been absent, but the point is that they do not constitute a cleavage that is generally reflected in existing patterns of party competition. Modern political processes are indeed likely to have been affected by a range of factors linked with different kinds of social cleavage, but none stemming from more distant periods has exerted a decisive influence on the overall shape of the post-communist party system.

This does not mean that contemporary east European party systems are unstructured or that they will not develop a clearer pattern of relations. The idea that the post-communist political landscape is a *tabula rasa* lacking structure and perceived in relatively random ways by its active constituents is certainly not generally confirmed.[73] New social cleavages have developed and there are limited signs of these being reflected in party alignments, but the question of their 'freezing' in line with the model advanced by Lipset and Rokkan must wait for some time before any answer is possible. Cleavages, indeed, appear to be more numerous than those commonly identified in the west and vary in the degree to which they fissure the politics of the region. As many as eight separate cleavage dimensions have been identified in one account, but the relevance of most of them remains open to considerable doubt.[74]

Overall three major lines of cleavage can identified as having some impact on party system development:

- one concerning the legacy of communist rule, different evaluations of the authoritarian past, and the varying appeals of decommunization;
- a major cleavage developing around the economic dimension and pointing to the emergence of a left-right broadly similar to that seen in western democracies; and
- the continuing salience of a clerical dimension and importance of religious issues in some countries, although with a strength that varies considerably according to time and context.

The profound experiences of the region in terms of communist rule thus impinge on emerging party structures in a variety of ways, but generally combine to form an overarching political division defined by contrasting evaluations of the communist past in most countries (it was, for example, particularly strong in presidential contests and the 1997 Polish elections). In the Czech Republic decommunization had a low salience for politicians as a whole and, while there was some variance in its prominence in Poland and Hungary, it was an issue that had greatly declined in prominence. Only in Bulgaria, where democratization and the crystallization of party positions have been less advanced, were struggles over contemporary economic issues found to be strongly linked with issues and individuals directly representative of the old regime.[75] In some situations the nature of communist authoritarianism and particular inheritances from the period of Soviet domination continue to play a highly significant part. One singular example was the prime importance of the 1956 revolution in subsequent Hungarian developments.[76]

But many writers see a primary cleavage in post-communist society developing around the economic dimension and a recognizable left-right axis emerging as a major structuring agency in east European party systems.[77] It varies in strength and takes particular forms in different countries, being most clearly articulated in the Czech Republic where it is as sharply defined as in western Europe.[78] While four distinct kinds of party have been identified by one analyst of contemporary east-central Europe (liberal, liberal-traditional, tradition/state-oriented, liberal/ state-oriented), there are quite striking differences across the region as to where they are located on the political spectrum.[79] Cleavages other than the socio-economic are also highly influential and the significance of religious issues has, for example, been considerable in Poland. They also continue to have an impact in areas of the more diverse party spectra of Slovakia and Slovenia, where agrarian organizations and elements of Christian Democracy have a significant parliamentary presence.

By way of summary of the different divisions, three distinctively post-communist dimensions of cleavage formation have been identified by Herbert Kitschelt.[80] One relates to resource allocation and distinguishes advocates of political principles of distribution (populism) from those committed to the market; a second concerns the extent and nature of democratic participation and differentiates modern libertarians from traditional authoritarians; whereas a third contrasts those holding a universal conception of citizenship rights from others making them contingent on ethnic, religious or national identity. Initial investigation confirmed that the *tabula rasa* view taken of the party systems in eastern Europe was indeed misleading – although the view taken here of party system was considerably more complicated than that based on just the number of parties and concerned the establishment of congruent relations between voters and party elites. It also demonstrated, on rather a different basis, the distinction already drawn between the increasingly pluralist countries of east-central Europe from the hegemonic systems of the Balkans. Bulgaria thus 'represents a different political world than the Central European countries' and was characterized by a legacy of the overwhelming strength of the communist elite in the transition. Party systems in east-central Europe were quite different, with that in the Czech Republic once more defined as giving voters the most distinctive choice of alternatives.[81]

In terms of concrete parties, the systems that have developed in eastern Europe are understandably quite diverse and stand in some contrast to those of the established democracies in western Europe (which, indeed, differ considerably among themselves). The growing prominence of the economic dimension in party competition and the emergence of a recognizable left-right arena of electoral contestation nevertheless show some structural similarities, at least in the more developed systems of east-central Europe, with the countries of western Europe. But they also show some distinctive common features in some parts of the spectrum:[82] they include the following.

- The prominence on the left of successfully democratized successors to former ruling parties such as the Hungarian Socialist Party and the Democratic Left Alliance in Poland. The Czech Republic, on the other had, provides the unusual case of a Social Democratic Party that has come to prominence from outside the old governing establishment.
- The strong showing of agrarian parties, such as the Polish Peasant Party and Independent Party of Smallholders in Hungary, whilst the conservative Slovene People's Party also has a major rural base.
- The absence, despite the important religious dimension to political life in all parts of east-central Europe apart from the Czech Republic, of Christian Democracy as an influential organized political force (although it has some presence in the more diverse Slovenian party spectrum and the still unconsolidated coalition that has governed Slovakia since 1998). Overall, however, the traditional and nationalist orientations of eastern Catholicism fit uncomfortably with the liberal economic policies that the right has little choice but to espouse, and this continues to produce strong political tensions that right-wing forces have yet to resolve.

Such forms of differentiation can be used to produce spatial models of east European systems that define parties according to their location on two axes, characterized broadly by economic liberalism or state interventionism on the one hand, and cultural liberalism counterposed to a nation-based traditionalism on the other. A model such as that produced by Kitschelt (see Figure 5.1) thus shows parties distributed throughout the four quadrants in a relatively uniform fashion, although few occupied the two left-hand quadrants representing support for state intervention (i.e. the standard left-wing position). The results are broadly in line with those produced by other analysts: although the socio-economic left-right division was most clearly marked in the Czech Republic, both Czech and Hungarian parties were more strongly associated with cultural liberalism with those in Poland more representative of traditional values.[83] Despite the fluidity of post-communist politics and the apparent weakness of most parties, then, major parties can be located in the political arena according to a few main characteristics,

According to Kitschelt (1995):

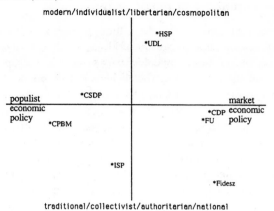

According to Herbut (1997):

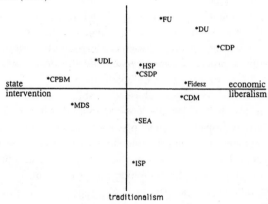

Figure 5.1 Parties in the east-central European political space

although the features of developing party systems in eastern Europe are linked less strongly with established social cleavages than those of the older democracies of western Europe.

Subsequent elections and later investigation showed a relatively strong association between different groups and party preferences little different from that in the west. Far from the fluidity argued for by many early observers, G. Tóka found that there was 'little in the direction of the links between social groups and parties that would appear chaotic or abnormal'.[84] Such sociological approaches certainly substantiate the basic form that party system development seems to be taking in eastern Europe, but it is by no means clear that they go very far to actually *explaining* its nature or the relative speed with which it is occurring in the more developed countries.

The relative autonomy of party systems

Influential though the Lipset and Rokkan thesis has been, and much discussed as it still is, its complexity and the wealth of ideas contained in it are such that its implications are by no means unambiguous. Its sociological approach and the stress it places on the role of deep-rooted historical factors on the formation of modern party systems suggest a kind of social determinism of party politics, but this is by no means all they propose. The authors also consider the possibility that parties themselves might 'produce their own alignments independently of the geographical, the social, and the cultural underpinnings of the movements'.[85] Parties themselves may be forces for political stability in a rapidly changing social and economic environment. Their own activity can help bring party systems into existence where the conditions for their emergence do not otherwise seem to exist. Equally, it has been suggested within the east European context, the apparent paradox of new democratic institutions performing 'normally' and with due effectiveness within a non-consolidated party system can be explained at actor level, it seems, by politicians behaving as if such a system had emerged and in accordance with some norms of 'transformational correctness'.[86]

Neither do the high levels of electoral volatility seen in eastern Europe *necessarily* mean that the emergence of party systems in the proper sense of the phrase lies far in the future or that electoral patterns must first fully stabilize before inter-party relations can become established. A shift away from such conventional assumptions can also help dispel the 'conventional idea that party system change is largely, if not exclusively, a function of, or even a synonym for, electoral change'. It is, equally, according to this view not so much the total number of parties in a system that is important or interesting as the structure of inter-party competition and the process of competition for government.[87]

A focus on differential patterns in the competition for government directs attention away from straightforward analysis of the number of parties that make up a given system and the moderation of their ideological commitments towards three other factors:

- the pattern of alternation in government, i.e. whether the turnover of parties is wholesale, partial or does not happen at all;
- the stability or consistency of governing alternatives, and the extent to which innovative recipes for coalition formation are adopted; and
- who actually governs, and the extent to which access to government is open to a wide range of parties or limited to a smaller subset.

Variations in each factor can be viewed as a whole to determine whether the structure of competition is generally a closed or open one. Examples of closed structures might be the United Kingdom, and Ireland and Japan for much of the post-war period.[88]

The closed structure of competition in those countries might indeed help explain why party systems have been so stable despite the pronounced weakening of religious and class identities in western Europe – and thus of the underlying cleavages that are supposed to keep the party systems frozen. The structure of party competition may therefore, such as the electoral mechanism or organizational activities undertaken by the parties themselves, itself be a 'freezing' agent. More open structures of competition have been seen in Denmark and the Netherlands, as well as in emerging party systems where stable patterns of any sort are yet to be formed. It may equally be argued that the structures of party competition in some east-central European countries have developed patterns of closure quite rapidly and that, in the wake of the 1998 elections, both Hungary and the Czech Republic were showing significant signs of party system stabilization in this respect. Changes of government in all three countries after the second and third elections were either wholesale or non-existent (as Klaus's CDP government stayed put after the 1996 election), which indicated a closing in of the structure of competition. Of the two cases where governing coalitions were returned to power after a period in opposition only one, in Poland, was characterized by an unfamiliar governing formula. Access to government, it is also argued, has only been closed in the Czech Republic, leaving Poland with a relatively open structure of competition but Hungary and the Czech Republic with structures closed on two of three counts. There are, then, also signs of party system stabilization in the more democratic countries of east-central Europe in this sense, even if the argument is not as yet wholly conclusive.

6 Conclusion: political parties in contemporary eastern Europe

Party development in post-communist Europe

After a decade and more of post-communist politics in eastern Europe reasonably strong and politically vibrant parties have developed in some countries, although such growth has by no means been uniform throughout the region. Party development has been particularly weak in some countries (Ukraine is an obvious example), and parties have faced major obstacles to growth as autonomous forces, where authoritarian tendencies have remained strong in states such as Belarus and Serbia. Even in east-central Europe, where party development has been more robust and party government has put down stronger roots, parties show several major weaknesses. They generally have fewer members and a lower level of regular support among the electorate than those in established western democracies, formal structures are quite weakly developed and the parties have little in the way of an organizational presence in local areas, while political identities are often diffuse and factional tendencies still strong in recently established parties.

Parties have not generally established a firm base among the post-communist electorates or secured a regular place in parliament sufficient to give them any predictable level of political representation in the few elections that have been held. New parties and electoral organizations of major parliamentary importance continue to be formed. Electoral volatility has been high and, arguably, shows few signs of declining. Relations between the parties have yet to become regularized, and well-defined party systems are not in evidence at this relatively early stage. On the other hand, electoral blocs of an identifiable right- or left-wing character have become more stabilized in some countries, and this helps produce a more productive context for the growth of individual parties and the establishment of working relations between them.

Any statement about parties in eastern Europe as a whole, though, must be general to the point of superficiality. One of the main features of the region during the post-communist period is the strong differentiation that has emerged between the range of countries it includes. Communist eastern Europe was always more differentiated than it seemed to the detached western observer, and throughout the post-1945 period there were marked differences between the countries that formed part of the Soviet Union itself and those that were subject to less strong forms of Moscow control or influence. Yugoslavia lay wholly out-side the Soviet sphere of influence from 1948, and more independent lines of pol-icy were followed by the communist leaders of countries as diverse as Albania, Poland, Hungary and Romania. But for more than 40 years after World War II eastern Europe remained subject to communist party rule within a framework of states whose borders were agreed not just with the Soviet Union but by the inter-national community as a whole. This has changed as all the countries have moved away from communist rule towards, in most cases, some agreed form of liberal or pluralist democracy.

Party development has been an important aspect of this process, but its pro-gress has been critically influenced by a number of broader political conditions. Basic conditions for party development in eastern Europe have included the fol-lowing.

- The establishment of a viable political community – which has involved both the building of new states out of the constituent republics of Czechoslovakia and Yugoslavia and the transformation of former Soviet states into indepen-dent political units, as well as the maintenance of a degree of civic order, which permits the peaceful resolution of conflicts through political institu-tions (Bosnia most obviously failed to meet the latter criterion for much of the 1990s, but it has also now become highly relevant for other states involved directly or indirectly in the Kosovo conflict).
- Decoupling of the exercise of political and economic power in such a way as to mark the effective end of totalitarian communist rule – this requires either privatization of the economy or full depoliticization of the administration of state economic assets, processes that are less advanced in countries of the Former Soviet Union (FSU) and closely associated with the limited develop-ment of party pluralism there.[1]
- Democratization of the political process to the extent that the principles of free association and organized competition for public office can be effectively implemented – which in turn rests on the development of a constitutional order and the establishment of a number of interconnected civic rights and freedoms.

The different parts of eastern Europe have had contrasting experiences in this respect, and the conditions for party development have been far more favourable in some areas than others.

- States deriving from the republics of the FSU (Belarus, Ukraine and Mol-dova) have been particularly slow to *decouple political and economic power* and, in close association with this fact, have continued to suffer massive economic dislocation and continuing decline. Communist parties with strong roots in the old regime are major political forces in these countries, and they contin-ued to win elections during 1998 in Ukraine and Moldova. In the wake of the degeneration of the Soviet system, however, it is not the old communist political organization that has held centre stage so much as national 'parties of power' representing an 'amorphous and non-ideological group consisting of a non-party president, a politicized bureaucracy, and a depoliticized government closely linked to non-official groups'.

They are parties only in a loose sense, and do not stand for office in elections on their own account, but rather act as a political buffer and stand between the more politicized forces of the reformed communists on the left and nationalists on the right.[2] Such an informal power-sharing body has been seen to lie behind the otherwise relatively fragmented Ukrainian legislature, with its large number of formally non-party deputies. In some ways it can also be identified as a presidential party, and it is certainly more characteristic of presidential than parliamentary systems. The close identification of Leonid Kravchuk with such forces did not, however, prevent him losing the Ukrainian presidential elections in 1994.[3] Despite winning a second term as president in 1999, too, Leonid Kuchma remained highly dissatisfied with his powers of political leadership and tabled a successful (if controversial and widely criticized) referendum proposal in April 2000 to further restrict the capacity of parliament to block the much-needed reform process. Growing friction between the legislature and President Lucinschi in Moldova has also prompted him to press for reforms towards a more closely organized presidential system in the country, which betrays more of a desire to strengthen existing power-sharing arrangements than to establish structures of effective democratic or party government.[4]

- The countries of the Balkans and south-east Europe have, in the context of the dissolution of the former Yugoslavia and the turbulence of the transition from stone-age communism in Albania, encountered particular problems in *building viable political communities* and avoiding various forms of warfare and civil violence. Slovenia, with its small and ethnically uniform population, achieved a clean break from the former Yugoslavia, but Croatia, Serbia and Bosnia were for years embroiled in vicious warfare and conflicts that were quite incapable of containment within political institutions and ruled out the development of parties as significant agencies of conflict resolution. The fate of Montenegro has in this respect been closely linked with that of Serbia in a reconstituted Yugoslav federation, while Macedonian political life was stabilized by the presence of a small (until the Kosovo war) but significant NATO presence. Processes through which parties could develop as central agencies of the democratic process were quite marginalized under such conditions. The autonomy of most of these countries as political units is now further circumscribed by the presence of massive NATO and other international forces.

Bulgaria and Romania were less involved by the Kosovo war, but have certainly suffered some of its consequences, if only in the economic field. Overall conditions for social and political development in both countries, and for the rise of independent parties, were also influenced by strong links with the former communist regime throughout the early 1990s and the slow start made to the decoupling of political and economic power, as in the FSU states. Only in the 1997 elections was Bulgaria's 'party of power' based on a partially reconstituted Socialist Party ousted from power. An equivalent transformation had taken place in Romania a few months earlier, but forces surrounding former President Iliescu continued to mount strong opposition. The more pluralistic form of party government embarked on in 1996 has only survived on the basis of a weak coalition whose achievements to date have been meagre in both economic and political terms.

Throughout the countries both of the Balkans and the FSU *democratization* has also made only limited progress (a generalization from which Slovenia may now be wholly excluded as being part only of the former Yugoslavia and effectively having lost its Balkan identity; Bulgaria also appears to have developed most strongly in this area since the change of government in 1997). The absence of democratic conditions for party development have been particularly marked in Belarus, where only one post-communist election was held throughout the 1990s (whose outcome was by no means clear) while President Lukashenka grew increasingly opposed to independent parties and unconstrained parliamentary activity in general. Serbia has also experienced major limitations on democratic practice during the unbroken period of leadership of Slobodan Milošević, the only east European leader to have stayed in power since 1987 during the communist period, although it should also be noted that the Serbian opposition has not always been strongly committed to promoting a more democratic alternative. Democratic party development has not been opposed so resolutely in the other countries of the Balkans and the FSU, but neither has it been pursued with great enthusiasm either by government leaders and the political elite – or, it must be said, by much of the population as a whole. Mass attitudes and the weak development of a civic culture also play an important part throughout the region. Only in the two other areas of eastern Europe have conditions overall been more favourable for party development.

- Despite weaknesses in structural consolidation and continuing political fluidity, the Baltic states of Estonia, Latvia and Lithuania have made considerable progress in building new parties and developing some kind of party system. A strong national consciousness, relatively high levels of socio-economic development and a shorter period of encapsulation within the Soviet Union all helped them cope with the problems of post-communist transition more successfully than other areas of the FSU. The challenge of incorporating the large Russian minorities in Latvia and Estonia into a democratically organized political community caused considerable problems but has been met with increasing success, while the traditions of inter-war independence have provided a reasonably solid basis for contemporary democratic practice.

  One major weakness has been the continuing fluidity of party structures, tendencies of parties to split and reform with disconcerting frequency, and the dominance of individuals and political leaders over party structures (a feature perhaps linked with the size of these mini-states and the personalized nature of the national community). Such problems have been less pronounced in Lithuania, where features of a two-party system have been emerging, and both electoral volatility and parliamentary fragmentation showed signs of reducing in later elections in Latvia and Estonia.

- Pluralist party development has been significantly stronger in east-central Europe (Hungary, Poland, Slovakia, Slovenia and the Czech Republic) where viable political communities and civic order have been maintained (the dissolution of the Czechoslovak state into its constituent parts occurred peacefully and was conducted according to agreed constitutional procedures), the dismantling of the centrally administered, state-dominated economy has proceeded quite swiftly (although by no means without major social dislocation), and democratic norms have been consistently applied (a feature initially affirmed by the accelerated EU accession procedures agreed in 1997 with four of the five countries concerned).

  The only major doubts to surface in the latter area have concerned Slovakia, where the style of government employed by Vladimìr Mečiar as much as its actual content raised concerns in the EU (which issued several 'démarches'), and the European community more generally as well as amongst the forces of domestic opposition. The defeat of Mečiar both in the parliamentary election of 1998 and the subsequent presidential contest, combined with the acceptance by Mečiar and his still numerous supporters of the legitimacy of these defeats, provided a broad reassurance of the fundamentally democratic trajectory of political change in Slovakia. But while the *conditions* for party development have been more positive in east-central Europe than in other parts of the post-communist area, that does not necessarily mean that the *course* of such development has run smoothly or met all initial expectations.

The prime weaknesses identified in the course of party development in east-central Europe have been summarized at the beginning of this section, and may be seen primarily (as discussed in Chapter 4) as those of *institutionalization*. This involves the accretion by organizations of value and stability, qualities as central to the consolidation of a democratic regime as to any other form of political order.[5] In comparative context, surveys of political attitudes as well as social outcomes of public sentiment like organizational membership suggest that the value assigned to contemporary parties remains limited. Equally, both organizational characteristics and election outcomes point to the establishment of some degree of stability, but, even where conditions have been conducive to the process of party development as a whole, party growth has been limited and there have been important discontinuities of structure and parliamentary representation.

From another perspective, east European parties continue to show signs of weak institutionalization in terms of their relative lack of autonomy and the general absence of systemness in their organization.[6] They remain open to social and individual pressure, and often show limited organizational staying-power. In conjunction with this, party system institutionalization in eastern Europe is also low in relation to that seen in other new democracies.[7] There is limited stability in perceptions both in the identity of the main parties and of how they behave. As well as the shallow roots parties have in society, their weakly developed organization and the low legitimacy accorded parties and elections, there have yet to emerge clear patterns of party competition. Even where the basic conditions for party development have been met in eastern Europe, the process has not necessarily progressed evenly or with great vigour, a pattern best defined as one of *partial institutionalization*. The partial formation at the current stage both of parties and the democratic political system as a whole is summed up in the title of a recent study of the Polish polity – 'protoparties in a protosystem'.[8]

Political parties and modern democracy

The problems of parties in the new democracies of eastern Europe, however, emerge against a background of related doubts about the efficacy of western democracy and its institutions as national forms of political organization.[9] One reflection of this situation has been the increasingly problematic status of the established west European political party, features of which include falling membership, funding problems and corruption scandals, the decline of traditional ideologies and shifts in fundamental political orientation, growing electoral volatility, declining turnout, and the prominent role played by single-issue politics and more informal social movements. Broad processes of post-industrial change and marginalization of traditional political structures were understood to underlie such shifts. In east European terms the operation of a recently restored political autonomy and national sovereignty similarly contrasts strongly with the constraints of global capitalism to which a new openness leaves post-communist democracy highly vulnerable.

Fundamental obstacles to defining the 'political' in contemporary life in general are understood in some cases to stem from the equivalent disappearance from the public arena of an identifiable ruling class.[10] This makes the location and meaning of the 'political' for newly enfranchized citizens highly problematic, and some see this as the cause of the wide-spread disillusion and alienation from new institutions of democratic rule seen in eastern Europe. Others link debate on the contemporary status of the political with the internal transformations of western democracy and the perceived inadequacy of its liberal underpinnings following the demise of the communist antagonist. Declaration of the 'end of history' has also been seen to place the political at stake and threaten the elimination of politics from public debate altogether.[11]

Liberal democracy, it is finally argued, has consistently found it difficult and at times impossible (as in the case of fascism) to confront the centrality of antagonism and the importance of elements of hostility in political life, factors that bear critically on the differentiation of social positions and the formation of collective identities. Outbursts of ethnic, religious and nationalist conflict in eastern Europe, similarly, cannot be comprehended by those welcoming the universal supremacy of the liberal principles, and they have thus been relegated to the sphere of the archaic or marginalized as a post-totalitarian legacy. The political dimension in modern democracies risks being overly identified with the rule of law, leaving much of the population excluded and available for mobilization by fundamentalist movements or attracted to anti-liberal, populist forms of democracy.[12] Conventional parties from this point of view, such as the other institutions of modern liberal democracy, are likely to be unable to cope with the acute tensions and virulent conflicts of post-communism.

But actual experience of the early post-communist period suggests a different conclusion. The pluralist party structures of the leading democratic countries have in fact been sufficiently robust and attractive to the electorate to create effective working legislative bodies and restrict extremist movements to the margins of political life. More concrete analysis shows that organized extremism has not occupied a prominent place in post-communist politics. The fascist Association for the Republic gained limited representation in early Czech parliaments, which it lost in the 1998 election, and illiberal forces in Hungary only succeeded in taking some seats in 1998 in the form of the Justice and Life Party, while in Poland – following the defeat of the colourful populist Tymiński in the 1990 presidential run-off – representatives of more extreme tendencies have been excluded from the political mainstream altogether. It is precisely where liberal forces failed to triumph over the communist antagonist and the rule of law was not established, where civil oppositions did not succeed in establishing even a temporary liberal ascendancy, that extremism has had its strongest impact. Milošević retained his dominance as communist party leader and then socialist president of Yugoslavia through to the debacle of the 1999 Kosovo war; Belarus was left politically marooned by the collapse of the Soviet Union and remained almost wholly untouched by the practices of liberal democracy before Lukashenka took power and mounted an intensified anti-parliamentary campaign to eliminate the embryo party organizations from public life.

Where they have succeeded in establishing themselves, the record of pluralist parties in eastern Europe has been a largely positive one. Experience of the brief post-communist period confirms the perception of parties as the prime political form and a major institutional basis of modern liberal democracy. Despite doubts about their role and the significance of their contribution to contemporary liberal democracy that surfaced in the west during the 1970s, too, the prime role of political parties has also survived relatively unscathed in established democracies and there are no real alternative ideas of how modern democracies might operate without them. They continue to play a major role in organizing political activity, channelling participation and providing the means to make it effective. Professionally organized parties are still essential to the establishment and continuity of a liberal democracy; in most practical senses, 'democracy in the modern world is representative democracy, and the contribution made by political parties is central'.[13]

Party systems effectively determine levels of citizen participation, the activities they sponsor in legislative and electoral arenas exercise a major influence on the nature and stability of political leadership, and the dynamics of party systems have a profound impact on prospects for political stability, the survival of particular regimes and the avoidance of social turmoil.[14] Neither does there seem to be much doubt about the importance of parties and their activities in the course of democratization and the consolidation of new democracies. The mark of a genuinely consolidated democracy, it is argued, is the degree to which the alternation of parties in power is regular and accepted, whereas the creation of strong parties is one of the main components of a civil society.[15] But there are still serious questions to be raised about the nature of the political party and the range of functions it performs in the established democracies of the developed world.

A comprehensive list of the functions traditionally performed by parties in a democracy is an extensive one, although not all possible tasks have been carried out by all parties. Apart from their basic function of structuring the vote and linking that process with broader forms of opinion structuring, parties also help to integrate citizens within the broader community and mobilize the public for political participation; facilitate the recruitment of political leaders; organize government; shape public policy by influencing public discussion, formulating programmes and bringing pressure to bear on the incumbent government; and aggregate social interests in ways that can range from simply noting their existence to the purposive structuring of social behaviour.[16] Clearly the range of functions and the intensity with which they are performed has varied over time, as has the importance of the different levels of party organization – modern parties being far more leadership dominated than their predecessors and correspondingly less inclined to perform historically important mediating functions.

Recent discussion, indeed, links the growing dominance of party leadership with changes that have taken place within political parties during the 1990s in response to what has been termed a 'fourth wave' of democratic party-building originating in eastern Europe. In this conception four major party functions are outlined: the identification of goals (ideology and programme), articulation and aggregation of social interests, mobilization and socialization of the general public, elite recruitment and government formation. Only the second of these, it is argued, cannot be performed by an individual party leader.[17] The functional range of the political party has certainly been slimmed down and it has become more specialized as an institution, ceasing to play such a pivotal role in the democratic process as a whole. But although changes in the overall role, structure and function of parties have occurred, they have not as institutions become as irrelevant to the central processes of modern democracy as many maintained during the 1970s and 1980s.

Much of the discussion about the apparent decline of the party on closer examination concerned the increasingly limited relevance of the mass party whose roots, as outlined in Chapter 4, lay very much in the nineteenth century.[18] The emergence of parties with hundreds of thousands of members, an extensive national organization and a well-developed internal structure represented an important contribution to the early formation and operation of contemporary mass democracies, but the conditions that gave rise to them soon began to erode and the consequences of this process were well recognized by the 1960s. On the basis of experiences during the 1990s, and from the perspective of developments during the first decade of post-communism, it would be more accurate to conclude that the nature of the political party has changed in association with the broader transformations of modern democracy.

In terms of political functions, this means that the modern party is:

- less prominent as an agency of societal *integration* – the enormous expansion of the electronic media and the overwhelming impact of television on politics and society over recent decades means that party organizations are now relatively minor agencies for integrating the citizen within the greater community, while modern media and electronics-based campaign techniques are equally decisive for the electoral success of individual parties;[19] political integration is achieved by the manipulation and projection of diffuse but often powerful symbols rather than the organization of concrete activity around specific goals, while individuals relate to the centres of power in modern society and exercise any influence they command primarily as consumers rather than on the basis of any civic identity.

- correspondingly less capable of *mobilizing* the population for political participation in terms of enrolling them as party members and securing their formal or informal support on any kind of permanent basis; voter turnout has declined during elections and volatility has increased to the extent that some parties have little in the way of a core base of electoral support on which to count and, in more extreme cases, may rapidly coalesce and become major political forces only to fade away and lose all electoral momentum prior to the next vote; thus of the 'faces' of party organization it is primarily the 'party on the ground' made of the members who provide the party with potentially loyal voters that can most accurately be said to be in decline (the party in public office and in central office make up the other 'faces').[20]

- less able also to perform the pivotal *mediating* role it has traditionally played in twentieth century politics and appear as the key bonding mechanism or buckle that holds state and civil society together in some kind of stable relationship;[21] in association with a diminished membership base, the weak structure it is able to develop in many contexts gives the party little capacity to act either as a powerful representative of social forces or as an autonomous force with regard to the state. Although common tendencies in most democracies this, such as other features, is particularly prominent in the recently liberalized regimes of eastern Europe. Even where political pluralism has put down stronger roots, its institutional development has been limited. The early 'over-particization' of the political process was intimately linked with the paucity of the parties' social ties and an overall organizational deficit.[22]

The diminished capacity of these aspects of the modern party has had particular implications for the new democracies of eastern Europe. Greater fluidity of party structures and the particular weakness of their electoral base in post-communist regimes affect the steering capacity of their governments, a condition that gives rise to a paradoxical emphasis amongst both electors and the elite on political leadership while creating poor conditions and a limited capacity for the actual performance of leadership functions in society as a whole. The strains of post-communist change in social and economic as well as political areas create a demand for stability and need for security that the whole current of liberal-democratization runs counter to. The resistance of those contemporary east European power-centres with strong links with the communist regime to democratic change and the development of party pluralism is quite understandable under these conditions, and there is considerable support for this response amongst the broader population.

In the countries (predominantly of east-central Europe) where democracy has put down stronger roots and party pluralism is most developed, what is most significant is not the sporadic outbreaks of political extremism and the elements of populism that impinge on the parliamentary arena but the relatively minor part they play in the political process as a whole. Parties with a slender social base and few organizational resources maintain not just a sizeable parliamentary presence and access to government power but also a reasonably strong capacity for responsible political behaviour and surprisingly high levels of commitment to democratic norms.

This feature became more prominent in east-central Europe after the sequence of elections in 1998 when the governments of all five countries came to be formed by parties with weaker ties to the old establishment and fewer resources inherited from the former regime. In 1999 it was noticeable that most of the parties with a greater number of members (Czech Communists, Socialists elsewhere) were precisely those with such old-regime organizational legacies but which were now less central to the parliamentary process and had little or no role in the governments then in office. The position of these parties with weaker historical links to the old regime and fewer inherited resources but a stronger contemporary political presence raises further questions as to how the parties that now dominate east European politics are best understood.

The nature of contemporary east European parties

The growing distance of the mass party from the realities of party politics in modern democracies has given rise to competing conceptions about the kind of party that succeeds it. Several models have emerged in the context of the changing conditions of modern party politics. The weakening link of parties with particular groups (especially the declining attraction of socialist parties for the working class, itself far less homogeneous and considerably diminished in size), the reduced prominence of ideology and growing reliance on the mass media and commercial public relations techniques all contributed to the idea of the catchall party.[23] On the basis of observations of similar trends, further analysis directed attention to the professionalization of party organization and led to the formulation of ideas of the electoral-professional party.[24] More recently, observation of the lengthy stability of most established democratic party systems, the regular alternation of most parties in government and their growing dependence on state resources has been responsible for the emergence of the concept of the cartel party.[25]

Debate continues about such theoretical proposals and their respective merits in helping to grasp the essentials of the modern party as a generic form. The novelty of the cartel party and questions concerning the level at which the concept might best operate (at system level or in relation to the individual party) are particular issues that have been aired in connection with the most recent formulation.[26] The models referred to above also derive primarily from analysis of west European party developments and have generally been limited in their historical and territorial relevance. Some clearly relate only partially to North American experience (which never saw the development of tightly organized mass parties and have not permitted state support of party activity). Their relevance to east European developments must also be demonstrated rather than assumed if they are to be accepted as useful tools for empirical analysis.

On the face of it, the models discussed in the western party literature seem to fit eastern Europe quite well. Some have argued that the eastern developments reflect a more general transformation of European parties, and that 'parties of a new type' have been emerging on this basis in established democracies.[27] Arguments for this kind of influence are not very convincing, though. The implication of the discussion so far has been that patterns of party representation in eastern Europe in fact quite closely resemble that of the west, and that lower levels of institutionalization and party development in the post-communist context tend to replicate characteristics of the relative decline detected in western parties and their selective weakening in established democracies. The *trajectory* of party development is nevertheless different and, while parties may share characteristics and seem to occupy similar positions within a political system, this may be for very different reasons.[28]

Many contemporary parties employ a catch-all electoral strategy but, while in the west this is largely a function of established parties' responses to changing class structures, in eastern Europe it is more a matter of poorly defined party identity and lack of certainty about a target electorate.[29] Early attempts to define the characteristics of the emerging catch-all party also turned out to be rather inconclusive. 'Professionalization' of party activity may appear to be a prominent feature in the absence of a mass membership and extensive rank-and-file involvement in eastern Europe, but there are few signs that such technical values really determine party activity and (on a very practical basis) there are just no funds to sustain professionalization as a general process.[30] Its influence on any party as a whole, then, is unlikely to be a strong one. Individual parties may, further, show characteristics of different party types. In Poland, the original Social Democracy could be characterized by its features both as a catch-all organization and a mass party; the Freedom Union was equally both a cadre and a catch-all party.[31]

As well as individual organizational characteristics, it is also important to link political development with changing external conditions of party activity, as these are likely to have a strong effect on the nature of the evolving party system as a whole. The influence of historical and political context is always important for the analysis of any single party or party system as a whole, but in relation to the cartel party differences in the political role and power of the state are particularly significant factors. In view of the fundamental consequences of the collapse of the communist state and integration within an increasingly globalized world system, this will count no less in the post-communist east European context than in that of recently democratized west and south European parties.[32] The reliance of the newly identified western cartel parties on state subventions equally strikes a ready chord with analysts of eastern Europe, who rightly identify this factor with the acute weakness of most new parties and their similar reliance on the resources of the post-communist state.[33]

Others have also seized on this apparent identity to argue more directly for the emergence of the cartel party as the dominant new form of east European political organization. There has, contends Ágh, been a very rapid shift in east-central Europe from loose movement parties to 'rigidly organized cartels as power parties, expressing a new separation of parties and society'.[34] But contrasting views have also been expressed on the applicability of the cartel concept, particularly in terms of its assumption of a 'fixed menu' of well-established parties with mutual interests and a smoothly functioning working relationship.[35] The context of radically changing state-civil society relations is indeed an important one, but it is a framework that needs analysis in terms of specific east European developments and the characteristics of both post-communist state and society. There is, to be sure, little disagreement about the central role played by the state and its diverse agencies in the development of east European parties. But this is not a sufficient condition for the existence of fully-fledged cartel parties in the sense recently proposed for western Europe.

The overall weakness of the new parties and their dependence on the state and its resources in a number of areas have indeed been fully recognized.[36] But this does not mean either that there is such a close symbiosis of state and party as suggested by the cartel model, or that any such relations have been established with the degree of stability that can be argued for quite convincingly in the case of some west European countries. There is certainly a widespread feeling throughout the region (as there is throughout much the modern world) that political life is carved up by the major parliamentary players, and that access to the leadership of the main parties opens the path to state power and the disposition of the extensive resources it still controls. This is very much a sentiment that the more established concept of overparticization also takes account of. But in eastern Europe such perceptions are as much, and probably more, a reflection of the gulf between population and the political class, the lack of identification of a diverse post-communist society with the processes of competitive politics, and popular suspicion of party leaders and the elite as a whole than any genuine process of 'cartelization' of party life.

Early public discussion of reform proposals of the electoral mechanism in

Poland following the major territorial restructuring of 1998 thus betrayed deep popular suspicion that the major parliamentary forces were simply preparing to carve up the representative arena between them more effectively. It was suspected that they were hoping to create larger constituencies that would erect yet greater barriers to new parties seeking to enter parliament – although early indications were that nothing like this was actually happening.[37] The idea of an established club of self-interested politicians overcoming their antagonism to the extent that all largely accepted the existing constellation of political forces was certainly exaggerated.

Perceptions of political life dominated by a cartel of established parties are far stronger than the brief experience of democratic party government in eastern Europe actually suggests they are in reality. Such tendencies have not been absent (and have certainly been detectable in the record of the post-1998 Social Democratic government in the Czech Republic), but party competition has also been strong and the electoral record shows a strong anti-incumbency bias in voting patterns and parliamentary outcomes (with Klaus's Civic Democratic Party actually being the only governing party in the main post-communist democracies of east-central Europe to win an election). This is precisely a tendency that reflects not just high levels of volatility and the weakness of party institutionalization, but also the diffuse but entrenched anti-political attitudes outlined above and otherwise linked with perceptions of an emerging cartel pattern.

Eastern Europe thus shows little in the way of the 'fixed menu' of parties deemed to be a major characteristic of the cartel model.[38] In terms of the monopolization of power by a narrow elite and the access of post-communist politicians to state resources, it is precisely where party development is less advanced and the political process more resistant to the activities of openly organized political associations that establishment privilege is more deeply entrenched. It is also in countries, such as those of the Balkans and the FSU, where this tendency is most commonly observed, that civil society is at its weakest. While shifting relations between state and society are indeed of critical importance for the nature of the modern party, and the dependence on state resources that characterizes many parties seems to be increasing throughout Europe, it is rather the relative weakness of new parties against a background of a similarly impoverished civil society that is the most salient feature of party politics in the east.

With this observation we return to the major condition of party development in post-communist eastern Europe highlighted in Chapter 1. The problematic social conditions of contemporary eastern Europe and its perceived lack of civility provide a weak basis of party development as a whole rather than fostering any specific kind of party in the way that the proponents of cartelization argue. The imperfect party democracy that has emerged in eastern Europe is closely linked with the conditions of what has been termed a minimal civic society.[39] The parameters of this situation in terms both of conditions for continued democratization and for future party development in eastern Europe remain unclear. While broad patterns of western democratic practice and west European models of party development offer some guidance they by no means provide a universal template.

The focus of attention on relations between parties and state, too, important though it is, is only one part of the story.

The weak social base of party politics in eastern Europe and the tenuous links of party leaders with identifiable social groupings are important factors in eastern Europe in ways closely analogous to patterns of development in the west over recent decades. But the context of post-communism and the broader cultural context of eastern Europe cannot be ignored. General discussion of 'civil society' masks important analytical differences within the region between the impact of domestic society and the emergence of political society in a more sharply defined sense.[40] The emergence of different models of party in western Europe is also linked with shifting configurations of society in general and more distinctive conceptions of a modern civil society.[41] The role of civil society, or different aspects of it, in undermining and seeing off communist rule in eastern Europe remains unclear, and it is hardly surprising that the relationship of the new parties with a rapidly changing post-communist social formation emerges as a highly ambiguous one. What is less uncertain is that pluralist parties are steadily developing in most countries of the region, and that the prospects of continuing democratization are strongly conditioned by the effectiveness of the party government they sustain.

Annex: party profiles (major parties in east-central European parliaments)

Czech Republic

Christian Democratic Union (KDU), founded in December 1989 with the intention to develop a pan-Czechoslovak party. It combines a Christian Socialist perspective with a rural orientation; leader Jozef Lux. Strongly opposed to supporting Social Democrats after 1998 election.

Civic Democratic Party (ODS), organized in April 1990 on basis of Civic Forum; merged with Christian Democratic Party (KDS) in 1996. Its leader Václav Klaus survived the corruption scandal that broke out in November 1997 and was re-elected chairman. The party is committed to economic liberalism and firmly located on right wing, with a strong sense of identity as a conservative force.

Communist Party of Bohemia and Moravia (KSCM), organized in March 1990 after dissolution of Czechoslovak Communist Party; stood as part of Left Bloc in first elections but separated prior to vote in 1996. Its popularity rose in 1999 as the problems of the minority Social Democratic government became apparent. Led by Miroslav Grebenicek.

Czech Social Democratic Party (CSSD): founded in 1878 and reorganized in December 1989, formerly Czechoslovak SDP. Under leader Milos Zeman it developed as the only successful Social Democratic party in the region without roots in a former ruling communist party. Formed a minority government after 1998 elections.

Freedom Union (US), founded in January 1998 by dissidents from Civic Democratic Party dissatisfied with Klaus's leadership after the corruption debacle of 1997. First leader Jan Ruml resigns in the face of growing dissatisfaction with personal animosities within unstable governing coalition. Chaired from December 1999 by Karel Kuehnl.

Hungary

Alliance of Free Democrats (SZDSZ), founded November 1988 as liberal anti-communist organization. One of main democratic forces (with Democratic Forum) during early transition period, and junior partner in Socialist-led coalition government after 1994 elections. Privatization and financial scandals led to a fall in public support and resignation of chairman Ivan Pett in 1996. Leader Gabor Kuncze.

Fidesz (Alliance of Young Democrats), to which title of **Hungarian Civic Party (MPP)** was added in 1995. Originally founded in 1988 as party of radical youth; embargo on membership of those over 35 removed in 1995 at same time as major – and electorally successful – relaunch of party as professional liberal-conservative organization was undertaken. Leader Lazlo Kover.

Hungarian Democratic Forum (MDF), founded in September 1987 it emerged as major leader (with Free Democrats) of anti-communist movement and scored a major electoral success in the 1990 elections. In government it became increasingly weakened by splits and internal divisions, and secured its parliamentary position in 1998 largely by virtue of alliance with Fidesz. Leader David Ibolya.

Hungarian Justice and Life Party (MIEP), founded in 1992 by István Csurka as offshoot of Hungarian Democratic Forum after Csurka was expelled from it for anti-Semitism. It failed to enter parliament in 1994, but gained enough seats in the 1998 election to form its own faction in the legislature.

Hungarian Socialist Party (MSZP), founded after dissolution of communist Socialist Workers' Party in October 1989. It was successfully transformed into a democratic socialist organization and became a major electoral force in 1994, maintaining a stable government coalition until 1998. Leader Laszlo Kovacs.

Independent Party of Smallholders (FKGP), rebuilt from 1988 on basis of historical party prominent in inter-war period. It maintained a steady parliamentary presence in successive post-communist elections, and entered a governing coalition led by Fidesz in 1998. Leader Balint Magyar.

Poland

Democratic Left Alliance (SLD) was the coalition headed by the **Social Democracy of the Polish Republic (SdRP)** that fought all elections as the main left-wing force from 1991. It was formed with the **Confederation of Polish Trade Unions (OPZZ)** and other left-wing groups. The Social Democracy was founded in January 1990 after the dissolution of the communist United Workers' Party and developed as a credible democratic socialist party. In 1999 the Social Democracy was disbanded and the Democratic Alliance was registered as a political party in its own right, with Leszek Miller as its chairman.

Freedom Union (UW), founded on the basis of the Democratic Union organized in 1990 by supporters of Tadeusz Mazowiecki after the presidential contest with Lech Wałęsa. The Freedom Union was formed in April 1994 by a merger of the Democratic Union with the Congress of Liberal Democrats (KLD), and continues to represent a political current that combines strong features of economic and political liberalism. Leader Leszek Balcerowicz.

Movement for the Reconstruction of Poland (ROP), registered in November 1995 by supporters of Jan Olszewski in his unsuccessful bid for the presidency in the election of that year. It drew on the support of a number of right-wing organizations but lost considerable ground following the emergence of Solidarity Electoral Action. As a party committed to the leadership of Olszewski it was unwilling to form an alliance with the Solidarity organization, which was necessarily led by the union's chairman, but it nevertheless failed to develop a distinctive right-wing identity of its own. It soon fell prey to the well-established factionalism of the Polish right and formally split with a rival faction led by Antoni Macierewicz less than 3 months after the 1997 election.

The Polish Peasant Party (PSL) was founded in May 1990, largely on the basis of the United Peasant Party that had been a junior partner of the ruling Polish United Workers' Party during the communist period. It formed part of the governing coalition led by the Social Democracy between 1993 and 1997 but did not perform well in the elections held in 1997. Leader Jarosław Kowalski.

Solidarity Electoral Action (AWS), founded in June 1996 following the exclusion from parliament of most right-wing forces after the elections of 1993 and defeat of former Solidarity leader Lech Wałęsa in the 1995 presidential elections. It was based on the organization of the still powerful Solidarity trade union (estimated membership of 1.8–2 million) and made up of forty different groups prior to the 1997 election. Steps were taken to organize an **Solidarity Action – Social Movement (AWS-RS)** that would act as a more organized form of political support for the Action's parliamentary representation. Prime Minister Jerzy Buzek was elected the Movement's leader at its first Congress in 1999, but it failed to attract many individual members or to develop as much of an autonomous political force.

Slovakia

Hungarian Coalition (MK), originally formed by three organizations founded between 1990 and 1992: Coexistence, the Hungarian Christian Democratic Movement and the Hungarian Civic Party. It has contested all elections as a separate entity, but joined the opposition coalition in 1998 to form a broad governing group. Leader Bela Bugar.

The Movement for Democratic Slovakia (HZDS) was founded by Vladimìr Mečiar in March 1991 and acted as the representative of a nationalist current within the Public Against Violence prior to the break-up of Czechoslovakia. It remained the leading political force in the republic until its defeat by the Democratic Coalition in the election of 1998 and consistently acted to sustain the rule and political dominance of its leader, but otherwise its political programme and ideological identity remained unclear.

Party of Civic Understanding (SOK), founded by popular politician Rudolf Schuster in the spring of 1998. The party is oriented to western values and the development of a civil society. Pavel Hamzik elected chairman in June 1999 after Schuster's election to the presidency.

Party of the Democratic Left (SDL) was formed in October 1990 by the Communist Party of Slovakia and organized a re-registration of its members in January 1991; in 1994 it stood in elections as part of the Common Choice electoral coalition but remained outside the opposition democratic coalition in 1998. Growing signs of factionalism and internal dissension appeared during 1999. Leader Jozef Migas.

Slovak Democratic Coalition (SDK), founded in July 1997 to offer concerted opposition to the continued rule of Mečiar and the MDS in elections due to be held the following year; it was made up of representatives of the Democratic Union, Christian Democratic Party, Social Democratic Party, Green Party and Democratic Party. Leader and prime minister was Mikulas Dzurinda. The problematic effectiveness and instability of the governing coalition was further threatened by Dzurinda's establishment of a separate Slovak Democratic and Christian Union in January 2000.

Slovak National Party (SNS), organized in February 1990 and partner of Mečiar's Movement in campaign for independence. Member of successive Mečiar governments until election defeat of 1998. Leader A. Malikova.

Slovenia

Democratic Party of Retired People (DeSUS), founding member of United List in 1992 but stood separately in 1996 elections.

Liberal Democracy of Slovenia (LDS), organized as such in the form of an expanded group on the basis of an existing Liberal Democratic Party, the original group that emerged from Slovenian Organization of Communist Youth. Under the leadership of Janez Drnovšek it remained the cornerstone of various government coalitions throughout the 1990s.

Slovene Christian Democrats (SKD), historical party re-established March 1989; under the leadership of Lozje Peterle the decision was taken in early 2000 to merge with the People's Party.

Slovene National Party (SNS), founded in March 1991 by nationalist faction of the Slovenian Farmers' Party.

Slovene People's Party (SLS), formally the Slovenian Farmers' Party (founded May 1988); in government as major coalition partner of the Liberal Democracy since 1996. Leader Marjan Podobnik was also deputy premier; the decision to merge with the Christian Democrats thus seriously destabilized the government.

Social Democratic Party of Slovenia (SDSS), historical party re-established in February 1989 and developed along right-wing lines; chair Janez Jansa.

United List of Social Democrats (SLSD), established as a coalition for the 1992 election on the basis of the Party of Democratic Renewal, which in turn had been formed in February 1990 as the League of Slovenian Communists was wound up.

Estonia

Centre Party (KESK), originally organized in October 1991 as Estonian Popular Front and fought 1992 election in alliance with Women's Union and Association of Nationalities; has leftist orientation and advocates preservation of relatively strong social safety net. Single most popular party after 1999 elections; leader Edgar Savisaar.

Coalition Party (EK), founded in 1993 and affiliated to Liberal International. Joined for 1995 election by **Country Peoples' Party and Farmers' Assembly (PK)**, after which it formed main component of governing coalition. Internal conflicts strengthened during 1998, but prime minister Mart Siiman re-elected leader that year. Andrus Oovel replaced him in May 1999 with a commitment to stop the infighting.

Country People's Party (EME) founded 1994, fought 1995 election with Coalition Party and became member of post-1995 coalition, led by Arnold Aruutel.

The Fatherland Union was formed after the 1995 election by major right-wing forces: the **Estonian National Independence Party (ERSP)**, which was organized in August 1988 and appeared as the largest party prior to 1992 election. It later joined with **Fatherland Party (Isammaa)**, led by Lennart Meri and which was formed in early 1992 by Christian and Liberal Democrats, Conservatives and Republican Coalition Party. Mart Laar elected leader in November 1998.

Moderates (M), first organized in 1990 as coalition of the Social Democratic Party (and member of Socialist International) and the Rural Centre Party, achieved closer union as party in 1996. Centrist orientation.

Our Home is Estonia (MKE), Russian bloc comprising Estonian United People's Party, Russian People's Party and Russian Party in Estonia, which nevertheless endorses Estonian independence.

Reform Party (ER), founded in 1994 as liberal rightist party; incorporates Liberal Democratic Party and is member of Liberal International. Partner in the post-1995 government until end of 1996 with a strong commitment to liberal market economy; led by Siim Kallas.

United People's Party (EUR) established in April 1998 by Farmers' Party merging with Rightists' Party, also called **Republican and Conservative People's Party (VKR/P)**; this originally formed in 1994 by a merger of Conservatives and Republican Coalition; led by Toomas Hendrick.

Latvia

The Conservative Union for Fatherland and Freedom was composed of two parties: one the **Latvian National Conservative Party (LNKP)**, founded as the National Independence Movement in 1988 and that changed its name to the Conservative Party in 1994. It fought the 1995 election with the Green Party and became part of a governing coalition. The second was

Fatherland and Freedom (TB), formally registered in January 1995, although its roots lay in movements of the late 1980s and the broad opposition ('Congress Movement') formed in 1990. An earlier organization had formed the centrepiece of the 1993 For Fatherland and Freedom electoral coalition. It joined forces with the Conservatives in June 1997 under the leadership of Guntars Krasts. As the leading right-wing nationalist force the alliance initiated a referendum on changes to the citizenship law held at the same time as the general election in October 1998.

Latvian Social Democratic Alliance (LSDA), formed in 1997 to support strong role for state in the economy and appeal to major losers of post-communist reform policies, it represents the values of the former Soviet regime. It is led by Juris Bojars, who as a former KGB employee who was barred from entry to parliament.

Latvia's Way (LC), centrist organization founded as an electoral coalition in February 1993, and it became a party in October. The party was victorious in the 1993 elections and became one of the main forces in a ruling coalition that carried a broad appeal but found it difficult to retain support as policy problems intensified. It was a strong advocate of the reforms to the citizenship law passed in October 1998. Chair Andrejs Pantelejevs.

National Harmony Party (TSP), combines in its membership former communists and independence activists though promotes policies more associated with the former element in terms of strong state control of the economy and opposition to NATO membership. Generally positioned to left-of-centre it derives from the Harmony for Latvia – Economic Rebirth coalition which fought the 1993 election and attempted to bridge the strong ethnic divisions articulated by other parties. Leader Alfreds Rubiks.

New Party (JP), formed in early 1998 by a popular entertainer, promotes a combined left-wing and centrist programme that favours state control over the economy and closer ties with Russia, as well as EU membership and tax cuts for private entrepreneurs. Also a supporter of NATO membership for Latvia. Leader Raimonds Pauls.

People's Party (TP), a right of centre organization founded in December 1997 by charismatic former prime minister Andris Skele after his removal from office; party intended to promote a strategy reflecting his success in achieving the country's first balanced budget and building a basis for subsequent policies promoting strong economic development.

Lithuania

Centre Union, formerly Centre Movement (LCJ), a pro-market party established in 1992, a relatively small organization but a vehicle for prominent politicians such as Bickauskas and Ozolas.

Christian Democratic Party (LKDP) was a major political force between the wars and was reconstituted in 1990; strong support from the Church hierarchy. Chair Povilas Katilius.

Homeland Union – Conservatives of Lithuania (TS – LK), founded as a relatively conventional (and, in comparison with the other Baltic republics, quite stable) right-wing political organization on the basis of Sajudis, the movement that had spearheaded the drive for Lithuanian independence. Party leader Vytautas Landesbergis was also first chairman of the post-communist Lithuanian Supreme Council.

Democratic Labour Party (LDDP), formed in December 1990 as the reformist majority (80 per cent of existing members) of the former Lithuanian Communist Party; it won the 1992 election as the first of the reformed communist parties to return to power in eastern Europe.

Social Democratic Party (LSDP), established in 1989 on the model of original party founded in 1896.

Notes

1 Political change in eastern Europe

1 For example G. Sartori (1976) *Parties and Party Systems: a Framework for Analysis*, Cambridge University Press: 'A party is any political group that presents at elections, and is capable of placing through elections, candidates for public office' (p. 64).
2 A. Ware (1996) *Political Parties and Party Systems*, Oxford University Press.
3 K. von Beyme (1985) *Political Parties in Western Democracies*, Aldershot, Gower.
4 M. Duverger, *Political Parties* (1954) London, Methuen.
5 L. Epstein, *Political Parties in Western Democracies*, London, Pall Mall Press, 1967, p. 4.
6 J. LaPalombara and M. Weiner (eds) (1966) *Political Parties and Political Development* Princeton University Press.
7 V. Randall, *Political Parties in the Third World*, London, Sage, 1988, p. 3.
8 Serbia and Montenegro still exist officially as a remnant or rump of the pre-1990 Yugoslavia and are treated internationally as a single state (although, in more realistic terms, it is actually a greater Serbia that they now constitute). In practice the old Yugoslavia died in 1990 and there are compelling political and analytical reasons to treat Serbia and Montenegro as separate entities for the purposes of this work.
9 A. Ágh, *The Politics of Central Europe*, London, Sage, 1998, p. 7. A more precise definition of central Europe should also, according to Ágh, include Austria but it was hardly appropriate to include the country in a text of that kind.
10 K. Crawford, *East-Central European Politics Today*, Manchester University Press, 1996.
11 L. Holmes (1997) *Post-Communism: an introduction*, Cambridge, Polity Press, p. 13.
12 For details of pre-1939 politics consult the classic account by J. Rothschild (1974) *East Central Europe Between the Two World Wars*, Seattle, University of Washington Press. A comprehensive view of the region is taken by R.J. Crampton (1997) in *Eastern Europe in the Twentieth Century*, London, Routledge. A briefer narrative is found in A. Polonsky (1975) *The Little Dictators: the history of Eastern Europe since 1918*, London, Routledge and Kegan Paul, and P.G. Lewis (1999) *Eastern Europe 1918–53: from Versailles to Cold War*, Bedford, Sempringham Press.
13 Developments during the communist period are covered in J. Rothschild (1993) *Return to Diversity: a Political History of East Central Europe Since World War II*, New York, Oxford University Press; G. Schöpflin (1993) *Politics in Eastern Europe, 1945–1992*, Oxford, Blackwell; and P.G. Lewis (1994) *Central Europe Since 1945*, London, Longman.
14 The intricacies of national and international communist rule in eastern Europe in its early years are best dealt with by Z. Brzezinski (1967) in *The Soviet Bloc: Unity and Conflict*, Cambridge, Harvard University Press.
15 Contemporary repercussions are examined in J. Bugajski (1995) *Nations in Turmoil, Conflict and Cooperation in Eastern Europe*, Boulder, Westview.
16 S. Berglund et al. (1998) *Handbook of Political Change in Eastern Europe*, Cheltenham, Edward Elgar, pp. 46–7.

17 The changing situation of eastern Europe and its international context are examined by K. Dawisha (1988) in *Eastern Europe, Gorbachev and Reform*, Cambridge University Press.
18 M. Gorbachev (1988) *Perestroika: New Thinking for our Country and the World*, London, Fontana, pp. 163–4.
19 A. Brown (1997) *The Gorbachev Factor*, Oxford University Press, p. 249.
20 J. Batt (1991) *East Central Europe from Reform to Transformation*, London, Pinter.
21 J.F. Brown (1991) presents a good overview of the process in *Surge to Freedom: the End of Communist Rule*, Durham, Duke University Press.
22 M. Glenny (1992) *The Fall of Yugoslavia: the Third Balkan War*, Harmondsworth, Penguin.
23 See K. Dawisha and B. Parrott (1994) *Russia and the New States of Eurasia: the Politics of Upheaval*, Cambridge University Press.
24 C. Offe (1991) 'Capitalism by democratic design? Democratic theory facing the triple transition in east central Europe', *Social Research* **58**: 865–92.
25 G. Szablowski and H.-U. Derlien (1993) 'East European transitions: elites, bureaucracies, and the European Community', *Governance* **6**: 307–10.
26 P.G. Lewis (1997) 'Theories of democratization and patterns of regime change in eastern Europe', *Journal of Communist Studies and Transition Politics* **13**: 20–1.
27 P.H. O'Neil (1998) *Revolution from Within: the Hungarian Socialist Workers' Party and the Collapse of Communism*, Cheltenham, Edward Elgar.
28 Details in B. Kamiński (1991) *The Collapse of State Socialism: the case of Poland*, Princeton University Press.
29 Z.D. Barany and L. Vinton (1990) 'Breakthrough to democracy: elections in Poland and Hungary', *Studies in Comparative Communism* **23**: 196–7.
30 G. Tóka, 'Political parties in east central Europe', in L. Diamond et al. (eds) *Consolidating the Third Wave Democracies: Themes and Perspectives*, Baltimore, Johns Hopkins Press, 1997, p. 94. Others hold quite different views and A. Ágh (1998), for example, argues that parties have been the chief actors of the democratization process as a whole, *Emerging Democracies in East Central Europe and the Balkans*, Cheltenham, Edward Elgar, p. 18.
31 G. Pridham and P.G. Lewis (eds) (1996) *Stabilizing Fragile Democracies*, London, Routledge, pp. 6–7.
32 G. Pasquino, 'Party elites and democratic consolidation: cross-national comparison of southern European experience', in G. Pridham (ed.) *Securing Democracy: Political Parties and Democratic Consolidation in Southern Europe*, London, Routledge, 1990, p. 53.
33 M. Cotta (1994) 'Building party systems after the dictatorship: the east European cases in a comparative perspective', in G. Pridham and T. Vanhanen (eds), *Democratization in Eastern Europe: Domestic and International Perspectives*, London, Routledge, p. 100.
34 S.M. Terry (1993) 'Thinking about post-communist transitions: how different are they?', *Slavic Review* **52**: 334–6.
35 H. Kitschelt (1992) 'The formation of party systems in East Central Europe', *Politics and Society*, **20**: 7–50, provided one of the earliest analyses of this theme.
36 G. Pridham (1996) 'Transnational party links and transition to democracy: Eastern Europe in comparative perspective', in P.G. Lewis (ed.) *Party Structure and Organization in East-Central Europe*, Cheltenham, Edward Elgar.
37 P.C. Schmitter (1986) 'An introduction to Southern European transitions from authoritarian rule', in G. O'Donnell et al. (eds) *Transitions from Authoritarian Rule*, vol. 1, Baltimore, Johns Hopkins Press, p. 6.
38 P.G. Lewis (ed.) (1992) *Democracy and Civil Society in Eastern Europe*, London, Macmillan, pp. 13–14.
39 B. Zhang (1994) 'Corporatism, totalitarianism, and transitions to democracy', *Comparative Political Studies* **27**: 108–36.
40 H.A. Welsh (1994) 'Political transition processes in central and eastern Europe', *Comparative Politics* **26**: 388.

41 P. Kopecký (1995) 'Developing party organizations in east-central Europe: what type of party is likely to emerge?', *Party Politics* **1**: 517–18; Lewis (1996) *Party Structure and Organization*, pp. 15–16.

42 Stemming in particular from M. Duverger (1964) *Political Parties*, London, Methuen.

43 O. Kirchheimer (1966) 'The transformation of the western European party system', in J. LaPalombara and M. Weiner (eds) *Political Parties and Political Development*, Princeton University Press, pp. 177–200; A. Panebianco (1988) *Political Parties: Organization and Power*, Cambridge University Press.

44 R.S. Katz and P. Mair (1995) 'Changing models of party organization and party democracy: the emergence of the cartel party', *Party Politics* **1**: 5–28.

2 Party origins and party development

1 C. Lapychak (1996) 'Ukraine', in *Building Democracy* (OMRI Annual Survey of Eastern Europe and the Former Soviet Union), New York, M.E. Sharpe, p. 92.1

2 A. Ágh (1996) 'From nomenclatura to clientura', in G. Pridham and P.G. Lewis (eds) *Stabilising Fragile Democracies*, London, Routledge, pp. 54–5.

3 K. Crawford (1996) *East Central European Politics Today*, Manchester University Press, p. 229.

4 P. Lewis, B. Lomax and G. Wightman (1994) 'The emergence of multi-party systems in East-Central Europe', in G. Pridham and T. Vanhanen (eds) *Democratization in Eastern Europe*, London, Routledge, pp. 158–9.

5 K. Henderson and N. Robinson (1997) *Post-Communist Politics: an Introduction*, London, Prentice Hall, p. 152.

6 J.A. Dellenbrant (1994) 'Romania: the slow revolution', in: S. Berglund and J.A. Dellenbrant (eds) *The New Democracies in Eastern Europe*, Aldershot, Edward Elgar, p. 212.

7 J. Seroka (1993) 'Yugoslavia and its successor states', in S. White, J. Batt and P.G. Lewis (eds) *Developments in East European Politics*, London, Macmillan, p. 115.

8 B. Parrott (1997) 'Perspectives on postcommunist democratization', in K. Dawisha and B. Parrott (eds) *The Consolidation of Democracy in East-Central Europe*, Cambridge University Press, p. 17.

9 J. Simon (1998) 'Electoral systems and regime change in Central and Eastern Europe, 1990–1994', *Representation* **35**: 123.

10 P. Mair (1997) 'What is different about post-communist party systems?', in *Party System Change: Approaches and Interpretations*, Oxford, Clarendon Press, pp. 175–98.

11 M. Mann (1993) *The Sources of Social Power, vol. II: The Rise of Classes and Nation-States*, Cambridge University Press, pp. 46–7.

12 R. Rose and W. Mishler (1997) 'Negative and positive partisanship in post-communist countries', *University of Strathclyde Studies in Public Policy* **286**: 4.

13 R. Gortat (1998) *Ukraińskie wybory*, Warsaw, Fundacja Polska Pracy, p. 96.

14 A. Ágh (1998) *Emerging Democracies in East Central Europe and the Balkans*, Cheltenham, Edward Elgar, p. 19.

15 K. Dawisha (1997) 'Democratization and political participation: research concepts and methodologies', in Dawisha and Parrott, *Consolidation of Democracy*, pp. 52, 57.

16 A.M. Cirtautas (1994) 'In pursuit of the democratic interest: the institutionalization of parties and interests in Eastern Europe', in C. Bryant and E. Mokrzycki (eds), *The New Great Transformation? Change and Continuity in East-Central Europe*, London, Routledge, p. 37.

17 P.G. Lewis (1993) 'Civil society and the development of political parties in East-Central Europe', *Journal of Communist Studies* **9**: 10.

18 M. Waller (1996) 'Party inheritances and party identities', in Pridham and Lewis, *Stabilising Fragile Democracies*, p. 38.

19 G. Wightman (ed.) (1995) *Party Formation in East-Central Europe*, Aldershot, Edward Elgar, p. 241.

20 Sanford (1991) 'Poland', in B. Szajkowski (ed.), *New Political Parties of Eastern Europe and the Soviet Union*, Harlow, Longman, p. 182.
21 K. Jasiewicz and S. Gebethner (1998) 'Poland', *European Journal of Political Research* **34**: 505.
22 *Donosy* 5 January 1998. Details of the new party law were given in *Rzeczpospolita* 10 – 11 May 1997; 1000 members were now needed for party registration. Provision for regular support from state financial sources was also made.
23 G. Wightman (1991) 'Czechoslovakia', in Szajkowski, *New Political Parties*, p. 59.
24 D.M. Olson (1997) 'Democratization and political participation: the experience of the Czech Republic', in Dawisha and Parrott, *Consolidation of Democracy*, p. 173.
25 R.L. Tokes (1997) 'Party politics and political participation in postcommunist Hungary', in Dawisha and Parrott, *Consolidation of Democracy*, p. 110.
26 A. Bozoki (1994) 'Party formation and constitutional change in Hungary', *Journal of Communist Studies and Transition Politics* **10**: 40–5.
27 N. Swain (1991) 'Hungary', in Szajkowski, *New Political Parties*, p. 133.
28 Ágh (1998) *Emerging Democracies*, p. 109.
29 S.P. Ramet (1997) 'Democratization in Slovenia – the second stage', in K. Dawisha and B. Parrott (eds) *Politics, Power, and the Struggle for Democracy in South-East Europe*, Cambridge University Press, p. 193.
30 R.J. Krickus (1997) 'Democratization in Lithuania', in Dawisha and Parrott, *Consolidation of Democracy*, p. 295.
31 R.J. Crampton (1994) *Eastern Europe in the Twentieth Century*, London, Routledge, p. 405.
32 S. White (1991), 'Latvia', in Szajkowski, *New Political Parties*, p. 170.
33 A. Plakans (1997) 'Democratization and political participation in postcommunist societies: the case of Latvia', in Dawisha and Parrott, *Consolidation of Democracy*, p. 256.
34 T.U. Raun (1997) 'Democratization and political development in Estonia, 1987–96', in Dawisha and Parrott, *Consolidation of Democracy*, p. 359.
35 D. Arter (1996) *Parties and Democracy in the Post-Soviet Republics: the Case of Estonia*, Aldershot, Dartmouth, pp. 17–18.
36 J.D. Bell (1997) 'Democratization and political participation in "post-communist" Bulgaria', in Dawisha and Parrott, *Politics, Power and the Struggle*, p. 365.
37 V. Tismaneanu (1997) 'Romanian exceptionalism? Democracy, ethnocracy, and uncertain pluralism in post-Ceausescu Romania', in Dawisha and Parrott, *Politics, Power, and the Struggle*, p. 407.
38 N.J. Miller (1997) 'A failed transition: the case of Serbia', in Dawisha and Parrott, *Politics, Power, and the Struggle*, pp. 146, 164.
39 J.B. Allcock (1991) 'Yugoslavia', in Szajkowski, *New Political Parties*, p. 339.
40 S.L. Burg (1997) 'Bosnia Herzegovina: a case of failed democratization', in Dawisha and Parrott, *Politics, Power, and the Struggle*, p. 127.
41 N. Pano (1997) 'The process of democratization in Albania', in Dawisha and Parrott, *Politics, Power, and the Struggle*, p. 304.
42 I. Prizel (1997) 'Ukraine between proto-democracy and "soft" authoritarianism', in Dawisha and Parrott (eds) *Democratic Changes and Authoritarian Reactions in Russia, Ukraine, Belarus, and Moldova*, Cambridge University Press, p. 342.
43 S. Birch (1998) 'Electoral reform in Ukraine: the 1998 parliamentary elections', *Representation* **35**: 149, 153.
44 K.J. Mihalisko (1997) 'Belarus: retreat to authoritarianism', in Dawisha and Parrot, *Democratic Changes and Authoritarian Reactions*, pp. 243–5.
45 W. Crowther (1997) 'The politics of democratization in postcommunist Moldova', in Dawisha and Parrott, *Democratic Changes and Authoritarian Reactions*, p. 291.
46 A. Panebianco (1988) *Political Parties, Organization and Power*, Cambridge University Press.
47 K. von Beyme, *Political Parties in Western Democracies*, Aldershot, Gower, 1985, p. 29

et seq. The *familles* and party groupings comprise: liberals and radicals, conservatives, socialists and social democrats, Christian Democrats, communists, agrarians, regional and ethnic parties, right-wing extremism, and ecologists.

48 K. von Beyme, *Transition to Democracy in Eastern Europe*, London, Macmillan, 1996, pp. 132–9.

49 Although he did not use quite this terminology, this is largely what H. Kitschelt (1992) was getting at when he saw the former ruling parties as likely to be trapped in a political ghetto populated by post-communist losers unless they espoused values beyond initial their initial anti-market, authoritarian responses, 'The formation of party systems in East Central Europe', *Politics and Society* **20**: 20, 41.

50 A. Ware (1996) *Political Parties and Party Systems*, Oxford University Press, p. 26.

51 *Polityka* 16 January 1999.

52 Crawford (1996) *East Central European Politics*, p. 236. But note that both were later registered as members of the CD Union: see G. Pridham, ' Transnational party links and transition to democracy: Eastern Europe in comparative perspective' in Lewis (1996) *Party Structure and Organization*, p. 217.

53 In a later formulation by K. von Beyme (1985) such parties mostly appear within a new category of national conservatives: parties in the process of consolidation in East Central Europe, *Budapest Papers on Democratic Transition*, no. 256.

54 Analogous typologies include up to ten variants of party, see H. Kitschelt (1995) 'Party systems in East Central Europe: consolidation or fluidity', *University of Strathclyde Studies in Public Policy* **241**, and Crawford (1996) *East Central European Politics*, pp. 233–41.

55 R. Markowski (1997) 'Political parties and ideological spaces in East Central Europe', *Communist and Post-Communist Studies* **30**: 227. See also Ware (1996) *Political Parties and Party Systems*, Oxford University Press, on the influence of nationalism and populism.

3 Parties, elections and parliaments

1 D.M. Olson, 'Political parties and party systems in regime transformation: inner transition in the new democracies of Central Europe', *The American Review of Politics*, 1993, **14**: 632.

2 S. Gebethner, 'Parliamentary and electoral parties in Poland', in P.G. Lewis (ed.), *Party Structure and Organization in East-Central Europe*, Cheltenham, Edward Elgar, 1996, p. 122.

3 J. Bielasiak, 'Substance and process in the development of party systems in East Central Europe', *Communist and Post-Communist Studies*, 1997, **30**: 28.

4 A. Ágh (1988) *Emerging Democracies in East Central Europe and the Balkans*, Cheltenham, Edward Elgar, pp. 203, 205.

5 L. Holmes (1997) *Post-Communism: an introduction*, Cambridge, Polity Press, pp. 154–5.

6 K.J. Mihalisko (1997) 'Belarus: retreat to authoritarianism', in K. Dawisha and B. Parrott (eds) *Democratic Changes and Authoritarian Reactions in Russia, Ukraine, Belarus, and Moldova*, Cambridge University Press, p. 263.

7 F. Schmidt (1997) 'Albania's Democrats consolidate power', in *Forging Ahead, Falling Behind: OMRI Annual Survey 1996*, New York, M.E. Sharpe, p. 144. Sharp conflict and radical divisions of opinion developed between some of the international organizations overseeing and evaluating the conduct of east European elections, relations being particularly bitter between both OSCE representatives and others associated with the International Helsinki Federation for Human Rights (IHF) and the British Helsinki Human Rights Group; see J. Druker (1999) 'War of the monitors', *Transitions* **6**: 14–21.

8 *OSCE Newsletter* (1997) **4**; OSCE, Report on Slovak Parliamentary Elections, 25 November 1998.

9 *OSCE Newsletter* (1997) **4** (December).

10 M. Glenny (1990) *The Rebirth of History: Eastern Europe in the Age of Democracy*, Harmondsworth, Penguin Books, p. 176.

11 M. Vickers and J. Pettifer (1997) *From Anarchy to a Balkan Identity*, London, Hurst, pp. 88–9.
12 R. Markowski (1992) 'Absencja wyborcza i bierność wyborcza', *Krytyka* **38**: 59.
13 L. Wade et al. (1994) 'Estimating participation and party voting in Poland: the 1991 parliamentary elections', *East European Politics and Society* **8**: 94–121.
14 J. Wasilewski et al. (1999) 'Stabilność zachowań wyborczych, in R. Markowski (ed.) *Wybory Parlamentarne 1997*, Warsaw, Instytut Studiów Politycznych/Fundacja Eberta, p. 95.
15 R. Gortat (1994) 'Partyjne *perpetuum mobile*', in S. Gebethner (ed.) *Pobocze Systemu Partyjnego*, Warsaw, Uniwersytet Warszawski Instytut Nauk Politycznych, p. 97.
16 D.M. Olson (1997) 'Democratization and political participation: the experience of the Czech Republic', in K. Dawisha and B. Parrott (eds) *The Consolidation of Democracy in East-Central Europe*, Cambridge University Press, p. 175.
17 *RFE/RL Newsline* 28 January 1999.
18 T.O. Raun (1997) 'Democratization and political development in Estonia, 1987–96', in Dawisha and Parrott, *Consolidation of Democracy, p. 359.*
19 R. Taagepera (1998) 'How electoral systems matter for democratization', *Democratization* **5**: 80.
20 For details see G. Sanford (1991) 'Poland', in B. Szajkowski (ed.) *New Political Parties of Eastern Europe and the Soviet Union*, Harlow, Longman.
21 J. Simon (1998) 'Electoral systems and regime change in Central and Eastern Europe, 1990–94', *Representation* **35**(2–3): 122–36.
22 R. Rose, N. Munro and T. Mackie (1998) 'Elections in Central and Eastern Europe since 1990', Studies in Public Policy no. 300, University of Strathclyde, pp. 122–3.
23 Holmes (1997) *Post-Communism*, p. 152; also Z.D. Barany and L. Vinton (1990) 'Breakthrough to democracy: elections in Poland and Hungary', *Studies in Comparative Communism* **23**: 191–212.
24 I. Prizel (1997) 'Ukraine between proto-democracy and "soft" authoritarianism', in Dawisha and Parrott, *Democratic Changes and Authoritarian Reactions*, pp. 351–3.
25 S. Birch (1998) 'Electoral reform in Ukraine: the 1998 parliamentary elections', *Representation* **35**: 149.
26 K. Henderson and N. Robinson (1997) *Post-Communist Politics: an Introduction*, London, Prentice Hall, p. 335.
27 Olson (1993) 'Political parties and party systems', p. 622.
28 K. Jasiewicz (1998) 'Elections and voting behaviour', in S. White, J. Batt and P.G. Lewis (eds) *Developments in Central and East European Politics*, London, Macmillan, p. 175.
29 Olson (1993) 'Political parties and party systems', pp. 620, 623.
30 G. Wightman (ed.) (1995) *Party Formation in East-Central Europe*, Aldershot, Edward Elgar, p. 241.
31 G. Evans and S. Whitefield (1995) 'Economic ideology and political success: communist-successor parties in the Czech Republic, Slovakia and Hungary compared', *Party Politics* **1**: 565–78.
32 A. Mahr and J. Nagle (1995) 'Resurrection of the successor parties and democratization in East-Central Europe', *Communist and Post-Communist Studies* **28**: 393–409.
33 J.T. Ishiyama (1995) 'Communist parties in transition: structures, leaders, and processes of democratization in Eastern Europe', *Comparative Politics* **27**: 147–66.
34 M. Waller (1995) 'Adaptation of the former communist parties of east-central Europe: a case of social-democratization?', *Party Politics* **1**: 473–90.
35 M. Orenstein (1998) 'A genealogy of communist successor parties in East-Central Europe and the determinants of their success', *East European Politics and Societies* **12**: 473–4.
36 H. Kitschelt (1995) 'Formation of party cleavages in post-communist democracies: theoretical propositions', *Party Politics*, **1**: 449.

37 H. Kitschelt (1992) 'The formation of party systems in East Central Europe', *Politics and Society* **20**: 41.
38 See P. Webb and P.G. Lewis (1998) 'The lessons of comparative politics: Russian political parties as independent variables?', *Journal of Communist Studies and Transition Politics* **14**: 260.
39 M. Waller (1996) 'Party inheritances and party identities', in G. Pridham and P.G. Lewis (eds) *Stabilizing Fragile Democracies: Comparing New Party Systems in Southern and Eastern Europe*, London, Routledge, p. 36.
40 Kitschelt (1995) 'Formation of party cleavages', pp. 456–7.
41 Radosław Markowski (1997) 'Polski system partyjny w środkowoeuropejskiej perspektywie', in M. Grabowska and S. Mocek (eds) *Pierwsza Sześciolatka 1989–1995, Próba Bilansu Polityki*, Warsaw, Instytut Studiów Politycznych, p. 110.
42 G. Tóka (1997) 'Political parties in East Central Europe' in L. Diamond et al. (eds) *Consolidating the Third Wave Democracies*, Baltimore, Johns Hopkins, p. 110.
43 G. Tóka (1996) 'Parties and electoral choices in east-central Europe', in Pridham and Lewis, *Stabilizing Fragile Democracies*, p. 111.
44 S. Oates (1999) 'The Soviet legacy in voting behaviour', Paper delivered to ECPR Joint Sessions, Mannheim.
45 J. Raciborski (1997) *Polskie Wybory: Zachowania Wyborcze Społeczeństwa Polskiego w Latach 1989–1995*, Warsaw, Wydawnictwo Naukowe 'Scholar', pp. 53–5.
46 A. Szczerbiak (1998) 'Electoral politics in Poland: the parliamentary elections of 1997', *Journal of Communist Studies and Transition Politics* **14**: 68.
47 G. Wightman and S. Szomolanyi (1995) 'Parties and society in Slovakia', *Party Politics* **1**: 613.
48 Orenstein (1998) 'A genealogy of communist successor parties', p. 485.
49 Henderson and Robinson (1997) *Post-Communist Politics*, p. 289.
50 P.G. Lewis (1998) 'Party funding in post-communist east-central Europe', in P. Burnell and A. Ware (eds) *Funding Democratization*, Manchester University Press, pp. 137–57.
51 P. Walewski (1999) 'Swój radzie', *Polityka* 6 November.
52 Rose et al. (1998) 'Elections', p. 118.
53 D. Olson (1998) 'Party formation and party system consolidation in the new democracies of Central Europe', *Political Studies* **46**: 460.
54 R. Rose et al. (1998) 'Elections', pp. 118–19.
55 S. Mainwaring (1998) 'Party systems in the third wave', *Journal of Democracy* **9**: 71.
56 R. Markowski (1999) 'Polish party system: institutionalization – political representation – issue structuring', Paper presented to ECPR Joint Sessions, Mannheim.
57 R. Taagepera and M. Sobert, *Seats and Votes*, New Haven, Yale University Press, 1989. It is derived by squaring the percentage of seats gained by each party, adding the totals and inverting the result (i.e. 1/x) to arrive at the effectiveness measure.
58 J. McGregor (1993) 'How electoral laws shape Eastern Europe's parliaments', *RFE/RL Research Report* **2**(4): 14.
59 D.L. Norden (1998) 'Party relations and democracy in Latin America', *Party Politics* **4**: 436.
60 A. Lijphart (1984) *Democracies: patterns of majoritarian and consensus government in twenty-one countries*, New Haven, Yale University Press, p. 122.
61 Olson (1998) 'Party formation', p. 459.
62 C.J. Anderson (1998) 'Parties, party systems, and satisfaction with democratic performance in the new Europe', *Political Studies* **46**: 586.
63 D.M. Olson and P. Norton (eds) (1996) *The New Parliaments of Central and Eastern Europe*, London, Frank Cass, p. 242.
64 A. Antoszewski (1997) 'Forma rządu', in A. Antoszewski and R. Herbut (eds) *Demokracje Europy Srodkowo-Wschodniej w Perspektywie Porównawczej*, Wydawnictwo Uniwersytetu Wrocławskiego, pp. 71–2.

178   *Notes*

65 D.M. Olson (1998) 'The parliaments of new democracies and the politics of representation', in White, Batt and Lewis (eds) *Developments in Central and East European Politics*, p. 129.
66 G. Ilonszki (1996) 'From marginal to rational parliaments: a Central European regional view', in A. Ágh and G. Ilonszki (eds) *Parliaments and Organized Interests: the Second Steps*, Budapest, Hungarian Centre for Democracy Studies, p. 452.
67 A. Ágh (1998) *The Politics of Central Europe*, London, Sage, p. 88.
68 Olson and Norton (1996) *The New Parliaments*, p. 241.
69 R. Taras (1998) 'The politics of leadership', in White, Batt and Lewis (eds) *Developments in Central and East European Politics*, p. 110.
70 A. Urbański (1998) 'Dwaj panowie K.', *Polityka* 15 May 1999.
71 R. Gortat (1996) 'Trudny egzamin: partie polityczne w wyborach prezydenckich '95', *Przegląd Społeczny* **1–2**: 104.
72 Olson (1998) 'The parliaments of new democracies', pp. 135, 137–8, 143.
73 Ilonszki (1996) 'From marginal to rational parliaments', p. 460.
74 Antoszewski (1997) 'Forma rządu', p. 72.
75 A. Offerdal et al. (1996) 'Elites and parties', in H. Baldersheim et al. (eds) *Local Democracy and the Processes of Transformation in East-Central Europe*, Boulder, Westview, p. 156.
76 A. Kroupa and T. Kostelecký (1996) 'Party organization and structure at national and local level in the Czech Republic since 1989', in P.G. Lewis (ed.) *Party Structure and Organization in East-Central Europe*, Cheltenham, Edward Elgar, p. 114.
77 A. Szczerbiak (1999) 'The impact of the October 1998 local elections on the emerging Polish party system', Paper presented to PSA Specialist Communist and Post-Communist Group, London.

4 Party organization and institutional development

1 P. Kopecky (1995) 'Developing party organizations in east-central Europe: what type of party is likely to emerge?', *Party Politics* **1**: 517–18.
2 P.G. Lewis (ed.) (1996) *Party Structure and Organization in East-Central Europe*, Cheltenham, Edward Elgar, pp. 15–16.
3 A. Ágh, *The Politics of Central Europe*, London, Sage, 1998, pp. 107–8.
4 A. Ware, *Political Parties and Party Systems*, Oxford University Press, 1996, p. 111.
5 K. von Beyme (1985) *Political Parties in Western Democracies*, Aldershot, Gower, pp. 160–1.
6 M. Duverger, *Political Parties*, London, Methuen, 1964, pp. 63, 427.
7 P. Mair (1994) 'Party organizations: from civil society to the state', in R.S. Katz and P. Mair (eds) *How Parties Organize: Change and Adaptation in Party Organizations in Western Democracies*, London, Sage, p. 2.
8 *Ibid*, pp. 2–6.
9 von Beyme (1985) *Political Parties in Western Democracies*, p. 168.
10 *The Observer* 25 May 1997, 29 March 1998. Von Beyme in fact suggests that the Conservatives' awareness of internal party affairs was little different in the 1970s (*Political Parties*, London, Methuen, 1964, p. 169).
11 H. Kitschelt et al. (1999) *Post-Communist Party Systems: Competition, Representation, and Inter-Party Cooperation*, Cambridge University Press, p. 396.
12 *Polityka* 13 November 1999.
13 Ágh, *Politics of Central Europe*, p. 106.
14 *Polityka* 16 January 1999.
15 M. Janicki (1999) 'Likwidacja według planu', *Polityka* 26 June 1999.
16 Kopecký (1995) 'Developing party organizations', p. 523.

17 *Polityka* 8 May 1999.
18 S.L. Wolchik (1997) 'Democratization and political participation in Slovakia', in K. Dawisha and B. Parrott (eds) *The Consolidation of Democracy in East-Central Europe*, Cambridge University Press, p. 228.
19 S.P. Ramet (1997) 'Democratization in Slovenia – the second stage', in K. Dawisha and B. Parrott (eds) *Politics, Power and the Struggle for Democracy in South-East Europe*, Cambridge University Press; A. Krašovec (1999) 'Cartelization of Slovene political parties', Paper presented at ECPR Joint Sessions, Mannheim.
20 I. Prizel (1997) ' Ukraine between proto-democracy and "soft" authoritarianism', in K. Dawisha and B. Parrott (eds) *Democratic Changes and Authoritarian Reactions in Russia, Ukraine, Belarus, and Moldova*, Cambridge University Press, pp. 354–5.
21 *RFE/RL Newsline* 27 April 1998.
22 A. Ágh (1997) 'Defeat and success as promoters of party change: the Hungarian Socialist Party after two abrupt changes', *Party Politics*, **3**: 428, 430.
23 M. Shafir (1999) 'The mind of Romania's radical right', in S.P. Ramet (ed.) *The Radical Right in Central and Eastern Europe Since 1989*, University Park, Pennsylvania State University Press, p. 214.
24 Duverger *Political Parties*, p. xv.
25 P.G. Lewis (1994) 'Political institutionalization and party development in post-communist Poland', *Europe-Asia Studies* **46**: 792.
26 P.G. Lewis and R. Gortat (1995) 'Models of party development and questions of state dependence in Poland', *Party Politics* **1**: 601.
27 Kopecký (1995) 'Developing party organizations', pp. 525–6.
28 B. Lomax (1996) 'The structure and organization of Hungary's political parties', in Lewis, *Party Structure and Organization*, pp. 20, 38.
29 *Polityka* 5 March 1994, 19 May 1994.
30 A. Szczerbiak (1999) 'Testing party models in east-central Europe: local party organization in postcommunist Poland', *Party Politics* **5**: 525–37.
31 M. Grabowski (1997) 'Partie polityczne: reprezentant społeczeństwa czy twórca nowego ładu', in M. Grabowska and S. Mocek (eds) *Pierwsza sześciolatka: Próba Bilansu Polityki*, Warsaw, Instytut Studiów Politycznych, p. 46.
32 G. Tóka (1998) 'Party appeals and voter loyalty in new democracies', *Political Studies* **46**: 607.
33 K. Janda and T. Colman (1998) 'Effects of party organization on performance during the "golden age" of parties', *Political Studies* **46**: 618, 630–2.
34 M. Waller and G. Karasimeonov (1996) 'Party organization in post-communist Bulgaria', in Lewis (ed.) *Party Structure and Organization*, p. 161.
35 A. Ágh, *Politics of Central Europe*, p. 109.
36 Lewis (1996) *Party Structure and Organization*, pp. 13–14.
37 Krašovec (1999) 'Cartelization',
38 Mair (1994) 'Party organizations', pp. 8–10.
39 *Polityka* 7 November 1998.
40 Krašovec (1999) 'Cartelization'.
41 Lewis (1998) 'Party funding', p. 139.
42 *Ibid*, pp. 143–9.
43 A. Szczerbiak (1999) 'Bureaucrats and professionals: the "party machine" in post-communist Poland', Paper presented at ECPR Joint Sessions, Mannheim.
44 A. Krupa (ed.) (1997) *Prawie Biała księga polskiej sceny politycznej*, Warsaw, ARS Print Production, p. 210.
45 *Transitions*, 1998, **5**(1): 10.
46 Kitschelt et al., 1999, *Post-Communist Party Systems*, pp. 203, 375.
47 *RFE/RL Newsline* 24 November 1999.

48 T. Gallagher (1998) 'The Balkans: Bulgaria, Romania, Albania and the former Yugo-slavia', in S. White, J. Batt and P.G. Lewis (eds) *Developments in Central and East European Politics*, London, Macmillan, p. 50.

49 R.J. Krickus (1997) 'Democratization in Lithuania', in Dawisha and Parrott, *The Conso-lidation of Democracy*, p. 310.

50 A. Plakans (1997) 'Democratization and political participation in postcommunist socie-ties: the case of Latvia', in Dawisha and Parrott, *The Consolidation of Democracy*, pp. 269–70.

51 S. Mainwaring and T.R. Scully (1995) *Building Democratic Institutions: Party Systems in Latin America*, Stanford University Press, pp. 471–2.

52 G. Wightman (1998) 'Parties and politics', in White, Batt and Lewis (eds), *Developments in Central and East European Politics*, p. 163.

53 K. Jakubowicz (1996) 'Media legislation as a mirror of democracy', *Transitions* **2**: 21.

54 I. Nikolchev (1996) 'Polarization and diversification in the Bulgarian press', *Journal of Communist Studies and Transition Politics* **12**: 129.

55 A. Školkay (1996) 'Journalists, political elites and post-communist public: the case of Slovakia', *Journal of Communist Studies and Transition Politics* **12**: 70–1.

56 D. Ionescu (1996) 'Former communists on the march', *Transitions* **2**: 41.

57 Z. Szilagyi (1996) 'Shady dealings and slow privatization', *Transitions* **2**: 44.

58 L. Sekelj (2000) 'Parties and elections: the Federal Republic of Yugoslavia – change without transformation', *Europe-Asia Studies* **52**: 61.

59 A.K. Milton (1996) 'News media reform in Eastern Europe: a cross-national compari-son', *Journal of Communist Studies and Transition Politics* **12**: 21.

60 K. Jakubowicz (1996) 'Media legislation as a mirror of democracy', *Transitions* **2**: 19.

61 B. Tatomir (1996) 'Croatian government calls certain media "enemies of the state"', *Transitions* **2**: 24–5.

62 *Polityka* 11 July 1998.

63 D. Olson (1998) 'Party formation and party system consolidation in the new democ-racies of Central Europe', *Political Studies* **46**: 445.

64 G. Sartori (1976) *Parties and Party Systems: a framework for analysis*, Cambridge University Press.

65 Janda and Colman (1998) 'Effects of party organization', pp. 618–19.

66 This is the meaning adopted by Laszlo Szarvas (1994) when he discusses 'Parties and party factions in the Hungarian parliament', *Journal of Communist Studies and Transition Politics* **10**: 120–36.

67 P.G. Lewis (1995) 'Poland and Eastern Europe: perspectives on party factions and fac-tionalism', in R. Gillespie, M. Waller and L.L. Nieto (eds) *Factional Politics and Democrati-zation*, London, Frank Cass, p. 107.

68 von Beyme (1985) *Political Parties in Western Democracies*, p. 229.

69 M. Waller and R. Gillespie (1995) 'Introduction: factions, party management and poli-tical development', in Gillespie et al. (eds) *Factional Politics*, p. 6.

70 Lewis (1995) 'Poland and Eastern Europe', p. 103.

71 Janda and Colman (1998) 'Effects of party organization', p. 629.

72 B. Lomax (1995) 'Factions and factionalism in Hungary's new party system', in Gille-spie et al., *Factional Politics*, p. 136.

73 Waller and Gillespie, 'Introduction', p. 5.

74 *RFE/RL Newsline* 17 July 1998.

75 V. Pettai and M. Kreuzer (1999) 'Party politics in the Baltic states: social bases and institutional context', *East European Politics and Societies* **13**: 7.

76 Lewis (1995) 'Poland and Eastern Europe', p. 120.

77 S.P. Huntington (1968) *Political Order in Changing Societies*, New Haven, Yale University Press, pp. 412–13.

78 *Ibid.*, p. 12.

79 A. Panebianco, *Political Parties: Organization and Power*, Cambridge University Press, 1988, pp. 63–5.
80 *Ibid*, pp. 50–2.
81 Ware (1996) *Parties and Party Systems*, p. 104.
82 Lewis (1994) 'Political institutionalization and party development', pp. 779–99.
83 See A. Szczerbiak (1999) 'Bureaucrats and professionals'.
84 I. Panków (1994) 'Responsibility of new elites: from the Solidarity movement to parliament building', in A. Ágh (ed.) *The Emergence of East Central European Parliaments: the First Steps*, Budapest, Hungarian Centre of Democracy Studies, p. 216.
85 G. Pridham (1996) 'Transnational party links and transition to democracy: Eastern Europe in comparative perspective', in Lewis (ed.) *Party Structure and Organization*, p. 187.
86 Recognition of Poland's Social Democracy as the country's sole socialist representative was, for example, a major setback for the Union of Labour; see *Polityka* 21 November 1998.
87 G. Pridham (1999) 'Patterns of Europeanization and transnational party co-operation: party development in Central and Eastern Europe', Paper presented at ECPR Joint Sessions, Mannheim.

5 Party systems and structures of representation

1 A. Ware (1996) *Political Parties and Party Systems*, Oxford University Press, p. 149.
2 H. Kitschelt et al. (1999) *Post-Communist Party Systems: Competition, Representation, and Interparty Cooperation*, Cambridge University Press, p. 15.
3 P. Mair (1996) 'Party systems and structures of competition', in L. LeDuc et al. (eds) *Comparing Democracies: Elections and Voting in Global Perspectives*, London, Sage, pp. 83–4.
4 G. Sartori, *Parties and Party Systems: a Framework for Analysis*, Cambridge University Press, 1976, p. 44.
5 M. Cotta (1996) 'Structuring the new party systems after the dictatorship', in G. Pridham and P.G. Lewis (eds) *Stabilizing Fragile Democracies: Comparing New Party Systems in Southern and Eastern Europe*, London, Routledge, p. 71.
6 M. Cotta (1994) 'Building party systems after the dictatorship', in G. Pridham and T. Vanhanen (eds) *Democratization in Eastern Europe*, London, Routledge, p. 100.
7 See R.A. Dahl (ed.) (1966) *Political Oppositions in Western Democracies*, New Haven, Yale University Press. His conclusion suggests a view of party systems that gives this dimension particular prominence.
8 P.G. Lewis (1997) 'The repositioning of opposition in east-central Europe', *Government and Opposition* **32**: 628–9.
9 Kitschelt et al. (1999) *Post-Communist Party Systems*, pp. 14, 40.
10 P. Pennings and J.-E. Lane (eds) (1998) *Comparing Party System Change*, London, Routledge, p. 5.
11 Sartori (1976) *Parties and Party Systems*, pp. 132–3.
12 *Ibid.*, p. 266.
13 *Ibid.*, p. 244. The notion of structural consolidation in this context 'lays the emphasis ... on the viscosity, resilience, and immobilizing impact of structures'.
14 S. Mainwaring and T.R. Scully (eds) (1995) *Building Democratic Institutions: Party Systems in Latin America*, Stanford University Press, pp. 19–20.
15 Although other accounts stress that neither a small number of parties nor an absence of polarization has been a *guarantee* of democratic stability; see D.L. Norden (1998) 'Party relations and democracy in Latin America', *Party Politics* **4**: 437.
16 Mainwaring and Scully (1995) *Building Democratic Institutions*, pp. 4–5.
17 P. Mair (1997) *Party System Change: approaches and interpretations*, Oxford, Clarendon Press, pp. 175, 183. Rather different estimates of volatility levels have been produced, as

182   *Notes*

discussed in Chapter 3, and those cited here in fact suggest a lower level of volatility than some others.

18 S. Mainwaring (1998) 'Party systems in the third wave', *Journal of Democracy* **9**: 80.
19 Mainwaring and Scully (1995) *Building Democratic Institutions*, pp. 20–1.
20 Sartori (1976) *Parties and Party Systems*, pp. 230–8; Ware (1996) *Political Parties and Party Systems*, pp. 246–51. Sartori's identification of a 'predominant-party system' is also relevant to the east European context in this respect and introduces further complications into his basic classification in terms of party numbers (Mair (1997) 'Party systems', p. 87).
21 G. Wightman (1998) 'Parties and politics', in S. White, J. Batt and P.G. Lewis (eds) *Developments in Central and East European Politics*, London, Macmillan, p. 147.
22 C. Gati (1996) 'The mirage of democracy', *Transitions* **2**: 6–12.
23 Sartori (1976) *Parties and Party Systems*, p. 127. The 'relevance' of parties is carefully defined in pp. 121–4.
24 *Ibid.*, p. 199.
25 Mainwaring and Scully (1995) *Building Democratic Institutions*, p. 20.
26 V. Pettai and M. Kreuzer (1999) 'Party politics in the Baltic states: social bases and institutional context', *East European Politics and Societies* **13**: 5–11. The marked divergence between the Baltic party systems and the emergence of a bipolar model in Lithuania are largely attributed to the varying effect of ethnic politics and different citizenship laws.
27 K. Henderson and N. Robinson (1997) *Post-Communist Politics: an Introduction*, London, Prentice Hall, p. 324.
28 P.G. Lewis (1994) 'Democratization and party development in eastern Europe', *Democratization* **1**: 393.
29 G. Schopflin (1998) 'Hungary's elections: the dilemma of the right', *RFE/RL Newsline* 29 April.
30 International factors were prominent in all cases of political destabilization, the ambiguous role of the US ambassador in supporting the unstable order created by Berisha's highly centralized presidential system in Albania being particularly well documented by M. Vickers and J. Pettifer (1997) *Albania: From Anarchy to a Balkan Identity*, London, Hurst, p. 74.
31 D. Chandler (1998) 'Democratization in Bosnia: the limits of civil society building strategies', *Democratization* **5**: 87.
32 Sartori (1976) *Parties and Party Systems*, p. 200.
33 O. Varfolomeyev (1998) 'Ukrainian party politics gets a boost', *Transitions* **5**: 80.
34 T. Kuzio (1995) 'The 1994 parliamentary elections in Ukraine', *Journal of Communist Studies and Transition Politics* **11**: 338–55.
35 Sartori (1976) *Parties and Party Systems*, pp. 230–8.
36 *RFE/RL Newsline* 2 April 1998.
37 M. Shafir (1998) 'Moldova's upcoming parliamentary elections', *RFE/RL Newsline* 19–20 March.
38 Henderson and Robinson (1997) *Post-Communist Politics*, p. 215.
39 Further reasons for not exaggerating the consequences of communist electoral success are given by P. Goble (1998) in 'When communists win elections', *RFE/RL Newsline* 6 April.
40 The extent to which both the Serbian Radical Party and Seselj were created by Milošević as political instruments to discredit parliament and undermine its capacity to oppose his rule is documented by S. Reljic (1998) 'Demagogue in waiting', *Transitions* **5**: 70–5.
41 Ware (1996) *Political Parties and Party Systems*, p. 249.
42 *Eastern Europe Newsletter* 23 January 1998. The Montenegrin socialists formally split with the establishment of a new party on 21 March 1998.
43 Henderson and Robinson (1997) *Post-Communist Politics*, p. 369.

44 Kitschelt et al. (1999) *Post-Communist Party Systems*, p. 390.
45 I. Krastev (1997) Back to the basics in Bulgaria', *Transition* **3**: 14.
46 M. Shafir and D. Ionescu (1997) 'Radical political change in Romania', *OMRI Annual Survey 1996*, New York, M.E. Sharpe, p. 157.
47 M. Shafir (1999) 'Two very different reshuffles', *RFE/RL Newsline* 23 December.
48 *Eastern Europe Newsletter* 11 April 1997.
49 'Getting priorities straight in Croatia', *RFE/RL Newsline* 19 April 2000.
50 Of the twenty-three established liberal democracies in the late 1950s, for example, only four had radically different party systems 30 years later; see A. Ware (1996) *Political Parties and Party Systems*, p. 213.
51 One interesting exception to this tendency, which interposed a stage in which an 'anti-party system' held the stage before institutionalized multi-partism developed, was represented by the work of David Arter (1996) *Parties and Democracy in the Post-Soviet Republics*, Aldershot, Dartmouth, pp. 17–18.
52 S. Berglund and J.A. Dellenbrant (eds) (1991) *The New Democracies in Eastern Europe: Party Systems and Political Cleavages*, Aldershot, Edward Elgar.
53 H. Kitschelt (1992) 'The formation of party systems in East Central Europe', *Politics and Society* **20**: 7–50; A. Ágh (1992) 'The emerging party systems in East Central Europe', Budapest Papers on Democratic Transition.
54 In terms of publications the leaders appeared to be M.G. Roskin (1993) 'The emerging party systems of Central and Eastern Europe', *East European Quarterly* **27**: 47–63, and D.M. Olson (1993) 'Political parties and party systems in regime transformation: inner transition in the new democracies of Central Europe', *American Review of Politics* **14**: 619–58.
55 G. Tóka (1997) 'Political parties in East Central Europe', in L. Diamond et al. (eds) *Consolidating the Third Wave Democracies*, Baltimore, Johns Hopkins, p. 93.
56 J. Bielasiak (1997) 'Substance and process in the development of party systems in East Central Europe', *Communist and Post-Communist Studies* **30**: 40–1.
57 D.M. Olson (1998) 'Party formation and party system consolidation in the new democracies of Central Europe', *Political Studies* **46**: 462–3.
58 In terms of a possible 'freezing moment' of new party systems (Olson (1993) 'Political parties and party systems', p. 620) or the 'partial consolidation of a partial system' (A. Ágh (1996) 'The end of the beginning: the partial consolidation of East Central European parties and party systems', Budapest Papers on Democratic Transition **156**: 2).
59 Kitschelt et al. (1999) *Post-Communist Party Systems*, p. 389.
60 Ware (1996) *Political Parties*, pp. 190–6.
61 W. Merkel (1998) 'The consolidation of post-autocratic democracies: a multi-level model', *Democratization* **5**: 50–1. A. Ágh (1998) also identifies the conflict between forming ruling parties and new opposition groups as one of three dominant cleavages in his genetic typology of east European parties (*The Politics of Central Europe*, London, Sage, pp. 115–21), but similarly suggests that this cleavage line has limited contemporary significance.
62 B. Crawford and A. Lijphart (1995) 'Explaining political and economic change in post-communist eastern Europe', *Comparative Political Studies* **28**: 171–99. This draws on Geddes's work on the Leninist legacy in the same volume.
63 S.W. Rivera (1996) 'Historical cleavages or transition mode? Reflections on the emerging party systems in Poland, Hungary and Czechoslovakia', *Party Politics* **2**: 177–208.
64 V. Pettai and M. Kreuzer (1999) 'Institutions and party development in the Baltic states', Paper delivered at ECPR Joint Sessions, Mannheim, p. 14.
65 S.M. Lipset and S. Rokkan (eds) *Party Systems and Voter Alignments: Cross National Perspectives*, New York, Free Press, 1967, pp. 1–64.
66 Mair (1994) 'Party systems and structures of competition', pp. 102–3.

67 Kitschelt (1992) 'Formation of party systems', p. 11.
68 K. Lawson (1999) 'Cleavages, parties, and voters', in K. Lawson, A. Römmele and G. Karasimeonov (eds) *Cleavages, Parties, and Voters*, Westport, Conn., Praeger, pp. 31–2.
69 Cotta (1994) 'Building party systems', pp. 118–22. S. Berglund et al. (eds) (1998) *The Handbook of Political Change in Eastern Europe*, Cheltenham, Edward Elgar, pp. 11–12, directly links early high levels of electoral volatility with the weakness of class cleavages.
70 H. Tworzecki (1996) *Parties and Politics in Post-1989 Poland*, Boulder, Westview, p. 191.
71 T. Żukowski (1993) 'Polska scena polityczna w latach 1991–92 w świetle wyników wyborów: ciągłość i zmiany', in S. Gebethner (ed.) *Polska scena polityczna a wybory*, Warsaw, 'Polska w Europie', pp. 240–1; Tworzecki (1996) *Parties and Politics*, also makes some note of this factor.
72 Kitschelt et al. (1999) *Post-Communist Party Systems*, p. 145.
73 R. Markowski (1997) 'Political parties and ideological spaces in East Central Europe', *Communist and Post-Communist Studies* **30**: 221–2.
74 K. von Beyme (1996) *Transition to Democracy in Eastern Europe*, London, Macmillan, pp. 128–30.
75 Kitschelt et al. (1999) *Post-Communist Party Systems*, p. 261.
76 A. Bozoki (1994) 'Party formation and constitutional change in Hungary', *Journal of Communist Studies and Transition Politics* **10**: 54.
77 J. Bielasiak (1997) 'Substance and process in the development of party systems in East Central Europe', *Communist and Post-Communist Studies* **30**: 39.
78 Markowski (1997) 'Political parties', p. 229.
79 R. Herbut (1997) 'Systemy partyjne krajów Europy Centralnej i Wschodniej oraz wzorce rywalizacji politycznej', in A. Antoszewski and R. Herbut (eds) *Demokracje Europy środkowo-Wschodniej w perspektywie porównawczej*, Wrocław, Wydawnictwo Uniwersytetu Wrocławskiego, pp. 144–7.
80 H. Kitschelt, 'Party systems in East Central Europe: consolidation or fluidity?', University of Strathclyde Studies in Public Policy 241, 1995, pp. 55.
81 *Ibid*, pp. 3–4, 80–2, 98.
82 J.D. Nagle and A. Mahr (1999) *Democracy and Democratization*, London, Sage, p. 199.
83 Herbut (1997) 'Systemy partyjny', pp. 145–7.
84 G. Tóka, 'Parties and electoral choices in east-central Europe', in Pridham and Lewis, *Stabilizing Fragile Democracies*, p. 113.
85 Lipset and Rokkan (1967) *Party Systems and Voter Alignments*, p. 3.
86 B. Mach and W. Wesolowski (1998) 'Politicians in times of transition: "transformational correctness" or genuine differences in perception?', WZB Papers, Berlin, p. 6.
87 Mair (1997) 'Party systems', pp. 89, 97.
88 *Ibid*, p. 95.

6 Conclusion: political parties in contemporary eastern Europe

1 See data on the role of the private sector presented by G. Blazyca (1998) 'The politics of economic transformation', in S. White, J. Batt and P.G. Lewis (eds) *Developments in Central and East European Politics*, London, Macmillan, p. 210.
2 P. Goble (1999) 'The approaching end of the "party of power"', *RFE/RL Newsline* 11 June.
3 S. Birch (1998) 'Electoral systems, campaign strategies, and vote choice in the Ukrainian parliamentary and presidential elections of 1994', *Political Studies* **46**: 99, 105. The discussion also describes the mythical character of the 'party of power' and defines it more simply as a survival of the former ruling establishment.
4 M. Shafir (1999) 'Moldova and presidential system: little country, big question', *RFE/RL Newsline* 15 July. See also *RFE/RL Newsline* 13 July 1999.

5 S.P. Huntington (1968) *Political Order in Changing Societies*, New Haven, Yale University Press.
6 A. Panebianco (1988) *Political Parties: Organization and Power*, Cambridge University Press.
7 S. Mainwaring (1998) 'Party systems in the third wave', *Journal of Democracy* **9**: 67–81.
8 E. Nalewajko (1997) *Protopartie i Protosystem? Szkic do Obrazu Polskiej Wielopartyjności*, Warsaw, Instytut Studiów Politycznych PAN.
9 D. Held (ed.) (1993) *Prospects for Democracy* , Cambridge, Polity Press, p. 37.
10 N. O'Sullivan (1997) 'Difference and the concept of the political in contemporary political philosophy', *Political Studies* **55**: 753.
11 F. Fukuyama (1989) 'The end of history?', *National Interest* **16**: 3–18.
12 C. Mouffe (1993) *The Return of the Political*, London, Verso, pp. 1–6.
13 P. Burnell (1994) 'Democratization and economic change worldwide – can societies cope?', *Democratization* **1**: 3.
14 G.B. Powell (1982) *Contemporary Democracies*, Cambridge, MA, Harvard University Press, p. 7.
15 J.A. Hall (1993) 'Consolidations of democracy', in Held (ed.), *Prospects for Democracy*, pp. 282–3.
16 A. King (1974) 'Political parties in western democracies', in L.J. Cantor (ed.) *Comparative Political Systems*, Boston, MA, Holbrook Press, pp. 303–3.
17 K. von Beyme (1996) 'Party leadership and change in party systems: towards a postmodern party state?', *Government and Opposition* **31**: 135.
18 P. Mair (1994) 'Party organizations: from civil society to the state', in R.S. Katz and P. Mair (eds) *How Parties Organize*, London, Sage, p. 2.
19 S. Mainwaring and T.R. Scully (1995) *Building Democratic Institutions: Party Systems in Latin America*, Stanford University Press, pp. 471–2.
20 Mair (1994) 'Party organizations', p. 4.
21 N. Bobbio (1989) *Democracy and Dictatorship*, Cambridge, Polity Press, p. 25.
22 A. Ágh (1998) *The Politics of Central Europe*, London, Sage, p. 105.
23 O. Kirchheimer (1966) 'The transformation of the western European party system', in J. LaPalombara and M. Weiner (eds) *Political Parties and Political Development*, Princeton University Press, pp. 177–200.
24 A. Panebianco (1988) *Political Parties: Organization and Power*, Cambridge University Press.
25 R.S. Katz and P. Mair (1995) 'Changing models of party organization and party democracy: the emergence of the cartel party', *Party Politics* **1**: 5–28.
26 R. Koole (1996) 'Cadre, catch-all or cartel? A comment on the notion of the cartel party', *Party Politics* **2**: 507–21.
27 von Beyme (1996) 'Party leadership and change', p. 135; S. Padgett (1996) 'Parties in post-communist society: the German case', in Lewis (ed.) *Party Structure and Organization*, p. 184.
28 P. Mair (1997) 'What is different about post-communist party systems?', in *Party System Change: Approaches and Interpretations,* Oxford, Clarendon Press.
29 S. Roper (1995) 'The Romanian party system and the catch-all party phenomenon', *East European Quarterly* **27**: 518–32.
30 A. Szczerbiak (1999) 'Bureaucrats and professionals: the "party machine" in post-communist Poland', Paper presented at ECPR Joint Sessions, Mannheim.
31 Nalewajko (1997) *Protopartie*, p. 212.
32 Koole (1996) 'Cadre, catch-all or cartel?', p. 520.
33 A. Ágh (1996) 'The end of the beginning: the partial consolidation of east central European parties and party systems', Budapest Papers on Democratic Transition, **156**: 9–10.
34 Ágh (1998) *The Politics of Central Europe*, London, Sage, p. 109.

35 P.G. Lewis (ed.) (1996) *Party Structure and Organization in East-Central Europe*, Cheltenham, Edward Elgar, pp. 12–14; Koole (1996) 'Cadre, catch-all or cartel?', pp. 508, 514, 520.
36 P.G. Lewis and R. Gortat (1995) 'Models of party development and questions of state dependence in post-communist Poland', *Party Politics* **1**: 599–608.
37 *Polityka* 17 July 1999.
38 Katz and Mair (1995) 'Changing models of party organization', p. 21.
39 K. von Beyme (1999) 'Parties in the process of consolidation in east central Europe', Budapest Papers on Democratic Transition no. 256, p. 22.
40 G. Ekiert (1990) 'Democratization processes in East Central Europe: a theoretical consideration', *British Journal of Political Science* **21**: 285–313.
41 Koole (1996) 'Cadre, catch-all or cartel', pp. 511–14.

Bibliography

Ágh, A. (1992) 'The emerging party systems in East Central Europe', *Budapest Papers on Democratic Transition*, Budapest Economics University.

—— (1994) 'The Hungarian party system and party theory in the transition of Central Europe', *Journal of Theoretical Politics* **6**: 217–38.

—— (1996) 'From nomenclatura to clientura', in G. Pridham and P.G. Lewis (eds) *Stabilizing Fragile Democracies*, London: Routledge.

—— (1996) 'The end of the beginning: the partial consolidation of east central European parties and party system', *Budapest Papers on Democratic Transition* **156**.

—— (1997) 'Defeat and success as promoters of party change: the Hungarian Socialist Party after two abrupt changes', *Party Politics* **3**: 427–44.

—— (1998) *The Politics of Central Europe*, London: Sage.

—— (1998) *Emerging Democracies in East Central Europe and the Balkans*, Cheltenham: Edward Elgar.

Allcock, J.B. (1991) 'Yugoslavia', in B. Szajkowski (ed.) *New Political Parties of Europe and the Soviet Union*, Harlow: Longman.

Anderson, C.J. (1998) 'Parties, party systems, and satisfaction with democratic performance in the new Europe', *Political Studies* **46**: 572–88.

Antoszewski, A. (1997) 'Forma rządu', in A. Antoszewski and R. Herbut (eds) *Demokracje Europy środkowo-Wschodniej w perspektywie porównawczej*, Wydawnictwo Uniwersytetu Wrocławskiego.

—— and Herbut, R. (eds) (1997) *Demokracje Europy środkowo-Wschodniej w perspektywie porównawczej*, Wydawnictwo Uniwersytetu Wrocławskiego.

Arter, D. (1996) *Parties and Democracy in the Post-Soviet Republics: the Case of Estonia*, Aldershot: Dartmouth Press.

Barany, Z.D. and Vinton, L. (1990) 'Breakthrough to democracy: elections in Poland and Hungary', *Studies in Comparative Communism* **23**: 191–212.

Batt, J. (1991) *East Central Europe from Reform to Transformation*, London: Pinter.

Bell, J.D. (1997) 'Democratization and political participation in "post-communist" Bulgaria', in K. Dawisha and B. Parrott, *Politics, Power, and the Struggle for Democracy in Southeast Europe*, Cambridge, UK: Cambridge University Press.

Berglund, S. and Dellenbrant, J.A. (eds) (1994) *The New Democracies in Eastern Europe: Party Systems and Political Cleavages*, Aldershot: Edward Elgar.

Berglund, S., Hellen, T. and Aarebrot, F.H. (eds) (1998) *The Handbook of Political Change in Eastern Europe*, Cheltenham: Edward Elgar.

Beyme, K. von (1985) *Political Parties in Western Democracies*, Aldershot: Gower Press.

—— (1996) *Transition to Democracy in Eastern Europe*, London: Macmillan.

—— (1996) 'Party leadership and change in party systems: towards a postmodern party state?', *Government and Opposition* **31**: 135–59.

—— (1999) 'Parties in the process of consolidation in East Central Europe', *Budapest Papers on Democratic Transition* **256**.

Bielasiak, J. (1997) 'Substance and process in the development of party systems in East Central Europe', *Communist and Post-Communist Studies* **30**: 23–44.

Birch, S. (1998) 'Electoral reform in Ukraine: the 1998 parliamentary elections', *Representation* **35**: 146–54.

—— (1998) 'Electoral systems, campaign strategies, and vote choice in the Ukrainian parliamentary and presidential elections of 1994', *Political Studies* **46:** 96–114.

Blazyca, G. (1998) 'The politics of economic transformation', in S. White, J. Batt and P.G. Lewis (eds) *Developments in Central and East European Politics*, London: Macmillan.

Bobbio, N. (1989) *Democracy and Dictatorship*, Cambridge, Polity.

Bozoki, A. (1994) 'Party formation and constitutional change in Hungary', *Journal of Communist Studies and Transition Politics* **10:** 40–55.

Brown, A. (1997) *The Gorbachev Factor*, Oxford: Oxford University Press.

Brown, J.F. (1991) *Surge to Freedom: the End of Communist Rule*, Durham: Duke University Press.

Brzezinski, Z. (1967) *The Soviet Bloc: Unity and Conflict*, Cambridge: Harvard University Press.

Bugajski, J. (1995) *Nations in Turmoil, Conflict and Cooperation in Eastern Europe*, Boulder: Westview.

Bukowski, C. and Racz, B. (eds) (1999) *The Return of the Left in Post-communist States: Current Trends and Future Prospects*, Cheltenham: Edward Elgar.

Burg, S.L. (1997) 'Bosnia Herzegovina: a case of failed democratization', in K. Dawisha and B. Parrott, *Politics, Power, and the Struggle for Democracy in South-east Europe*, Cambridge, UK: Cambridge University Press.

Burnell, P. (1994) 'Democratization and economic change worldwide – can societies cope?', *Democratization* **1**: 1–7.

Chandler, D. (1998) 'Democratization in Bosnia: the limits of civil society building strategies', *Democratization* **5**: 78–102.

Cirtautas, A.M. (1994) 'In pursuit of the democratic interest: the institutionalization of parties and interests in Eastern Europe', in C. Bryant and E. Mokrzycki (eds) *The New Great Transformation? Change and Continuity in East-Central Europe*, London: Routledge.

Cook, L.J., Orenstein, M.A. and Rueschemeyer, M. (eds) (1999) *Left Parties and Social Policy in Postcommunist Europe*, Boulder: Westview.

Cotta, M. (1994) 'Building party systems after the dictatorship: the East European cases in a comparative perspective', in G. Pridham and T. Vanhanen, *Democratization in Eastern Europe: Domestic and International Perspectives*, London: Routledge.

—— (1995) 'Structuring the new party systems after the dictatorship', in G. Pridham and P.G. Lewis, *Stabilising Fragile Democracies*, London: Routledge.

Crampton, R.J. (1997) *Eastern Europe in the Twentieth Century*, London: Routledge.

Crawford, B. and Lijphart, A. (1995) 'Explaining political and economic change in post-communist eastern Europe', *Comparative Political Studies* **28:** 171–99.

Crawford, K. (1996) *East-Central European Politics Today*, Manchester: Manchester University Press.

Crowther, W. (1997) 'The politics of democratization in postcommunist Moldova', in K. Dawisha and B. Parrott, *Democratic Changes and Authoritarian Reactions in Russia, Ukraine, Belarus, and Moldova*, Cambridge, UK: Cambridge University Press.

Dahl, R.A. (ed.) (1966) *Political Oppositions in Western Democracies*, New Haven: Yale University Press.

Dawisha, K. (1988) *Eastern Europe, Gorbachev and Reform*, Cambridge University Press.

—— (1997) 'Democratization and political participation: research concepts and methodologies', in K. Dawisha and B. Parrott, *The Consolidation of Democracy in East-central Europe*, Cambridge, UK: Cambridge University Press.

—— and Parrott, B. (1994) *Russia and the New States of Eurasia: the Politics of Upheaval*, Cambridge University Press.

—— and Parrott, B. (eds) (1997) *The Consolidation of Democracy in East-Central Europe*, Cambridge University Press.

—— and Parrott, B. (eds) (1997) *Politics, Power, and the Struggle for Democracy in South-East Europe*, Cambridge University Press.

—— and Parrott, B. (eds) (1997) *Democratic Changes and Authoritarian Reactions in Russia, Ukraine, Belarus, and Moldova*, Cambridge University Press.

Dellenbrant, J.A. (1994) 'Romania and the slow revolution', in S. Berglund and J.A. Dellenbrant, *New Democracies of Eastern Europe: Party Systems and Political Cleavages*, Cheltenham: Edward Elgar.

Druker, J. (1999) 'War of the monitors', *Transitions* **6**: 14–21.

Duverger, M. (1954) *Political Parties*, London: Methuen (2nd edn 1964, 1st edn pub. in French 1951).

Ekiert, G. (1990) 'Democratization processes in East Central Europe: a theoretical consideration', *British Journal of Political Science* **21**: 285–313.

Epstein, L. (1967) *Political Parties in Western Democracies*, London: Pall Mall Press.

European Bank for Reconstruction and Development (1999) *Transition Report*, London.

Evans, G. and Whitefield, S. (1995) 'Economic ideology and political success: communist-successor parties in the Czech Republic, Slovakia and Hungary compared', *Party Politics* **28**: 565–78.

Fukuyama, F. (1989) 'The end of history?', *National Interest* **16**: 3–18.

Gallagher, T. (1998) 'The Balkans: Bulgaria, Romania, Albania and the former Yugoslavia', in S. White, J. Batt and P.G. Lewis (eds) *Developments in Central and East European Politics*, London: Macmillan.

Gati, C. (1996) 'The mirage of democracy', *Transition* **2**(6): 6–12.

Gebethner, S. (1996) 'Parliamentary and electoral parties in Poland', in P.G. Lewis, *Party Structure and Organization in East-Central Europe*, Cheltenham: Edward Elgar.

Gillespie, R., Waller, M. and Nieto, L.L. (eds) (1995) *Factional Politics and Democratization*, London: Frank Cass.

Glenny, M. (1990) *The Rebirth of History: Eastern Europe in the Age of Democracy*, Harmondsworth: Penguin Books.

—— (1992) *The Fall of Yugoslavia: the Third Balkan War*, Harmondsworth: Penguin.

Goble, P. (1998) 'When communists win elections', *RFE/RL Newsline* 6 April.

—— (1999) 'The approaching end of the "party of power"', *RFE/RL Newsline* 11 June.

Gorbachev, M. (1988) *Perestroika: New Thinking for Our Country and the World*, London: Fontana.

Gortat, R. (1994) 'Partyjne *perpetuum mobile*', in S. Gebethner (ed.) *Pobocze Systemu Partyjnego*, Warsaw: Uniwersytet Warszawski Instytut Nauk Politycznych.

—— (1996) 'Trudny egzamin: partie polityczne w wyborach prezydenckich '95', *Przegląd Społeczny* pp. 6–107.

—— (1998) *Ukraińskie Wybory*, Warsaw: Fundacja Polska Pracy.

Grabowska, M. (1997) 'Partie polityczne: reprezentant społeczeństwa czy twórca nowego ładu?', in M. Grabowski and S. Mocek, *Pierwsza sześciolatka 1989–1995, Próba Bilansu Polityki*, Warsaw: Instytut Studiów Politycznych.

Grabowska, M. and Mocek, S. (eds) (1997) *Pierwsza sześciolatka 1989–1995, Próba Bilansu Polityki*, Warsaw: Instytut Studiów Politycznych.

Grzymala-Busse, A. (1998) 'Reform efforts in the Czech and Slovak Communist parties and their successors, 1988–1993', *East European Politics and Societies* **12**: 442–70.

Hall, J.A. (1993) 'Consolidations of democracy', in D. Held, *Prospects for Democracy*, Cambridge: Polity Press.

Hayward, J. and Page, E.C. (1995) *Governing the New Europe*, Cambridge: Polity Press.

Held, D. (ed.) (1993) *Prospects for Democracy*, Cambridge: Polity Press.

Henderson, K. and Robinson, N. (1997) *Post-Communist Politics: an Introduction*, London: Prentice Hall.

Herbut, R. (1997) 'Systemy partyjne krajów Europy Centralnej i Wschodnej oraz wzorce rywalizacji politycznej', in A. Antoszewski and R. Herbut, *Demokracje Europy środkowo-Wschodniej w perspektywie porównawczej*, Wydawnictwo Uniwersytetu Wrocławskiego.

Holmes, L. (1997) *Post-Communism: an Introduction*, Cambridge: Polity Press.

Huntington, S.P. (1968) *Political Order in Changing Societies*, New Haven: Yale University Press.

Ilonszki, G. (1996) 'From marginal to rational parliaments: a Central European regional view', in A. Ágh and G. Ilonszki (eds) *Parliaments and Organized Interests: the Second Steps*, Budapest: Hungarian Centre for Democracy Studies.

—— (1998) 'Representation deficit in a new democracy: theoretical considerations and the Hungarian case', *Communist and Post-Communist Studies* **31**: 157–70.

Innes, A. (1997) 'The breakup of Czechoslovakia: the impact of party development on the separation of the state', *East European Politics and Societies* **11**: 393–435.

Ionescu, D. (1996) 'Former communists on the march', *Transition* **21**(2): 40–1.

Ishiyama, J.T. (1995) 'Communist parties in transition: structures, leaders, and processes of democratization in Eastern Europe', *Comparative Politics* **27**: 147–66.

—— (1997) 'The sickle or the rose? Previous regime types and the evolution of the ex-communist parties in post-communist politics', *Comparative Political Studies* **30**: 299–330.

—— (1999) 'Sickles into roses: the successor parties and democratic consolidation in post-communist politics', *Democratization* **6**: 52–73.

Jakubowicz, K. (1996) 'Media legislation as a mirror of democracy', *Transition* **21**(2): 17–21.

Janda, K. and Colman, T. (1998) 'Effects of party organization on performance during the "golden age" of parties', *Political Studies* **46**: 611–32.

Janicki, M. (1999) 'Likwidacja według planu', *Polityka* 26 June.

Jasiewicz, K. (1998) 'Elections and voting behaviour', in S. White, J. Batt and P.G. Lewis (eds) *Developments in Central and East European Politics*, London: Macmillan.

—— and Gebethner, S. (1998) 'Poland', *European Journal of Political Research* **34**: 493–506.

Kamiński, B. (1991) *The Collapse of State Socialism: the case of Poland*, Princeton University Press.

Karatnycky, A. (ed.) (1999) *Freedom in the World: Annual Survey of Political Rights and Civil Liberties*, New York: Freedom House.

Katz, R.S. and Mair, P. (1995) 'Changing models of party organization and party democracy: the emergence of the cartel party', *Party Politics* **1**: 5–28.

King, A. (1974) 'Political parties in western democracies', in L.J. Cantor (ed.) *Comparative Political Systems*, Boston: Holbrook Press.

Kirchheimer, O. (1966) 'The transformation of the western European party system', in J. LaPalombara and M. Weiner, *Political Parties*, Princeton University Press.

Kitschelt, H. (1992) 'The formation of party systems in East Central Europe', *Politics and Society* **20:** 7–50.

—— (1995) 'Formation of party cleavages in post-communist democracies: theoretical propositions', *Party Politics* **1**: 447–72.

—— (1995) 'Party systems in East Central Europe: consolidation or fluidity', *University of Strathclyde Studies in Public Policy*, no. 241.

—— Mansfeldova, Z., Markowski, R. and Tóka, G. (1999) *Post-Communist Party Systems: Competition, Representation, and Inter-Party Cooperation*, Cambridge, UK: Cambridge University Press.

Koole, R. (1996) 'Cadre, catch-all or cartel? A comment on the notion of the cartel party', *Party Politics* **2**: 507–21.

Kopecký, P. (1995) 'Developing party organizations in east-central Europe: what type of party is likely to emerge?', *Party Politics* **1**: 515–34.

Krašovec, A. (1999) 'The cartelization of Slovene political parties', Paper presented to Joint Sessions of the *European Consortium for Political Research*, Mannheim.

Krastev, I. (1997) 'Back to the basics in Bulgaria', *Transition* **3**(4): 12–15.

Krause, K.D. (2000) 'Public opinion and party choice in Slovakia and the Czech Republic', *Party Politics* **6**: 23–46.

Krickus, R.J. (1997) 'Democratization in Lithuania', in K. Dawisha and B. Parrott, *The Consolidation of Democracy in East-Central Europe*, Cambridge, UK: Cambridge University Press.

Kroupa, A. and Kostelecký, T. (1996) 'Party organization and structure at national and local level in the Czech Republic since 1989', in P.G. Lewis, *Party Structure and Organization in East-Central Europe*, Cheltenham: Edward Elgar.

Krupa, A. (ed.) (1997) *Prawie Biała ksiga Polskiej Sceny Politycznej*, Warsaw: ARS Print Production.

Kuzio, T. (1995) 'The 1994 parliamentary elections in Ukraine', *Journal of Communist Studies and Transition Politics* **11**: 338–55.

LaPalombara, J. and Weiner, M. (eds) (1966) *Political Parties and Political Development*, Princeton University Press.

Lapychak, C. (1996) 'Ukraine', in J. Schmidt (ed.) *Building Democracy*, 1995 OMRI Annual Survey of Eastern Europe and the Former Soviet Union, New York: M.E. Sharpe.

Lawson, K. (1999) 'Cleavages, parties, and voters', in K. Lawson, A. Römmele and G. Karasimeonov (eds) *Cleavages, Parties, and Voters*, Westport, Conn.: Praeger.

Lewis, P.G. (ed.) (1992) *Democracy and Civil Society in Eastern Europe*, London: Macmillan.

—— (1993) 'Civil society and the development of political parties in East-Central Europe', *Journal of Communist Studies* **9**(4): 5–20.

—— (1994) *Central Europe Since 1945*, London: Longman.

—— (1994) 'Democratization and party development in eastern Europe', *Democratization* **1**: 391–405.

—— (1994) 'Political institutionalization and party development in post-communist Poland', *Europe–Asia Studies* **46:** 779–99.

—— (1995) 'Poland and Eastern Europe: perspectives on party factions and factionalism', in R. Gillespie, M. Waller and L.L. Nieto, *Factional Politics and Democratization*, London: Frank Cass.

—— (ed.) (1996) *Party Structure and Organization in East-Central Europe*, Cheltenham: Edward Elgar.

—— (1997) 'The repositioning of opposition in east-central Europe', *Government and Opposition* **32:** 614–30.

—— (1997) 'Theories of democratization and patterns of regime change in Eastern Europe', *Journal of Communist Studies and Transition Politics* **13**: 4–26.

—— (1998) 'Party funding in post-communist east-central Europe', in P. Burnell and A. Ware (eds) *Funding Democratization*, Manchester University Press.

—— (1999) *Eastern Europe 1918–53, from Versailles to Cold War*, Bedford: Sempringham Press.

—— and Gortat, R. (1995) 'Models of party development and questions of state dependence in Poland', *Party Politics* **1**: 599–608.

—— Lomax, B., and Wightman, G. (1994) 'The emergence of multi-party systems in East-Central Europe', in Pridham and Vanhanen, *Democratization in Eastern Europe: Domestic and International Perspectives*, London: Routledge.

Lijphart, A. (1984) *Democracies: Patterns of Majoritarian and Consensus Government in Twenty-one Countries*, New Haven: Yale University Press.

Lipset, S.M. and Rokkan, S. (eds) (1967) *Party Systems and Voter Alignments: Cross National Perspectives*, New York: Free Press.

Lomax, B. (1995) 'Factions and factionalism in Hungary's new party system', in R. Gillespie, M. Waller and L.L. Nieto, *Factional Politics and Democratization*, London: Frank Cass.

—— (1996) 'The structure and organization of Hungary's political parties', in P.G. Lewis, *Party Structure and Organization in East-Central Europe*, Cheltenham: Edward Elgar.

McGregor, J. (1993) 'How electoral laws shape Eastern Europe's parliaments', *RFE/RL Research Report* **2**(4): 11–18.

Mach, B. and Wesołowski, W. (1998) 'Politicians in times of transition: "transformational correctness" or genuine differences in perception?', *WZB Papers*, Berlin.

Mahr, A. and Nagle, J. (1995) 'Resurrection of the successor parties and democratization in East-Central Europe', *Communist and Post-Communist Studies* **28**: 393–409.

Mainwaring, S. (1998) 'Party systems in the third wave', *Journal of Democracy* **9**: 67–81.

—— and Scully, T.R. (eds) (1995) *Building Democratic Institutions: Party Systems in Latin America*, Stanford University Press.

Mair, P. (1994) 'Party organizations: from civil society to the state', in R.S. Katz and P. Mair (eds) *How Parties Organize: Change and Adaptation in Party Organizations in Western Democracies*, London: Sage.

—— (1996) 'Party systems and structures of competition', in L. LeDuc (ed.) *Comparing Democracies: Elections and Voting in Global Perspectives*, London: Sage.

—— (1997) *Party System Change: Approaches and Interpretations*, Oxford: Clarendon Press.

Mann, M. (1993) *The Sources of Social Power, vol. II: The Rise of Classes and National-states*, Cambridge University Press.

Markowski, R. (1992) 'Absencja wyborcza i bierność wyborcza', *Krytyka* **38**: 57–71.

—— (1997) 'Political parties and ideological spaces in East Central Europe', *Communist and Post-Communist Studies* **30**: 221–54.

—— (1997) 'Polski system partyjny w środkowoeuropejskiej perspektywie', in M. Grabowska and S. Mocek, *Pierwsza sześciolatka1989–1995, Próba Bilansu Polityki*, Warsaw: Instytut Studiów Politycznych.

—— (1999) 'Polish party system: institutionalization – political representation – issue structuring', Paper presented at Joint Session of *European Consortium of Political Research*, Mannheim.

Merkel, W. (1998) 'The consolidation of post-autocratic democracies: a multi-level model', *Democratization* **5**(3): 33–67.

Mihalisko, K.J. (1997) 'Belarus: retreat to authoritarianism', in K. Dawisha and B. Parrott, *Democratic Changes and Authoritarian Reactions in Russia, Ukraine, Belarus, and Moldova*, Cambridge, UK: Cambridge University Press.

Miller, N.J. (1997) 'A failed transition: the case of Serbia', in K. Dawisha and B. Parrott, *Politics, Power, and the Struggle for Democracy in South-east Europe*, Cambridge, UK: Cambridge University Press.

Miller, W.L., White, S. and Heywood, P. (1998) *Values and Political Change in Postcommunist Europe*, London: Macmillan.

Milton, A.K. (1996) 'News media reform in Eastern Europe: a cross-national comparison', *Journal of Communist Studies and Transition Politics* **12:** 7–23.

Mouffe, C. (1993) *The Return of the Political*, London: Verso.

Nagle, J.D. and Mahr, A. (1999) *Democracy and Democratization*, London: Sage.

Nalewajko, E. (1997) *Protopartie i Protosystem? Szkic do Obrazu Polskiej Wielopartyjności*, Warsaw: Instytut Studiów Politycznych PAN.

Nikolchev, I. (1996) 'Polarization and diversification in the Bulgarian press', *Journal of Communist Studies and Transition Politics* **12:** 124–44.

Norden, D.L. (1998) 'Party relations and democracy in Latin America', *Party Politics* **4**: 423–43.

Oates, S. (1999) 'The Soviet legacy in voting behaviour', Paper delivered at Joint Sessions of *European Consortium for Political Research*, Mannheim.

Offe, C. (1991) 'Capitalism by democratic design? Democratic theory facing the triple transition in East Central Europe', *Social Research* **58:** 865–92.

Offerdal, A., Hanspach, D. Kowalczyk, A. et al. (1996) 'Elites and parties', in H. Baldersheim, M. Illner, A. Offerdal et al. (eds) *Local Democracy and the Processes of Transformation in East-Central Europe*, Boulder: Westview.

Olson, D.M. (1993) 'Political parties and party systems in regime transformation: inner transition in the new democracies of Central Europe', *American Review of Politics* **14:** 619–58.

—— (1997) 'Democratization and political participation: the experience of the Czech Republic', in K. Dawisha and B. Parrott, *The Consolidation of Democracy in East-Central Europe*, Cambridge, UK: Cambridge University Press.

—— (1998) 'Party formation and party system consolidation in the new democracies of Central Europe', *Political Studies* **46:** 432–64.

—— (1998) 'The parliaments of new democracies and the politics of representation', in S. White, J. Batt and P.G. Lewis, *Developments in Central and East European Politics*, London: Macmillan.

—— and Norton, P. (eds) (1996) *The New Parliaments of Central and Eastern Europe*, London: Frank Cass.

OMRI (1997) OMRI Annual Survey of Eastern Europe and the former Soviet Union 1996. *Forging Ahead, Falling Behind*, New York: M.E. Sharpe.

O'Neil, P.H. (1998) *Revolution from Within: the Hungarian Socialist Workers' Party and the Collapse of Communism*, Cheltenham: Edward Elgar.

Orenstein, M. (1998) 'A genealogy of communist successor parties in East-Central Europe and the determinants of their success', *East European Politics and Societies* **12:** 472–99.

Organization for Security and Cooperation in Europe (OSCE), *Newsletter* and *Election Reports*.

O'Sullivan, N. (1997) 'Difference and the concept of the political in contemporary political philosophy', *Political Studies* **55:** 739–54.

Padgett, S. (1996) 'Parties in post-communist society: the German case', in P.G. Lewis (ed.) *Party Structure and Organization in East-Central Europe*, Cheltenham: Edward Elgar.

Panebianco, A. (1998) *Political Parties: Organization and Power*, Cambridge University Press.

Panków, I. (1994) 'Responsibility of new elites: from the Solidarity movement to parliament building', in A. Ágh (ed.) *The Emergence of East Central European Parliaments*, Budapest: Hungarian Centre of Democracy Studies.

Pano, N. (1997) 'The process of democratization in Albania', in K. Dawisha and B. Parrott, *Politics, Power, and the Struggle for Democracy in Russia, Ukraine, Belarus, and Moldova*, Cambridge, UK: Cambridge University Press.

Parrott, B. (1997) 'Perspectives on postcommunist democratization', in K. Dawisha and B. Parrott, *The Consolidation of Democracy in East-Central Europe*, Cambridge, UK: Cambridge University Press.

Pasquino, G. (1990) 'Party elites and democratic consolidation: cross-national comparison of southern European experience', in G. Pridham (ed.) *Securing Democracy: Political Parties and Democratic Consolidation in Southern Europe*, London: Routledge.

Pennings, P. and Lane, J.-E. (eds) (1998) *Comparing Party System Change*, London: Routledge.

Pettai, V. and Kreuzer, M., 'Institutions and party development in the Baltic states', Paper delivered at the Joint Sessions of the *European Consortium for Political Research*, Mannheim.

—— (1999) 'Party politics in the Baltic states: social bases and institutional context', *East European Politics and Societies* **13:** 148–89.

Plakans, A. (1997) 'Democratization and political participation in postcommunist societies: the case of Latvia', in K. Dawisha and B. Parrott, *The Consolidation of Democracy in East-Central Europe*, Cambridge, UK: Cambridge University Press.

Polonsky, A. (1975) *The Little Dictators: the History of Eastern Europe Since 1918*, London: Routledge and Kegan Paul.

Polska Agencja Informacyjna (1991) *Partia Polityczne w Polsce*, Warsaw.

Powell, G.B. (1982) *Contemporary Democracies*, Cambridge, MA: Harvard University Press.

Pridham, G. (1996) 'Transnational party links and transition to democracy: eastern Europe in comparative perspective', in P.G. Lewis, *Party Structure and Organization in East-Central Europe*, Cheltenham: Edward Elgar.

—— (1999) 'Complying with the European Union's democratic conditionality: transnational party linkages and regime change in Slovakia, 1993–1998', *Europe-Asia Studies* **51**: 221–44.

—— (1999) 'Patterns of Europeanization and transnational party co-operation: party development in Central and Eastern Europe', Paper presented at Joint Sessions of *European Consortium for Political Research*, Mannheim.

—— and T. Vanhanen (eds) (1994) *Democratization in Eastern Europe: Domestic and International Perspectives*, London: Routledge.

—— and Lewis, P.G. (eds) (1996) *Stabilising Fragile Democracies*, London: Routledge.

Prizel, I. (1997) 'Ukraine between proto-democracy and "soft" authoritarianism', in K. Dawisha and B. Parrott, *Democratic Changes and Authoritarian Reactions in Russia, Ukraine, Belarus, and Moldova*, Cambridge, UK: Cambridge University Press.

Raciborski, J. (1997) *Polskie wybory: zachowania wyborcze społeczeństwa polskiego w latach 1989–1995*, Warsaw: Wydawnictwo Naukowe 'Scholar'.

Ramet, S.P. (1997) 'Democratization in Slovenia – the second stage', in K. Dawisha and B. Parrott, *Politics, Power, and the Struggle for Democracy in South-East Europe*, Cambridge, UK: Cambridge University Press.

Randall, V. (ed.) (1988) *Political Parties in the Third World*, London: Sage.

Raun, T.U. (1997) 'Democratization and political development in Estonia, 1987–96', in K. Dawisha and B. Parrott, *The Consolidation of Democracy in East Central Europe*, Cambridge, UK: Cambridge University Press.

Reljic, S. (1998) 'Demagogue in waiting', *Transitions* **5**(3): 70–5.

Rivera, S.W. (1996) 'Historical cleavages or transition mode? Reflections on the emerging party systems in Poland, Hungary and Czechoslovakia', *Party Politics* **2**: 177–208.

Rose, R. (1995) 'Mobilizing demobilized voters in post-communist societies', *Party Politics* **1**: 549–63.

—— and Mishler, W. (1997) 'Negative and positive partisanship in post-communist countries', *University of Strathclyde Studies in Public Policy* **286**.

—— Munro, N. and Mackie, T. (1998) 'Elections in Central and Eastern Europe since 1990', *University of Strathclyde Studies in Public Policy* **300**.

Roskin, M.G. (1993) 'The emerging party systems of Central and Eastern Europe', *East European Quarterly* **27**: 47–63.

Rothschild, J. (1974) *East Central Europe Between the Two World Wars*, Seattle: University of Washington Press.

—— (1993) *Return to Diversity, a Political History of East Central Europe Since World War II*, New York: Oxford University Press.

Sanford, G. (1976) 'Poland', in B. Szajkowski, *New Political Parties of Eastern Europe and the Soviet Union*, Harlow: Longman.

Sartori, G. (1976) *Parties and Party Systems: a Framework for Analysis*, Cambridge University Press.

Schmidt, F. (1997) 'Albania's Democrats consolidate power', in OMRI Annual Survey 1996, Armonk: New York.

Schmitter, P.C. (1986) 'An introduction to Southern European transitions from authoritarian rule', in G. O'Donnell et al. (eds) *Transitions from Authoritarian Rule*, vol. 1, Baltimore: Johns Hopkins Press.

Schöpflin, G. (1993) *Politics in Eastern Europe 1945–1992*, Oxford: Blackwell.

—— (1998) 'Hungary's elections: the dilemma of the right', *RFE/RL Newsline* 29 April.

Sekelj, L. (2000) 'Parties and elections: the Federal Republic of Yugoslavia – change without transformation', *Europe–Asia Studies* **52**: 57–75.

Seroka, J. (1993) 'Yugoslavia and its successor states', in S. White, J. Batt and P.G. Lewis (eds) *Developments in East European Politics*, London: Macmillan.

Shafir, M. (1998) 'Moldova's upcoming parliamentary elections', *RFE/RL Newsline* 19–20 March.

—— (1999) 'The mind of Romania's radical right', in S.P. Ramet (ed.) *The Radical Right in Central and Eastern Europe Since 1989*, Pennsylvania: Pennsylvania State University Press.

—— (1999) 'Moldova and presidential system: little country, big question', *RFE/RL Newsline* 15 July.

—— (1999) 'Two very different reshuffles', *RFE/RL Newsline* 23 December.

—— and Ionescu, D. (1996) 'Radical political change in Romania', in OMRI Annual Survey, Armonk: New York.

Simon, J. (1998) 'Electoral systems and regime change in Central and Eastern Europe, 1990–1994', *Representation* **35**: 122–36.

Swain, N. (1991) 'Hungary', in B. Szajkowski, *New Political Parties of Eastern Europe and the Soviet Union*, Harlow: Longman.

Szablowski, G. and Derlien, H.-U. (1993) 'East European transitions: elites, bureaucracies, and the European Community', *Governance* **6**: 304–24.

Szajkowski, B. (ed.) (1991) *New Political Parties of Eastern Europe and the Soviet Union*, Harlow: Longman.

—— (ed.) (1994) *Political Parties of Eastern Europe, Russia and the Successor States*, Harlow: Longman.

Szarvas, L. (1994) 'Parties and party factions in the Hungarian parliament', *Journal of Communist Studies and Transition Politics* **10**(3): 120–36.

Szczerbiak, A. (1998) 'Electoral politics in Poland: the parliamentary elections of 1997', *Journal of Communist Studies and Transition Politics* **14**(3): 58–83.

—— (1999) 'Testing party models in east-central Europe: local party organization in post-communist Poland', *Party Politics* **5**: 525–37.

—— (1999) 'The impact of the October 1998 local elections on the emerging Polish party system', *Journal of Communist Studies and Transition Politics* **15:** 80–100.

—— (1999) 'Bureaucrats and professionals: the "party machine" in post-communist Poland', Paper presented at Joint Sessions of the *European Consortium for Political Research*, Mannheim.

Szilagyi, Z. (1996) 'Shady dealings and slow privatization', *Transition* **2**(21): 44–5.

Školkay, A. (1996) 'Journalists, political elites and post-communist public: the case of Slovakia', *Journal of Communist Studies and Transition Politics* **12**: 61–81.

Taagepera, R. (1998) 'How electoral systems matter for democratization', *Democratization* **5**(3): 68–91.

—— and Sobert, M. (1989) *Seats and Votes*, New Haven: Yale University Press.

Taras, T. (1998) 'The politics of leadership', in S. White, Batt, J. and Lewis, P.G. (eds) *Developments in Central and East European Politics*, London: Macmillan.

Tatomir, B. (1996) 'Croatian government calls certain media "enemies of the state"', *Transition* **2**(21): 24–6.

Terry, S.M. (1993) 'Thinking about post-communist transitions: how different are they?', *Slavic Review* **52:** 333–7.

Tismaneanu, V. (1997) 'Romanian exceptionalism? Democracy, ethnocracy, and uncertain pluralism in post-Ceausescu Romania', in K. Dawisha and B. Parrott (eds) *Politics, Power, and the Struggle for Democracy in South-East Europe*, Cambridge, UK: Cambridge University Press.

Tóka, G. (1996) 'Parties and electoral choices in east-central Europe', in G. Pridham and P.G. Lewis, *Stabilising Fragile Democracies*, London: Routledge.

—— (1997) 'Political parties in East Central Europe', in L. Diamond et al. (ed.) *Consolidating the Third Wave Democracies: Themes and Perspectives*, Baltimore: Johns Hopkins Press.

—— (1998) 'Party appeals and voter loyalty in new democracies', *Political Studies* **46:** 589–610.

Tokes, R.L. (1997) 'Party politics and political participation in postcommunist Hungary', in K. Dawisha and B. Parrott, *The Consolidation of Democracy in East-Central Europe*, Cambridge, UK: Cambridge University Press.

Tworzecki, H. (1996) *Parties and Politics in Post-1989 Poland*, Boulder: Westview.

United Nations, *Economic Survey of Europe*, at www.unece.org/stats/ trend/svn.htm.

Urbański, A. (1999) 'Dwaj panowie K.', *Polityka* 15 May.

Varfolomeyev, O. (1998) 'Ukrainian party politics gets a boost', *Transitions* **5**(1): 80–5.

Vickers, M. and Pettifer, J. (1997) *Albania: from Anarchy to a Balkan Identity*, London: Hurst.

Wade, L., Groth, A.J. and Lavelle, P. (1994) 'Estimating participation and party voting in Poland: the 1991 parliamentary elections', *East European Politics and Society* **8**: 94–121.

Walewski, P. (1999) 'Swój radzie', *Polityka* 6 November.

Waller, M. (1995) 'Adaptation of the former communist parties of east-central Europe: a case of social-democratization?', *Party Politics* **1**: 473–90.

—— (1996) 'Party inheritances and party identities', in G. Pridham and P.G. Lewis, *Stabilising Fragile Democracies*, London: Routledge.

—— and Gillespie, R. (1995) 'Introduction: factions, party management and political development', in R. Gillespie, M. Waller and L.L. Nieto, *Factional Politics and Democratization*, London: Frank Cass.

——— and Karasimeonov, G. (1996) 'Party organization in post-communist Bulgaria', in P.G. Lewis, *Party Structure and Organization in East-Central Europe*, Cheltenham: Edward Elgar.

Ware, A. (1996) *Political Parties and Party Systems*, Oxford University Press.

Wasilewski, J., Kopczynski, M and Szczur, S. (1999) 'Stabilność zachowań wyborczych', in R. Markowski (ed.) *Wybory Parlamentarne 1997*, Warsaw: Instytut Studiów Politycznych/ Fundacja Eberta.

Webb, P. and Lewis, P.G. (1998) 'The lessons of comparative politics: Russian political parties as independent variables?', *Journal of Communist Studies and Transition Politics* **14:** 253–64.

Welsh, H.A. (1994) 'Political transition processes in central and eastern Europe', *Comparative Politics* **26:** 379–94.

Wenzel, M. (1998) 'Solidarity and Akcja Wyborcza "Solidarnosc". An attempt at reviving the legend', *Communist and Post-Communist Studies* **31:** 139–56.

White, S. (1991) 'Latvia', in Szajkowski, B. (ed.) *New Political Parties or Eastern Europe and the Soviet Union*, Harlow: Longman.

——— Batt, J. and Lewis, P.G. (eds) (1998) *Developments in Central and East European Politics*, London: Macmillan.

Wightman, G. (1991) 'Czechoslovakia', in Szajkowski, B. (ed.) *New Political Parties of Eastern Europe and the Soviet Union*, Harlow: Longman.

——— (ed.) (1995) *Party Formation in East-Central Europe*, Aldershot: Edward Elgar.

——— (1998) 'Parties and politics', in S. White, Batt, J. and Lewis, P.G. (eds) *Developments in Central and East European Politics*, London: Macmillan.

——— and Szomolanyi, S. (1995) 'Parties and society in Slovakia', *Party Politics* **1:** 609–18.

Wolchik, S.L. (1997) 'Democratization and political participation in Slovakia', in K. Dawisha and B. Parrott, *The Consolidation of Democracy in East-Central Europe*, Cambridge, UK: Cambridge University Press.

World Bank, *Report* at www.worldbank.org/cgi.bin.

Zhang, B. (1994) 'Corporatism, totalitarianism, and transitions to democracy', *Comparative Political Studies* **27:** 108–36.

Ziblatt, D.F. (1998) 'The adaptation of ex-communist parties to post-communist East Central Europe: a comparative study of the East German and Hungarian ex-communist parties', *Communist and Post-Communist Studies* **31:** 119–37.

Żukowski, T. (1993) 'Polska scena polityczna w latach 1991–92 w świetle wyników wyborów: ciągłość i zmiany', in S. Gebethner (ed.) *Polska scena polityczna a wybory*, Warsaw: 'Polska w Europie'.

Index

Albania 4; Democratic Party 47, 68, 89; elections 30, 67–8, 72, 75, 76, 87, 89; historical background 8; party development 47, 77, 90, 134, 141, 151, 152; party formation 36; Party of Labour 30, 47; transition from communism 14, 18

Balkans, the 4, 5; democratic transition 21, 89–90; elections 74, 79

Baltic states 3, 5; elections 26–7, 30, 31; historical background 8; party formation 34; party systems 132–3; post-communist parliaments 91; transition from communism 15–16, 83

Belarus 3, 4; elections 30, 40, 667, 68, 70, 75, 76, 89; emergence of political parties 25; historical background 6, 10; party development 40, 48, 73–4, 82, 83, 150, 151, 152; party systems 125, 129, 134, 135, 141, 156; transition from communism 16

Berisha, President 68

Berov, Liuben 138

Bosnia 4; elections 29, 30, 61, 75; finance and party funding 112; party development 46, 134, 151, 152; transition from communism 15, 76

Brazil, democratic transition 18, 23

Bulatović, Momir 137

Bulgaria 4; elections 29, 30, 31, 64, 68, 75, 77, 87, 89, 106; finance and party funding 112; historical background 7, 8; media relations 113; party development 45, 77, 81, 102, 106, 152–3; party formation 36; party systems 129, 134,

137, 138, 139, 145; Socialist Party 29, 37, 45, 102, 112, 138; Stamboliiski government 7; transition from communism 14, 18; Union of Democratic Forces 45, 68, 106, 138

Ceausescu, Nicolae 14, 28, 31, 37, 45, 137

Central Electoral Commission 135

Chornovil, Viacheslav 47

Cold War, the 21, 22

Croatia 4; Democratic Union 28, 45, 94, 112, 139, 140; elections 28, 31, 61, 66, 75, 89; historical background 10; media relations 115–16; party development 44–5, 80–1, 82, 94, 112, 152; party systems 125, 129, 134, 139–40; transition from communism 15, 76

Csurka, István 82, 118, 165

Czechoslovakia 11; elections 29, 31, 75, 76, 87; historical background 7, 8, 9, 10, 11, 12, 23, 32, 33, 151; party development 40, 41, 77, 154; post-communist parliament 91; Prague Spring of 1968 9; transition from communism 14, 18

Czech Republic 4, 5; Civic Democratic Party 41, 94–5, 101, 109, 111, 112, 115, 117, 149, 162, 164; Civic Forum 29, 36, 41, 49, 76, 108; Communist Party 101, 102, 103, 108, 124, 159; Communist Party of Bohemia and Moravia 54, 164; elections 61, 70, 72, 76, 80, 87; emergence of political parties 22; finance and party funding 107, 108, 109, 110, 111–12; Freedom Union 111, 112, 117, 164; major parties 164; media relations